Child Neglect

Also by Jan Horwath:

The Child's World: Assessing Children in Need and their Families
Working for Children on the Child Protection Register: An Inter-agency Practice Guide
　(Ed. with M. Calder)
Effective Staff Training in Social Care: From Theory to Practice (With T. Morrison)
Trust Betrayed: Munchausen Syndrome by Proxy: A Multidisciplinary Approach
　(Ed. with B. Lawson)
Making Links across Specialisms: Understanding Modern Social Work Practice
　(Ed. with S. Shardlow)

Child Neglect: Identification and Assessment

Jan Horwath

First published 2007 by
PALGRAVE MACMILLAN
Houndmills, Basingstoke, Hampshire RG21 6XS and
175 Fifth Avenue, New York, N.Y. 10010
Companies and representatives throughout the world

PALGRAVE MACMILLAN is the global academic imprint of the Palgrave Macmillan division of St. Martin's Press, LLC and of Palgrave Macmillan Ltd. Macmillan® is a registered trademark in the United States, United Kingdom and other countries. Palgrave is a registered trademark in the European Union and other countries.

ISBN-13: 978–1–4039–3346–1
ISBN-10: 1–4039–3346–4

This book is printed on paper suitable for recycling and made from fully managed and sustained forest sources.

A catalogue record for this book is available from the British Library.

Library of Congress Cataloging-in-Publication Data
Basarab-Horwath, Janet Anne, 1952–.
    Child neglect : identification and assessment / Jan Horwath.
        p. cm.
    Includes bibliographical references and index.
    ISBN 1–4039–3346–4 (pbk.)
      1. Child abuse. 2. Child abuse—Investigation. 3. Abused children—Health risk assessment. I. Title.

    HV6626.5.B37 2007
    362.76'2—dc22   2006051500

10 9 8 7 6 5 4 3 2 1
16 15 14 13 12 11 10 09 08 07

Printed in China

This book is dedicated to my grandmother
Elspbeth Asch 1898–1979 who valued and believed
in me.

Contents

List of Figures, Tables and Boxes

Preface

Although signs of physical abuse such as broken bones, bruises, cuts and scars are observable (and obvious), the less overt and more subtle persistent omission of parental care resulting in neglect does, at least, as much damage to the growing and developing child. In spite of the widespread recognition of neglect and its high prevalence amongst maltreated children, it itself has been neglected and marginalised by many practitioners, policymakers, managers of resource allocation and the Courts.

Literature dealing with research and practice, which the author explores in detail in Chapter 2, has shown that persistent neglect can have a devastating effect on both physical and emotional development and well-being and that its consequences can be long-lasting – which in turn can impact on the neglected child's ability to parent. A paucity of longitudinal studies examining the short- and long-term outcomes of neglect and the vagueness of operational definitions have not made the task of identifying and dealing in a confident manner with neglect cases any easier. The key problem in identifying neglect is in establishing what may be considered minimally adequate levels of care, and what constitutes inadequate care. However, confusion and controversy still cloud the issues when it comes to defining at what point neglect should be considered as unacceptable and harmful to the child. Problems in establishing criteria for the threshold of minimal care make decision-making and planning difficult, as these may vary upon the child's age, resilience, vulnerability and the values prevalent in a particular community. Worryingly, as evidenced by the publicity given to the horrific death of Victoria Climbié, even now public attention focuses on sensational cases of severe physical neglect and injuries which are easily observable. However, less attention is given to other forms of neglect which do not show obvious physical marks such as emotional neglect. Yet, this is considered to be even more damaging than physical neglect if consistent and persistent.

As the author discusses in Chapter 1, the 1960s was a time when practitioners did focus on identifying and assessing neglect and indeed providing services to meet the child and family's needs. However, as growing attention was given through the 1970s and 1980s to physical abuse, and in the late 1980s and early 1990s to sexual abuse, neglect became marginalised. One of the key issues contributing to this marginalisation was that practice became increasingly forensically driven with practitioners focusing on incidents of abuse to demonstrate the child had suffered significant harm. The fact that the consequences of neglect may not be obvious and immediate (but damaging in the long-term) was not acknowledged. There was a lack of obvious knowledge, skills and confidence in how to assess neglect and furthermore how to provide proof of its harmful effects on children. The introduction of the *Framework for the Assessment of Children in Need and their Families* (Department of Health et al., 2000) in England and the *Framework for the Assessment of Vulnerable Children and their Families* (Buckley et al., 2006), which is used in parts of the Republic of Ireland, have sought to address this gap in knowledge and skills and has indeed assisted practitioners in identifying the factors that contribute to the neglect of a child. The English Common Assessment Framework (Department for Education and Skills, 2004) should take this further and assist practitioners in identifying vulnerable children. Yet despite the introduction of assessment frameworks and assessment tools (discussed in Chapter 7) practitioners still have to use their professional judgement to determine standards of acceptable care whilst recognising that resources are limited to meet any identified need. Moreover, the current systems for both assessing and intervening in cases of neglect do not take account of the multifaceted and long-term assessments and interventions required if we are to really make a difference to the life of neglected children and their families.

Jan Horwath recognises the dilemmas and challenges encountered by practitioners when identifying child neglect against this background. In this comprehensive text she assists the reader to make sense of neglect and explores practical and realistic ways of assessing neglect, taking account of the current working context. The author presents a painstaking analysis of the assessment tasks and processes based on a thorough literature review and empirical data generated from her own research and supported by other studies and relevant theories. Each chapter includes practical suggestions as to how to apply the theories and research evidence to practice ensuring that practitioners and the family keep a clear focus on the needs of the child.

Written for practitioners from a diverse range of disciplines the approach is elegant, scholarly and yet accessible and user-friendly. This book provides a wealth of information for those who are familiar with neglect issues and those who are new to the field. What sets this book apart from others is the attention to detail and the full exploration of the factors that contribute to and maintain neglect of a child. The comprehensive and non-judgemental approaches to discussing neglected children, their carers' behaviour and the communities in which they live is presented in a helpful problem-recognition and problem-solving way which is useful for busy and often stressed practitioners. The author pays particular attention to children who can be particularly vulnerable to neglect such as disabled children, the child perceived to be 'difficult to parent', adolescents and children from asylum-seeking and refugee families.

Readers from different professional backgrounds will find this book an invaluable daily companion on an often long journey of understanding and responding to the many needs of neglected children. Jan Horwath does not just talk about how to assess neglected children and their families: her practice experience is apparent as she brings the families to us in rich and graphic detail, so we experience the fate of these children as we progress through the book. Practitioners involved in child welfare and child protection work, students and policymakers will greatly benefit from the admirable and good sense evident in this work.

Emeritis Professor Dorota Iwaniec
Queen's University
Belfast
Northern Ireland

Acknowledgements

This book would never have been written without the support and encouragement of my family, friends and colleagues. I am particularly grateful to Peter Castleton, John Fox, Sarah Glennie, Tony Morrison, Dr Catherine Powell and Dr Jean Price who gave generously of their time and expertise. I would also like to thank the senior managers of what was the North Eastern Health Board (now the Health Service Executive) who commissioned the research study referred to in this book. Worthy of a special mention are Liz Coogan and Nuala Doherty and the staff who provided me with valuable advice through membership of the steering groups. I would also like to thank the practitioners and managers who participated in the research in such an honest and enthusiastic manner: without their contribution this book would never have been written. I am also indebted to the researchers who worked on the Health Board Studies, Beverley Bishop and Teela Saunders and to Sue Plummer who provided excellent administrative support and calming words throughout the research project and the preparation of this book. Most importantly I would like to thank my family who have lived with this book for the past two years and I am sure will breathe a sigh of relief now that it is finished. I regret that my mother, Eva Lasota, died before she saw this book published. I would, however, like to acknowledge the support and enthusiasm she brought to this work. Her confidence in my ability to write this book, as has been the case throughout my life, kept me going when I was full of self-doubt.

Introduction

I've had sleepless nights worrying about some of the children in my class that I guess you would say are neglected. The problems are insurmountable. It goes on from generation to generation I'm now teaching the children of children I'd had concerns about.
(A primary school teacher)

I always feel guilty about the child neglect cases. It seems so harsh making judgements about parents who are living in abject poverty.
(A social worker)

Child neglect – it's the worst kind of child abuse and yet the one that gets the least attention.
(A community paediatrician)

I came across a neglectful family with a history as long as your arm. I was really concerned and I rang up social services but they said the parenting seemed to be good enough at the moment and would not accept a referral.
(A health visitor)

If I referred every child in this school that I thought was being neglected, then at least half the children would be referred. It's inevitable you teach in an area like this you expect children to be neglected.
(A headteacher)

If only we had the resources to manage these cases properly. The problems are so entrenched and yet we only offer short-term solutions.
(A family centre manager)

It's difficult knowing where you draw the line with neglect. My 14 year old says he's neglected if he doesn't get the same trainers as everyone else in the class.
(A community mental health nurse)

These are a selection of comments made by practitioners that I know, when they learnt that I was writing a book about child neglect. These comments are not unusual: they reflect the frustration and confusion felt by many professionals faced with identifying and assessing child neglect. For example, the health visitor above described a negative experience of referring a case to social services. This experience would seem to be common-place according to studies which highlight differences in perceptions between cases that should be referred to social work services (Birchall & Hallett, 1995; Horwath, 2005; Stone, 1998; Taylor & Daniel, 1999). Moreover, once cases are referred the

1

focus of assessment can vary; with different practitioners emphasising various aspects of neglect, such as physical safety or, as was the case with the social worker above, not wishing to make a judgement between poverty and neglect (Scourfield, 2000; Daniel & Baldwin, 2001; Stevenson, 1998; Thoburn et al., 2000). Graham (1996), in a study reported by Buckley (2002), summarises the situation well. He concludes that workers are either 'over-whelmed' by the enormous and impervious problems presented by neglectful families, as is reflected in the feelings of the primary school teacher and the family centre manager, or 'under-whelmed' to the point where the practitioners normalise neglect, as is the case with the headteacher.

These attitudes and practices are concerning as they can lead to a loss of focus on the child and their needs. They are particularly worrying bearing in mind that child neglect is currently, and has for the past ten years, been the most frequently reported form of maltreatment in the developed world (Childhelp USA, 2003; Trocme et al., 2003; Australian Institute of Health and Welfare, 2004; Department for Education and Skills, 2004b).This is discussed in Chapter 2. However, what I have found most striking about these attitudes and practices, is that the confusion concerning child neglect, reported both by my colleagues and in the studies above, is similar to that which I experienced when I began practising as a social worker 30 years ago. Why is it that despite an ever increasing amount of government guidance and research in the field, this confusion remains? And why is it practitioners are so often 'under-whelmed' or 'over-whelmed' by child neglect? It is an attempt to answer these questions and begin to clarify both the assessment task and process in cases of neglect that has been my impetus for writing this book. However, before attempting to seek some clarity about identifying and assessing neglect, which is the focus of the book, I think it is useful to consider the reasons why there is such confusion about child neglect.

Confusion about Child Neglect: The Causes

In my opinion there are three reasons why there is such confusion about what constitutes child neglect and how possible concerns should be managed. These reasons are considered below.

Child Neglect Research

Despite the prevalence of child neglect, incidents of abuse, such as sexual and physical abuse, receive far more attention in both the literature and research (Hobbs & Wynne, 2002). For example, Behl et al. (2003) reviewed the research on child maltreatment published in the past 22 years. They found a decline in studies of physical abuse and an increase in research on sexual abuse. However, the percentage of papers reporting work on child neglect and emotional abuse remained low at 9 per cent and 4.2 per cent respectively. In addition, most published studies refer to 'child abuse and neglect' failing to distinguish between the two. In this situation, other forms of abuse, which are arguably less complex and easier to identify than neglect, take centre stage with neglect being minimised or ignored (Burke et al., 1998). As Garbarino and Collins (1999, p. 11) conclude, 'research on child maltreatment has a hole in the middle, where the concept of neglect should be filled'.

There are a number of reasons why this has occurred. First, there are definitional issues associated with child neglect, which are explored in detail in Chapter 1. The definitional issues centre on a lack of agreement about standards of appropriate care of children. For example, personal and community perspectives may vary depending on cultural, faith and class beliefs, which are considered in detail in Chapter 5 (Garbarino & Collins, 1999; Tanner & Turney, 2003). Second, there is no standard theoretical framework to inform neglect research. Hence, researchers often fail to distinguish between descriptions of seemingly neglectful behaviour and possible causes influencing these behaviours (Stone, 1998; Tanner & Turvey, 2003). Finally, much of the literature on child neglect is American based, which raises issues of transferability and interpretation across nations with different welfare systems (Tanner & Turney, 2003).

Neglect and Changing Perspectives

The problems associated with researching and writing about child neglect reflects a fundamental issue: neglect is not a static phenomenon. Attitudes towards child neglect in a society alter over time and are influenced by changing cultural, economic and ideological values (Garbarino et al., 1986; Reder et al., 1993; The Bridge Child Care Consultancy Service, 1995). These changing attitudes inform our expectations of parents and influence child welfare policy and practice (Reder et al., 1993). These changing attitudes have been noted in many developed countries over the last 30 years. (For further information on the USA see Gelles, 1999; Wattenberg & Boisen (no date); Canada see Sullivan, 2000; Australia see Thorpe, 1994; Tomison, 1995; and Ireland see Buckley et al., 1997; Ferguson & O'Reilly, 2001; Lavan, 1998). These changing attitudes and their impact on policy and practice in relation to child neglect will be explored using England as an example.

The Benevolent Approach

In the 1950s and 1960s, in the light of the newly formed Welfare State, a benevolent approach was taken to carers who failed to meet the needs of their children. Professional advice and practical assistance was generally offered to neglectful families. The aim of these interventions was to preserve the family unit and compensate for social injustices (Jordan & Jordan, 2000; Packman & Jordan, 1991; Parton et al., 1997; Stevenson, 1998). By the 1970s, the complex relationship between deprivation and neglect was beginning to be recognised. Policymakers and professionals began to express concern about families who, despite opportunities, remained disadvantaged from generation to generation caught, in what the Secretary for State for Health at the time, Sir Keith Joseph, referred to as, the 'cycle of deprivation'. The concern with generational neglect raised questions about existing child welfare systems which were increasingly perceived to be fostering client dependence and releasing parents from taking responsibility for their actions (Foster & Wilding, 2000).

The Forensic Approach

Further questions, about parental responsibility, were raised in light of the work of Henry Kempe and colleagues in the USA on 'battered babies' (Kempe & Helfer, 1968). This work emphasised that parents were capable of harming their children. The consequence was an attitudinal shift away from earlier benevolence towards maltreating parents, to perceiving these parents as possible criminals or scroungers (Foster & Wilding, 2000).

Governments responded, over the following 20 years, by introducing a plethora of child protection guidance that emphasised a forensic approach to practice and increased control over the way in which professionals worked with cases of child maltreatment. Systems, at national and local level, became incident-driven, with a focus on 'investigating, assessing and weighing forensic evidence' (Parton et al., 1997, p. 19). These systems lent themselves more readily to identifying sexual abuse and physical injury rather than neglect or emotional abuse. However, by the mid 1990s research studies, not surprisingly, showed that professionals working within the child protection system were focusing on a particular group of children: those children who were suffering or likely to suffer significant harm where forensic evidence was available. The result was that many neglected children, in situations where there was not specific forensic evidence of harm, were not receiving appropriate services, if they received any services at all (Department of Health, 1995; Parton, 2005; Gibbons et al., 1995). In addition, the studies indicated that a narrow focus on incidents meant that the impact of parenting issues, such as domestic violence and mental health issues, on the carer's ability to meet the needs of a child were often minimised or ignored.

The Early Intervention Approach

The findings from these research studies informed a change in approach in the mid to late 1990s, with a shift in focus towards early intervention and family support services as well as a recognition that safeguarding children is the responsibility of practitioners in both adult and children's services (Audit Commission, 1994; Rose, 2001; Cm (5860) 2003). This approach has continued into the 21st century with the Children Act 2004, which emphasises the importance of all professionals safeguarding and promoting better outcomes for children. In addition, professionals have become increasingly aware of the impact that such parenting issues as drug misuse can have on negatively affecting parenting capacity. The result of this shift away from a restricted, incident-based, forensic approach, together with a recognition of the impact that parenting issues can have on parenting capacity, has resulted in an increase in cases of child neglect coming to the attention of child welfare professionals.

The Organisational Context

Changes in policy alone will not necessarily improve practice in cases of child neglect. This will only occur if organisations are adequately funded and resourced by a skilled workforce, as is discussed in Chapter 9. As Lord Laming noted in his report, following the death of Victoria Climbié from physical abuse and neglect:

> Agencies were underfunded, inadequately staffed and poorly led ... scarce resources were not being put to good use. Bad practice can be expensive. For example, had there been a proper response to the needs of Victoria when she was first referred ... it may well be that the danger to her would have been recognised and action taken which may have avoided the need for the involvement of the other agencies. (Cm '5730', 2003, para 1.18)

The management of Victoria Climbié's case does not appear to be unique. For example, Cleaver and Walker (2004) found the availability of services and legal duties, rather than the developmental needs of the child, in some cases, notably multi-problem families, dictated outcomes following an Initial Assessment of need.

As we can see from the above, limited research, changing child welfare policy and inadequate resources have set the current context for working with cases of child neglect. Taking these into account, it is not surprising that practitioners express the type of feelings described at the beginning of the introduction and struggle with identifying and assessing child neglect.

The Aims of the Book

My purpose in writing this book is to assist professionals manage the ambiguity, vagueness and anxiety associated with identifying and assessing possible cases of child neglect against a backcloth of limited research, changing welfare policy and inadequate resources. More specifically, the aims of this book are three-fold. First, to explore the available research, policy and practice develop-ments that provide a theoretical framework for defining, identifying and assess-ing child neglect. Second, to recognise the ways in which the personal, professional and organisational tensions and dilemmas encountered by practi-tioners working with child neglect can influence the application of theory to practice. Third, to consider ways in which the tensions and dilemmas can be managed by practitioners and managers to ensure practice remains child focused and evidence-based. With this in mind, the book is designed to offer practitioners, managers and educators ideas for developing practice that inspire whilst being attainable.

This book will be of particular value to professionals who are working regularly with children and young people and their carers and those who have a particular responsibility for safeguarding children. Most specifically it should assist social workers, health visitors, designated health and educational professionals. It is written to inform professional practice in cases of child neglect and is designed as a comprehensive reference source for practitioners and managers who are involved in identifying and assessing child neglect. The book lends itself to professionals undertaking post-qualifying programmes of study in child welfare and will be a useful source for qualify-ing social work students and other students completing placements in child welfare settings.

The legislative framework referred to primarily in this book is English. However, the book draws on international research and literature to inform professional understanding of child neglect and to highlight the factors that can result in practitioners losing the focus on the child. Hence, the lessons learnt will be of relevance to practitioners, managers and students irrespective of juris-diction.

Overview of Contents

Those writing for a professional audience usually make links between theory and practice. In this book I intend to go beyond this to consider the current working context and discuss the routine blocks and barriers encountered by practitioners working with child neglect within child welfare and associate settings. My intention is to consider ways in which lessons from research and the literature can inform practice in the 'real world'. To this end, I have attempted to apply theory to practice by offering tools and assessment prompts, based on the literature, that are designed to assist practitioners identify and assess neglect in a diverse range of practice settings.

The book is divided into four parts, which are described below.

Part I Identifying Neglect: What It Is and What It Does to Children

The first part of the book focuses on what practitioners should consider when trying to identify neglect and the possible impact of neglect on children. In Chapter 1 I consider definitional issues associated with child neglect. The Chapter begins with a discussion of the way in which child neglect is interpreted in contemporary society. Drawing on international literature, I explore the variations in definitions of neglect and the dilemmas for professionals working with these definitions. For example, recognising cultural filters, personal standards and the problem of differentiating between neglect and deprivation. A working definition of child neglect is provided. This definition will be used throughout the book. Chapter 1 also includes an overview of the different forms of neglect, including supervisory neglect, physical, nutritional, emotional, medical and educational neglect. The statistical data about prevalence of neglect is interrogated and issues regarding under and over-representation identified.

Having established what is meant by child neglect, Chapter 2 focuses on the impact of neglect on children. Particular attention is given to the effects on the development of the child's brain, socio-emotional development and attachment strategies. The signs and indicators of neglect in terms of the impact on the child's emotional, cognitive and physical development and resilience at different stages through childhood and adolescence are discussed in detail.

Part II Assessing the Care-Giver and the Care-Giving Context

In the following three chapters I argue that parenting capacity consists of three components – parenting ability, motivation and opportunity. These are then explored in detail. In Chapter 3 I begin with an analysis of the knowledge and skills required for effective parenting, including a discussion of the role of both male and female carers. The antecedents for neglect are discussed and the impact of the parents' own relationships with their carers, partners and their child are explored in terms of the effects on ability and motivation to parent.

In Chapter 4 I consider the possible impact of parenting issues on the carer's ability and motivation to meet the needs of the child. The effects of learning disability, mental illness, drug and alcohol misuse and domestic violence on parenting ability and motivation are discussed. Key common themes are considered, such as the possible impact of these issues on the child's emotional and cognitive development, carer pre-occupation with their own problems, and the implications for care-giving.

In the final chapter, in this part of the book, I focus on parenting opportunities. Assessing the impact of socio-economic factors in cases of child neglect can be complex. A common dilemma for most practitioners is differentiating between neglect and deprivation. Therefore, I consider ways in which poor housing and poverty can influence a carer's ability to meet the needs of their child and how practitioners can differentiate between society's failure to provide adequate resources and neglect on the part of carers. I also pay attention to the tensions encountered by practitioners when attempting to assess child neglect amongst members of ethnic minority groups and faith communises. The final section of this chapter centres on informal support networks in the community and ways in which these can be both a stress factor and also a buffer against stress for neglectful families.

Part III Referral and Assessment: Practice Reality

The first two parts of the book focused on the assessment task, in the next two chapters I concentrate on the referral and assessment process. Drawing on the findings of two studies I completed in the Republic of Ireland, I describe the dilemmas encountered by practitioners and their managers when referring and assessing possible cases of child neglect. In Chapter 6 the focus is on identifying and referring neglect. This chapter takes the discussion into the territory of professionals' roles and responsibilities in identifying neglect. Particular emphasis is placed on the roles of education and health workers and the police. Factors influencing practitioners' decisions to work with the case, or refer suspected cases of child neglect to social work services, are explored. Particular attention is given to blocks to referral, such as poor perceptions of social work practice, personal fears and anxieties of referral, and the 'battle of thresholds'.

Chapter 7 takes the process a stage further and considers the assessment process, once a case has been referred to social work services. The chapter includes a discussion of various frameworks and tools available to assist in assessing child neglect. A specific framework for assessing child neglect that I developed, as part of the Irish research studies, is provided. Drawing on the Irish research, attention is given to factors that distort assessment such as poor communication with the child, family and other professionals. The complexity of making judgements and decisions at different stages of the assessment process is explored.

Part IV Moving Practice Forward

In the final part of the book I attempt to draw on the topics covered in the previous sections to consider how to move practice forward, based on 'what works'. In Chapter 8 I consider some specific aspects of the assessment process that practitioners find particularly challenging in cases of child neglect. These include, assessing the carer's capacity to change, and factors that should be considered when planning interventions. I also explore forms of neglect which are particularly complex. These include chronic neglect; failure to thrive; lack of supervision; identifying neglect amongst refugee and asylum-seeking families and assessing neglect if the child is disabled or has complex health needs.

The final chapter moves us away from the family to consider practitioner capacity to identify and assess neglect. Drawing on findings from serious case reviews and inquires into child deaths from neglect; consideration is given to the personal, professional and organisational blocks that affect professional motivation. In this chapter, consideration is also given to practitioner ability: the knowledge and skills practitioners require to work effectively with these cases. If practitioners are to work effectively with child neglect they also need appropriate support from their organisation. Thus the role of training, the supervisor, and senior managers within agencies, in promoting effective practice and preventing professional neglect, is also discussed.

Terminology

Throughout the book, the term 'carer' is used in preference to 'parent'. The reason for this is that the term 'carer' acknowledges that adults other than parents may have parenting responsibility for a child. Unless reference is made to specific study findings the language used seeks to be gender neutral. An attempt has been made to use the term 'practitioner' to describe all staff who work directly with service users. The term seeks to be inclusive whilst recognising the current diversity among members of the child care workforce: in terms of qualifications and work settings. However, to avoid repetition on occasion the term 'professional' is used. In this context, it is used to include all staff who work on the front-line.

Part I

Identifying Neglect: What It Is and What It Does to Children

The following two chapters set the context for the rest of the book by determining first what we mean by neglect at the beginning of the 21st century in affluent nation states and second the ways in which neglected children are likely to present. Unless there is clarity about what constitutes neglect and the impact that it has on children practitioners will not be able to identify possible cases of child neglect effectively or undertake child-centred assessments.

In the first chapter, we discuss the definitions of neglect from the literature. The definitions are scrutinised to establish common themes, differences and gaps. Based on this discussion a working definition is constructed. This definition is included to ensure readers recognise what is being referred to throughout this book as 'child neglect' and to provide clarity for practitioners who are in situations where they may be identifying possible neglect.

The second chapter centres on the impact of neglect on children. In this chapter, consideration is given to the way in which neglect affects brain development and attachment strategies. The consequences of child neglect for physical, socio-emotional, cognitive and behavioural development are discussed. We also consider children who are particularly vulnerable to child neglect. This includes children born to mothers who use drugs during pregnancy, low birth weight babies; children with disabilities and complex health needs and the 'difficult-to-parent' child.

1

Defining Child Neglect: The Influence of Time and Place

Introduction

In competition gymnastics, there are clearly defined moves, such as a backward summersault. When a gymnast completes a backward summersault, they are told in minute detail what they should do. The coach and the competition judge know the components of a perfect move. The standards are the same the world over and are constant. Unfortunately, this is not the case with child neglect. The word 'neglect' originates from the Latin *neglectus* 'the fact of taking no notice' (Oxford University Press, 2003 cited in Lawrence & Irvine, 2004). However, neglect is not, of itself, a fact. How we define 'taking no notice' is influenced by time and place (Erickson & Egeland, 2002). As the concept of neglect is both constantly changing, and also interpreted differently in different communities, it makes conceptualising neglect difficult; particularly for practitioners who need to decide what constitutes child neglect in a particular setting at a specific time.

The aim of this chapter is to seek clarification as to how we conceptualise child neglect in the 21st century in developed countries. The chapter begins with an exploration of different definitions of child neglect, taken from government guidance and literature in the field. The commonalities and differences between these definitions are explored and the categorisation of the different types of neglect, included in the definitions, is considered in detail. The implications for practice are discussed. Informed by this discussion, a working definition of child neglect is provided. This working definition will be used throughout the book.

What is Child Neglect?

When I made the decision to collate definitions of child neglect, to explore themes and differences in conceptualising neglect, I thought it would be an easy task. I was wrong. Although there is a growing body of literature on child neglect, I was surprised at the number of publications that do not offer the reader a definition of neglect. What tends to happen is that reference is made to the complexity of attempting to conceptualise and define neglect. This may be the case, but how can we begin to work together, as practitioners or researchers, if we are not explicit about our understanding of neglect? Box 1.1 shows the definitions I obtained from government guidance, government websites and literature in the field.

An analysis of these definitions indicates that there is general agreement that child neglect is an omission, or failure on the part of the parent or carer, to provide adequate care for the child. However, what is adequate care? What is an act of omission? Does the failure have to be deliberate? If we go further and explore the terminology used within the definitions, then commonalities and conceptual differences begin to emerge. It is these very differences which can lead to practitioners talking at cross-purposes with each other when identifying and assessing child neglect.

Child Neglect as an Act of Omission

The definitions included in Table 1.1, make reference to 'omission', 'an inherent omission of a behaviour', 'failure to act', 'inadequate care', 'failure to provide' and 'failure to care for on the part of a parent or care-giver'. All these phrases indicate that neglect is, as is explicit in its Latin root, (discussed in the Introduction) an act of failure to notice on the part of the carer. Other forms of child maltreatment, such as hitting a child, are acts of commission. The New Zealand definition specifically differentiates between the two acts and Schumacher et al. (2001, p. 232) conclude 'neglect occurs when there is a deficiency in appropriate parenting behaviour, rather than when an inappropriate parenting behaviour occurs'.

Culpability

Little attention is paid in the definitions to culpability. Golden et al., (2003) argue that to fail to consider this can blur the boundaries between abuse and neglect. They argue that neglect has its roots in ignorance and competing carer priorities. Moreover, they argue the carer is without motive and unaware of the damage being caused, whilst child abuse has an element of

Box 1.1 Definitions of Child Neglect

Organisation/Author	Definition
World Health Organisation (2002, p. 60)	Neglect refers to the failure of a parent to provide for the development of the child – where the parent is in a position to do so – in one or more of the following areas: health, education, emotional development, nutrition, shelter and safe living conditions. Neglect is thus distinguished from circumstances of poverty in that neglect can occur only in cases where reasonable resources are available to family and caregiver.
USA Federal Law – Child Abuse Prevention and Treatment Act (CAPTA) (National Clearing House on Child Abuse and Neglect, no date para 1.31)	An act or failure to act which presents an imminent risk of serious harm. This provides a minimum definition for State Laws.
USA State Laws (general) (National Clearing House on Child Abuse and Neglect, no date p. 2)	Neglect is frequently defined in terms of deprivation of adequate food, clothing, shelter, or medical care. Several States distinguish between failure to provide based on the financial inability to do so and the failure to provide for no apparent financial reason. The latter constitutes neglect.
USA State Laws (specific) Arkansas, Florida, Louisiana, Pennsylvania, West Virginia, Wisconsin 30 states (National Clearing House on Child Abuse and Neglect, no date p. 3–4)	Financial inability to provide for a child is exempted from the definition of neglect. Provide an exemption from the definition of neglect for parents who choose not to seek medical care for their children due to religious beliefs.
England (HM Government, 2006, p. 9 para 1.33)	The persistent failure to meet a child's basic physical and/or psychological needs, likely to result in serious impairment of the child's health or development. Neglect may occur during pregnancy as a result of maternal substance abuse. Once a child is born, neglect may involve a parent or carer failing to provide

⊃

	adequate food and clothing, shelter including exclusion from home or abandonment, failing to protect a child from physical and emotional harm or danger, failure to ensure adequate supervision including the use of inadequate carer-takers or the failure to ensure access to appropriate medical care or treatment. It may also include neglect of, or unresponsiveness to, a child's basic emotional needs.
Republic of Ireland *Children First* (Department of Health and Children, 1999, p. 31, para 3.2.1–3)	Neglect can be defined in terms of an *omission*, where the child suffers significant harm or impairment of development by being deprived of food, clothing, warmth, hygiene, intellectual stimulation, supervision and safety, attachment to and affection from adults, medical care . . . Neglect generally becomes apparent *over a period of time.*
New Zealand Family Violence Clearing House (No date)	Neglect is defined as a failure to care for. As a point of differentiation from the wider definition of abuse, neglect can be viewed as an act of omission, rather than of commission.
Canada (Trocme et al., 2005, p. 120)	The child has suffered harm or the child's safety or development has been endangers as a result of the care-giver(s) failure to provide for or protect the child. Terminology is not consistent across provincial and territorial statutes, but interchangeable concepts include 'failure to care and provide or supervise and protect', 'does not provide', 'refuses or is unavailable or unable to consent to treatment'. Neglect covers failure to supervise, permitting criminal behaviour, physical neglect, medical neglect, failure to provide psychological treatment, abandonment, educational neglect, non-organic failure to thrive, emotional neglect and exposure to domestic violence.
Australia (Lawrence & Irvine, 2004, p. 4)	No uniform legal definition. Overall there are eight aspects of neglect covered by different states and territories. These include abandonment, physical neglect, medical neglect, psychological neglect, developmental neglect, supervisory neglect, failure to provide guidance (fostering delinquency), educational neglect.
Stowman, and Donohue, (2005, p. 492)	Child neglect is considered an act of omission in contrast to child abuse, which is an act of commission.

For instance, child neglect is often indicated by inadequate nutrition, clothing, hygiene, supervision, medical, dental or mental health care, unsafe environments, and abandonment or expulsions from the home and these neglect situations are influenced by the perpetrator's lack of care-taking behaviours. Indeed there is considerable agreement that it is important for care-givers to provide for the physical needs of their children, including food, clothing, shelter, supervision, medical care and education.

Connell-Carrick (2003, p. 390)

What most broadly distinguishes neglect from other forms of maltreatment is its inherent omission of a behaviour rather than a commission of behaviour as in the case of physical or sexual abuse.

Dubowitz, Black, Starr and Zuravin (1993, p. 9)

The persistent failure to meet a child's essential needs by omitting basic parenting tasks and responsibilities. The basic needs that are not usually met are those for adequate food, clothing, shelter, cleanliness, stimulation, medical care, safety, education and love and control, *in spite of parents having the economic resources to meet these needs at a basic level.*

Erickson and Egeland (2002, p. 3)

Typically defined as an act of omission rather than commission, neglect may or may not be intentional. It is sometimes apparent and sometimes nearly invisible until it is too late. Neglect is often fatal, due to inadequate physical protection, nutrition or health care. Sometimes, as in the case of 'failure to thrive' it is fatal. In some cases, neglect slowly and persistently eats away at children's spirits until they have very little will to connect with others or explore the world.

Rosenberg and Cantwell (1993, p. 186)

The child has the right to expect, and the adult care-taker has a duty to provide: food, clothing, shelter, safekeeping, nurturance and teaching. Failure to provide these constitutes neglect.

Minty and Pattinson (1994, p. 736)

A severe and persistent failure by a person having care for a child to provide food, hygiene, warmth, clothing, stimulation, supervision, safety precautions, affection and concern appropriate to the age and needs of the child to such an extent that the child's well-being and development are severely affected.

Garbarino and Collins (1999, p. 3)	Child neglect is a pattern of behaviour or a social context that has a hole in the middle where we should find the meeting of basic developmental needs.
Wolock and Horowitz (1984, p. 531)	The failure on the child's parent or care-taker who has the material resources to do so, to provide minimally adequate care in areas of health, nutrition, shelter, education, supervision, affection or attention and protection.
Strauss and Kaufman Kantor (2005, p. 20)	Neglectful behaviour by a care-taker is behaviour that constitutes a failure to act in ways that are presumed by the culture of a society to be necessary to meet the developmental needs of a child and which are the responsibility of a caregiver to provide.
English el al., (2005, p. 193)	Neglect is defined in terms of child needs that are potentially unmet and the subsequent impact on child functioning or development.

intentionality. However, if practitioners become over-exercised by determining whether the carer intended to harm the child the underlying causes and the implications of the act for the child may be lost (Erickson & Egeland, 2002).

An alternative approach is to conclude that intentionality is not of significance; what is of concern is the *impact* of the carer's behaviour on the child. This approach underpins the Irish Government's definition of neglect (Department for Health and Children, 1999, 3.2.1, p. 31). Dubowitz et al. (2005) argue that this approach is more appropriate for three reasons. First, it fits with our current interest in ensuring a child's health and well-being rather than blaming parents. Second, this emphasis is more likely to promote working with parents. Third, as neglect is multi-faceted there are likely to be other contributory causes over and above the parents' behaviour.

Abuse by Whom?

It would seem obvious that when we refer to neglect we are describing acts by carers towards children. But it is not so straightforward. Indeed, different emphasis is placed in the definitions in Table 1.1 on both various carers as perpetrators and also different developmental needs of children.

The Perpetrators

The majority of definitions, included in the Box 1.1, do refer to neglect as an act of omission committed by a parent or care-giver. Rosenberg and Cantwell (1993) refer specifically to adult caregivers. However, several statutes in the USA identify persons who are reportable for neglect. This includes parents, guardians, foster-parents, relations and other care-takers (National Clearing House on Child Abuse and Neglect, no date). Whilst the English government guidance recognises that carers have a responsibility, not only to meet the needs of their child, but also to ensure, if leaving the child that it is with other care-takers who will provide adequate supervision.

The Focus on Mothers

No reference is made, in the definitions, to the gender of the care-givers. Yet, reading the research literature on child neglect, one could easily presume that only neglectful mothers are capable of becoming neglectful carers. (For further discussion, see Chapter 3, also Forna, 1998; Swift, 1995; Turney, 2000; Turney, 2005.) This is reinforced in the research and literature, which is dominated by a focus on mothers, as perpetrators of child neglect (Schumacher et al., 2001). For example, Scourfield (2000), in a study of a social work team, concluded that *maternal* failure to adequately physically care for a child dominated the team's construction of child neglect. The focus on mothers goes beyond direct acts of omission to include indirect acts or possibly incidents for which they are not responsible. For example, Feldman et al., (1993), in a study of drowning, found professionals tended to blame the child's mother for the death, irrespective of the culpability of other carers. Whilst Scourfield (2001) found although social workers recognised the oppressed state of many women in neglectful families, and acknowledged they were often victims of domestic violence from their partners, they were still held responsible for protecting children.

Parenting Issues

Although, as discussed in Chapter 4, we are becoming increasingly aware of the impact of parenting issues, such as a learning disability or mental health issues, on a carer's ability and motivation to meet the needs of their child, only two definitions refer to the possibility of parenting issues influencing carer-giving behaviour, which may result in neglect. Polansky, (1998, p. 98) identify 'constant friction in the home, martial discord, mentally ill parents and [exposure] to unwholesome and demoralising circumstances' as jeopardising the welfare of the child. Whilst the English definition recognises that maternal substance misuse can affect an unborn child.

Collective or Societal Neglect

It is all too easy to presume that it is only carers who are responsible for neglect. However, the WHO (World Health Organisation, 2002) definition of child neglect, as well as those of some USA states, such as Arkansas, raises issues for practitioners and policymakers as to whether child neglect is always the result of a failure to act on the part of the parent or carer. Garbarino and Collins (1999) make reference to the social context in which neglect takes place. While the WHO (2002, p. 60) definition goes further and refers to neglect as 'the failure of a parent to provide for the development of the child – where the parent is in a position to do so'. Some American states recognise the need to distinguish between neglect, which is within the carer's control, and deprivation that is beyond their control. These states define neglect as a failure of the carer to meet the needs of the child, in spite of the availability of financial resources (National Clearing House on Child Abuse and Neglect, 2001). The failure of a society to provide support and services enabling parents to adequately meet the needs of children can be defined as societal or collective (Erickson & Egeland, 2002). Although societal neglect is not explicit in the English definition, the *Framework for the Assessment of Children in Need and their Families* (Department of Health et al., 2000) recognises that family and environmental factors may affect the carer's capacity to meet the needs of their child. Why do they have it in the first place?

The term societal neglect is rather vague. However, WHO (2002, p. 69) outlines the society-level factors that have important influences on the well-being of children and a carer's ability to meet the needs of their child. These include:

- The role of cultural values and economic forces in shaping family choices and their possible range of responses. These can influence the number of children parents have; expectations about working/non-working parents and opportunities for child-care. Families' choices about housing, health care, education and food are also influenced by economic forces. Cultural norms associated with gender roles, parent–child relationships and attitudes towards the family can influence expectations about approaches to parenting, supervision, health care, etc, as well as the division of the parenting tasks amongst male and female carers and the role of the extended family.
- Inequalities related to gender and income. This can result in certain groups in society, such as women and those living on state benefits, being more likely to live in poverty than the rest of the population. Discrimination towards women, particularly mothers, can increase stress and pressures on these women.

- Availability of preventative health care for children. Such services as routine dental, optical and health care checks can be used to identify early or emerging problems, not only in terms of the child's medical needs, but the carer's ability to physically care for their children.
- The quality of the social welfare system. This will determine whether the funding and services are sufficient to enable carers to meet the needs of their children, most notably to support vulnerable families.
- The nature and extent of social protection and the responsiveness of the criminal justice system. This will influence the ways in which issues of child neglect and other forms of maltreatment are identified and addressed.
- Larger social conflicts and wars. These will inevitably place tremendous strains on society and families affecting the ability to meet the needs of the child.

The influence of these factors on a carer's capacity to meet the needs of their child is explored in detail in Chapter 5.

Neglect in Affluent Families

As described above, conceptualising neglect means distinguishing poverty, and deprivation from neglect. This is discussed in detail in Chapter 5. However, a further challenge lies in recognising that neglect is not necessarily always associated with poverty. In the same way as there is a tendency to focus on mothers as perpetrators of child neglect, we also tend to focus on poorer families, when we think about neglect. It is important to remember that neglect can also occur in seemingly affluent families. As Garbarino and Collins (1999) note, neglect is not all about outward appearance, it is also about carers being psychologically there for their children. Increasingly we are becoming aware that children from affluent families can be deprived of their carers' attention. These carers often feel forced to work longer and longer hours in order to pursue their careers, spending less and less time with their children. Indeed, when they are with the children they are so exhausted that it is of little benefit to the child. The message children can receive in these homes is that they are not the main priority. For example, the carers may provide children with money to get their own food instead of preparing evening meals or school lunches, and offer material gifts or organised activities, instead of individual attention from the carer (Briggs & Hawkins, 1998). These parents or carers may also leave children at home unsupervised while they are at work. In summary, features of neglect in middle class families may include parental lack of interest in the child and putting the carers' own needs, such as furthering careers, before those of the children to the extent that they are never available for the child.

This is uncomfortable territory for practitioners. To a greater or lesser extent, any working practitioner who is also a carer, can identify with the tensions of balancing the demands of work with the needs of the children at home. However, Berliner (1994) questions whether this identification makes professionals reluctant to judge harshly parents from similar backgrounds managing similar circumstances to their own. Moreover, professionals may feel uneasy about criticising parents for acts of omission, such as inadequate supervision after school, which they themselves may commit. As practitioners, it is all too easy to hold stereotypical images of the neglecting family as poor, living in dirty homes with smelly children. These images can prevent us from recognising that chronic neglect can occur in a diverse range of settings. (This is discussed in further detail in Chapter 5.)

The Needs of the Child

A number of the definitions, included in Box 1.1, focus on the actual acts of omission paying little attention to the impact on the child. Other definitions refer to imminent risk of serious or significant harm, noting that at its worst neglect can result in the death of the child. Further definitions provide a list of the types of harm associated with neglect, such as emotional or physical harm. An additional set of definitions are more encompassing, recognising that neglectful acts and behaviours may not only cause significant harm but they can affect the health and development of the child. Focusing on the health and development of the child is most helpful as it enables practitioners to be explicit about the way in which the neglect is affecting the child. For example, The *Framework for the Assessment of Children in Need and their Families* (Department of Health et al., 2000) uses seven dimensions of children's developmental needs. These dimensions describe the different developmental needs of a child, which must be met during the different stages of childhood if the child is to develop into a healthy adult. These dimensions are important for children irrespective of race, gender, culture or ability (Ward, 2001). Drawing on the seven dimensions of developmental need and the literature on neglect, Box 1.2 summarises the different forms of neglect that can affect the health and development of a child.

What is concerning, about the definitions included in Box 1.1, is that little explicit attention is given to the child as an individual. Every child is unique and the needs of each child will vary depending on their age, gender, ethnicity, level of resilience and sources of support (See Chapter 2 for further detail). In addition, children may have supplementary needs such as special education or health needs. This is not recognised in the definitions in Box 1.1. However, it is crucial that practitioners take into account the particular needs of each individual child within a family (Department of Health et al., 2000). One cannot always predict a child's response to neglect. For example, the author recently read a case file, which recorded a situation where an eight-year-old child had returned home from school to an empty house. The child had become very distressed and the neighbours had contacted social work services. The mother returned home three hours later having been delayed at work and failed to organise suitable care arrangements. No further action was taken at the time. However, the child began to have nightmares about being left alone and refused to let the mother out of his sight. An assessment indicated that the child's father had left for work one morning and failed to return: he had gone to live with another woman. The child was frightened that his mother would also abandon him.

One-Off Incidents, Chronic and Episodic Neglect

The example above can be described as a one-off incident of neglect. However, the majority of definitions, included in Box 1.1, focus on continuing neglect with such phrases as 'chronic', 'persistent', 'severe' and 'ongoing'. The emphasis is on repeated neglect, which is indeed associated with cumulative developmental problems for children (Stone, 1998; Truman, 2004). This focus marginalises the two other possible forms of neglect: episodic neglect and one-off incidents. Episodic neglect may occur when there is a family crisis such as the parents separating or a carer suffering from physical or mental ill health. These episodic forms of neglect should not be ignored as they can have a detrimental effect on children (Nelson et al., 1993; Stevenson, 1998). They may also be indicative of an ongoing pattern of neglect and raise questions as to when episodic neglect becomes chronic. A good example of this dilemma is binge drinking by carers. The carer may well meet the needs of the child for most of the time. However, the child's experience will be very different when the carer is drinking. Although the periods of binge drinking may be short-lived they can contribute to a pattern of neglect at particular times which has a cumulative negative effect on the child.

An Accident or Neglect?

Neglect can also manifest itself through one-off incidents. Coincidentally, when writing this section of the book, a relevant article appeared in the English press. A headline read *'Mother on drinking binge left baby in car'* (Carter, 2004). The article described a situation where a mother left her 18-month-old daughter inappropriately dressed in a car outside a nightclub for five hours on a night when the temperature fell to $-2°C$. She was prosecuted and her solicitor argued

Box 1.2   Examples of Forms of Child Neglect Linked to the Child's Developmental Needs

Child's Developmental Need	Form of Child Neglect
Health: growth and development as well as physical and mental well-being	Health and development maybe affected through lack of: Sanitation causing disease Physical care Shelter Nutritious diet (this can lead to failure to thrive or obesity) Neglect of medical care can occur through: Refusal or delay of medical care for physical injury, illness or medical condition or impairment Not getting timely medical advice Not giving regular medication or treatment to control chronic disease Medical care inadequately provided for acute illnesses Lack of dental or optical treatment Neglect of the unborn child may occur through the use of drugs and alcohol, poor diet, lack of anti-natal care
Education: covers all areas of a child's cognitive development which begins from birth	Neglect of cognitive development includes: Inattention to general and special educational needs Failure to teach child acceptable language usage and comprehension Lack of toys, books or age appropriate activities to stimulate children In relation to education it covers: Permitted truancy Failure to enrol in school or pre-school Homework disregarded Lack of interest in child's school life
Emotional and behavioural development: concerns the appropriateness of response demonstrated in feeling and actions by a child	This includes inadequate nurturance or affection such as: Failure to promote attachment to carer Lack of consistent availability of carer Child placed in situation of unnecessary risk

	of emotional harm, e.g. witnessing domestic violence Child expected to take on parental role Failure to provide consistent messages about behaviour
Identity: concerns the child's growing sense of self as a separate and valued person	Lack of attention by carers to developing a positive self-image or sense of self-identity in child
Family and social relationships: development of empathy and the capacity to place self in someone else's shoes	Neglect concerns: Failure to enable child to develop a sense of empathy Giving no guidance regarding social or anti-social interactions Failing to provide opportunities to mix with peers
Social presentation: concerns child's growing understanding of the way in which appearance, behaviour and any impairment are perceived by the outside world and the impression being created	Lack of attention to personal hygiene so: Child dirty or smelly Clothing and shoes inappropriate for weather or unclean and in poor repair Lack of attention to personal hygiene
Self-care skills: concerns the acquisition by a child of practical, emotional and communication competencies required for increasing independence	These tend to relate to expecting too much of a child in terms of their self-care skills and include: Lack of age appropriate and consistent limit setting Lack of age appropriate supervision Making child vulnerable to foreseeable or avoidable injuries Placing child in situation of danger Making inappropriate judgements regarding danger to a child It also includes: Lack of attention to developing age appropriate self-care skills

(Rosenberg, 1993; Iwaniec, 1995; NCANDS, 1997; Stevenson 1998; Dubowitz 1999b; Sullivan 2000; Hobbs and Wynne 2002; Iwnaniec, 2002)

in court that it 'was a one-off occurrence'. Clearly, this situation was serious and could have been fatal for the child. Other one-off occurrences may appear minor and insignificant but they can still have a considerable impact on the child. The example of the eight-year-old boy above is a good example. One-off incidents, like episodic neglect may also be symptomatic of a pattern of neglect-ful behaviours. Stevenson (1998) argues that multiple minor accidents may be indicative of inadequate supervision and neglect and should be considered in that context. The kind of accidents that can be indicative of abuse and neglect include falls, choking on food, suffocation, drowning, residential fires and motor vehicle accidents (Bonner et al., 1999; Childhelp USA, 2003). In the overwhelming majority of deaths from neglect, recorded in the USA the care-giver was simply absent at a critical moment when the child was exposed to a hazard (Margolin, 1990). Official recording categories of 'accidental, natural or undetermined death' may obscure the prevalence of fatality from child neglect. Deaths attributed to such 'accidents' as drowning, suffocation, falls and poisoning are often classified as unintentional 'accidental' injuries. For example, between 7% and 27% of child deaths from abuse and neglect in the USA are believed to have been inaccurately classified as 'unintentional' (UNICEF, 2001). UNICEF (2001) in their report *'Child Deaths by Injury in Rich Nations'*, highlight how difficult it is to distinguish between accidental deaths and those caused by neglect. They describe how factors associated with neglect, such as poverty and poor housing, are also associated with injury and death from such causes as road traffic accidents and fire in the home.

Decisions as to whether an incident should be classed as an accident or neglect appear to be influenced by personal and professional beliefs. For example, Feldman et al., (1993) studied the factors that led medical profes-sionals, in the USA, to distinguish accidents involving drowning which they considered were indicative of neglect. They found a decision to report the family to Children's Protective Services, with concerns about neglect, was significantly more likely to occur if the child was young, non-white and from a poor family already known to social work services. In addition, cases where the injury occurred in a bathtub were the most commonly referred. However, an incident involving a four-year-old who wandered off at a church picnic and drowned in a lake was seen by respondents as an unfortunate accident. The professionals did not consider this to be a case of neglect although there was indication of possible lack of supervision by the carers and others present. This raises issues regarding ways in which professionals make a distinction between an accident and neglect. One way forward is to ascertain the child's perception of the isolated act/s of omission and their response to these acts and to note the similarities and differences between the child and carer's account of the incident. Moreover, the way in which the carer responds to the incident can be telling. Do they recognise that lack of supervision or their failure to ensure the safety of the child could have contributed to the accident? Do they blame others inappropriately? What efforts are the carers prepared to make to ensure the future safety and well-being of the child?

Types of Neglect

Although Garbarino and Collins (1999) describe neglect as a hole in the middle where there is a failure to meet the needs of the child. What is evident from the various definitions, included in Box 1.1, is that neglect does not take a single form. Rather, carers may neglect their children in very different ways. These include failure to:

- Meet basic physical needs for food, clothing, shelter and warmth.
- Provide appropriate health care including dental and mental health care.
- Meet the emotional developmental needs of the child.
- Ensure the child is adequately supervised and protected from harm.
- Provide appropriate cognitive stimulation both at home and in school.

However, different organisations and authors emphasise different aspects of care-taking behaviours. For example, the generalised term 'basic needs' is used in a number of definitions. In other definitions, specific reference is made to groups of needs such as physical, psychological and emotional. Other definitions include lists of the type of behaviours that constitute neglect such as denying the child normal feelings of being loved inadequate or dangerous housing Nelson et al. (1993).

Based on the definitions the following types of neglect have been identified:

- Medical neglect.
- Nutritional neglect.
- Emotional neglect.
- Educational neglect.
- Physical neglect.
- Lack of supervision and guidance.

Each of these are explored in detail below.

Medical Neglect

Medical neglect occurs when carers minimise or deny a child's illness or health needs, fail to seek appropriate medical attention or neglect to administer medication and treatments (Boxer et al., 1988; Ertem et al., 2002). Medical neglect includes neglect of all aspects of health care, including dental and optical care, speech and language therapy and physiotherapy. This form of neglect can be ongoing, such as a carer failing to take the child for regular medical or dental checks, and immunisations, ignoring tooth decay and possible hearing or sight problems. However, failure to make use of preventative services is not usually considered to be a reason for intervening because of neglect. Physicians are most likely to refer cases to child welfare services if they are concerned that failure to provide medical treatment is likely to have a serious effect on the child's health (Johnson, 1993). Whilst failing to take a child for regular health checks may appear less concerning than failing to provide treatment for an ill child, it can have a significant long-term effect on the health and well-being of the child. For example, a child who is short- or long-sighted but whose sight problems have not been identified and does not have spectacles may struggle at school reading what is written on white boards or computer screens. This in turn can affect their educational progress.

A group of children who are particularly vulnerable to medical neglect are children with complex needs. These children are often more dependent than other children on their carer being able to recognise and meet their specific health needs. This group of children may require intensive and extensive medical support for many years. These medical demands can place a strain on carers, particularly those living in poverty and without support systems. This in turn can result in some or all aspects of their medical care being neglected. (These issues are considered in detail in Chapter 8.)

When considering whether a case is medical neglect, Johnson (1993) found that physicians took into account economic, religious and intellectual variables that could affect the carers' approach. In addition, the physicians recognised that some treatments were controversial or had side effects that could influence the carer's behaviour. As shown in Box 1.1 a number of definitions of neglect exclude carers' failure to provide medical assistance to their child on the basis of religious beliefs. In the USA 24 states recognise a carer's right to refuse medical treatment on religious grounds. In most states, this must be a recognised religion and failure to give medical treatment must be in line with the beliefs of that religion (Iwaniec & McSherry, 2002). The challenge for practitioners, in these situations, is determining whether the rights of the carers to freedom to practice their religious beliefs should take precedence over the rights of the ill child to treatment (Dubowitz, 1999b). In England, the focus in such cases is on safeguarding and promoting the welfare of the child with the needs of the child being the primary consideration. Bross (1982 cited in Dubowitz, 1999b) suggests that in these type of cases practitioners should consider whether the lack of or delay in receiving medical attention, involves actual or potential harm to the child's health. Moreover, they should assess whether the recommended medical care offers significant benefits outweighing the side effects and risks of not receiving this care. In these situations in England if the child is 'Gillick competent', that is considered mature enough to give an informed opinion, it is also important to establish their wishes and feelings.

Medical neglect can also be linked to societal neglect. The reduction in preventative services for children, such as home visiting by health visitors, regular medical checks at school and free dental checks, which is occurring in some countries such as England, means that the health needs of the child may only be detected when they are already suffering.

What are the parents doing?

Nutritional Neglect

Nutritional neglect is usually associated with the child or infant being provided with inadequate calories for normal growth (Hobbs & Wynne, 2002). Whilst practitioners are often concerned about this within the first few months of a child's life it may only become a problem as the child is weaned. For example, carers who are not particularly tuned into the needs of their baby may manage during the first few months of the baby's life, as the baby just requires milk. However, after 6 months the baby needs additional nourishment. This can be time consuming and messy and may be neglected or rushed resulting in a decline in growth velocity. In addition, as the child develops, carers may pay little attention to balancing the child's diet or noting what the child eats, with children being given 'a bit of this and a bit of that but not given an adequate meal at any time' (Rosenberg & Cantwell, 1993, p. 193). Nutritional neglect is frequently associated with failure to thrive but increasingly we are recognising the link to obesity. These two forms of nutritional neglect are considered below.

Failure to Thrive

Failure to thrive 'is defined as failure to grow physically (in terms of weight, height and head circumference) as well as psychologically (including cognitive and psychosocial development)' (Iwaniec & Sneddon, 2002, p. 285). The view commonly held by professionals, up to the early 1990s, was that non-organic failure to thrive was a form of nutritional neglect. Indeed non-organic failure to thrive was included in the 1991 English definition of child neglect in *Working Together under the Children Act 1989: A Guide of Inter-Agency Co-operation for the Protection of Children* (Department of Health et al., 1991). However, further research in the field indicates that whilst neglect may be associated with failure to thrive, for many children this is not the case (Wright, 1995; Batchelor, 1999; Iwaniec, 2004). Increasingly, failure to thrive is recognised as resulting from a number of interconnected causes relating to the child, the carer and the context in which the child and carer live. For example,

Batchelor (1999), in a review of the research, summarises the causal factors, which are consistently highlighted in studies as contributing to failure to thrive. These include:

- Baby's feeding inefficiency.
- Feeding skills disorders and oral-motor problems.
- The carer's IQ.
- Feeding practices.
- Carer's eating attitudes and habits.
- The carer's ability to recognise and adapt their feeding to address the child's feeding problems.

While only a small number of cases of failure to thrive are linked to neglect, when neglect and failure to thrive are both present the effect on the child can be devastating. Mackner and Starr (1997) found children experiencing both failure to thrive and neglect performed less well cognitively than children who were either neglected or failing to thrive.

The dilemma for the practitioner is how to differentiate failure to thrive, caused by neglect on the part of the carer, from failure to thrive originating from other causes. Iwaniec (2004) suggests this can be achieved by considering the different *routes* that result in failure to thrive. In the case of child neglect, this is likely to be linked to carers' lack of understanding about the nutritional needs of the child. Or, the carer may understand what the child needs but lack the motivation to meet these needs. Mental health issues, drug and alcohol misuse may also influence the ability and motivation of the carer, resulting in a failure to meet the needs of the child. (The assessment challenges associated with failure to thrive and neglect are explored in Chapter 8.)

Obesity

Traditionally, neglect has been associated with failing to provide children with sufficient calories. There is however, another form of nutritional neglect that is becoming more common place and can have severe long-term consequences for children, heightening risks to health as adults and increasing the development of 'diseases of age' such as type 2 diabetes, in the children themselves (The International Obesity TaskForce, 2005). That is providing children with an unhealthy diet and lack of exercise that result in childhood obesity.

The International Obesity TaskForce (2005) reports that overweight and obesity is increasing rapidly in many European countries, with one in five children being overweight. The steepest rises are in England and Poland. The Department of Health, 2005, found between 1995 and 2003 the prevalence of obesity amongst children 2 to 10 rose from 9.9% to 13.7%, with the percentage of those overweight rising from 22.7% to 27.7%. Jay (2004) notes a similar increase in childhood obesity in the USA with 11% to 19% of adolescents estimated to be obese. There are twice the number of overweight children and three times the number of overweight adolescents, in the USA, as there were 30 years ago (CDC, 2003).

Childhood obesity in both England and the USA is also more prevalent amongst the lowest socio-economic groups (Livingstone, 2000; Department of Health, 2005). It has a physical consequence increasing risk of heart disease and diabetes and can also have psychological and social effects on children; leaving them with a low sense of self-esteem, isolated and vulnerable to bullying by their peers (Valios, 2004a). Carers have a crucial part to play in terms of influencing the quality and quantity of food intake and activity patterns in preschool children. As children grow up they are not so much under parents control, however those early habits are likely to influence subsequent eating patterns (Jeor et al., 2002). The particular early eating patterns associated with overweight status includes regular consumption of sweetened beverages, sweets, energy dense foods, snacking and fast foods replacing regular meals (Nicklas et al., 2003; Sabin et al., 2004). Lack of exercise also contributes to obesity.

The Role of Society in Nutritional Neglect

Society has a part to play in nutritional neglect. For example, food 'deserts' exist in many densely populated deprived urban areas and small rural communities, meaning families do not have access to affordable nutritious food. These families cannot reach the out of town superstores and are dependent on the more expensive, limited choice of local convenience stores or takeaway outlets (Valios, 2004a). Therefore, access to fresh and nutritious food is restricted. Parents not only need to have access to food they also need to know how to provide nutritious meals. Sadly, changes to the education curriculum in England and other countries means that many young people are not taught how to prepare meals. This is illustrated by the following example. Recently in a supermarket, I overheard two young mothers. One had picked up a packet of dried spaghetti and was attempting to read the instructions. She asked her friend if the spaghetti was similar to what was in tins and was wondering whether it would be more economical. Her friend turned around and said she was not sure but there was no point buying it as they did not know how to cook it.

There are some indicators that society's role is being recognised and changes are taking place. For example, as a result of the endeavours of a celebrity chef in England, the Government has introduced initiatives to improve the nutritional value of school dinners and attempts are being made in schools to educate children to eat healthily and exercise regularly.

Emotional Neglect

A number of the definitions, included in Box 1.1, refer to 'emotional develop-ment', 'emotional harm' 'unresponsiveness to a child's basic emotional needs' and indeed 'emotional neglect'. Iwaniec (1995, p. 5) defines emotional neglect as the 'hostile or indifferent parental behaviour which damages a child's self-esteem, degrades a sense of achievement, diminishes a sense of belonging and stands in the way of healthy, vigorous and happy development'. While Erickson and Egeland (2002, p. 6) refer to carers being 'psychologically unavailable'. Iwaniec (1995) helpfully makes a distinction between emotional neglect and abuse, describing the former as non-deliberate and the latter as deliberate acts of parental action. Hence, emotional neglect is a non-deliberate consequence of a carer's neglectful behaviour.

Carers, who emotionally neglect the child fail to interact with the child, do not provide physical or emotional affection and do not develop the child's sense of self-worth and positive identity. Iwaniec (ibid) argues that emotional neglect frequently originates from the carer's lack of awareness and ignorance of appropriate child-rearing models and their failure to understand the conse-quences of lack of attention to the emotional needs of a child. This lack of awareness is often linked to the carers own childhood experiences, depression, chaotic lifestyles and lack of support and is discussed in Chapter 3. Whatever the cause, emotional neglect can have a significant impact on the child's ability to feel positive about themselves and others as described in Chapter 2. In its extreme form, it can result in failure to thrive, stunted growth and physical illness (Erickson & Egeland, 2002; Iwaniec, 1995).

Educational Neglect

Educational neglect is often interpreted as carers failing to comply with state requirements regarding school attendance (Erickson & Egeland, 2002). Across the world more than 130 million children between 6 and 11 years of age are not in school and 60% of them are girls (World Health Organisation, 2002). However, educational neglect does not just mean complying with state require-ment for school attendance. It includes broader aspects of education, for example providing a stimulating environment for the child, including the infant and pre-schooler; showing an interest in the child's education at school; supporting their learning and ensuring that any special educational needs are met. An abiding memory for me is of a five-year-old child, starting school. For weeks beforehand she had talked enthusiastically about going to school. Although her father took her to school on her first day, albeit late, no one was there to collect her at the end of the day. Her teacher described how she had stood by the school entrance desperate to show her parents the picture she had painted. The following day, on a visit to the home, I noted the picture torn and tattered in the corner of the room, muddy paw prints all over it. A month later that five-year-old was miserable and reluctant to go to school. Her parents were the only parents in the class who had not attended an open day. Her reading pack was the only one returned to school each day unread but dirty with pages torn and missing. Her attendance was poor. She was late on a regular basis and frequently not collected on time. She became aware that she was dressed differently from the other children and smelt. When she went home from school no one asked her what she did at school; there were no toys or books in the home to stimulate her, and no one to answer the long list of questions a five-year-old wants answered. She quickly gained the impression that taking her to school was a burden to her parents and what she did there was not to be talked about. She learnt not to mention school or ask her parents to help her with her reading. She also kept quiet at school about the lack of support at home. By the time she was six she was falling behind educationally, she had no friends, her attendance was erratic and on the occasions when she was taken to school she would run away or try and hide in a store cupboard.

This is more than emotional neglect – this child was heated up in one very easy.

Physical Neglect

This type of neglect is the one most familiar to practitioners. At its worst the smell of dirt, decay and excrement hits you as you enter the home. The floor is filthy and your shoes stick to the surface. There are children, dogs and cats everywhere. Clothes, stale food and the general detriment of daily living lie around you. There is little furniture and what is there is broken or damaged. The rooms are poorly decorated with evidence of damp and other health hazards in every room. Some practitioners do not look beyond these physical conditions and become preoccupied with 'dirt, mess and smell in the identification of neglect' (Scourfield, 2000, p. 372). Other practitioners minimise physical neglect, describing the children as 'dirty but happy'.

Based on the definitions included in Box 1.1, physical neglect is the form of neglect that is most easy to describe and would include 'failure to provide an adequate hygienic living environment', 'ill-clad', dirty clothing', 'without proper shelter or sleeping arrangements', lack of 'cleanliness' and poor 'hygiene', to select but a few terms used in the definitions.

Despite the ease with which we can describe physical neglect, identifying and assessing physical neglect is complex. Practitioners can become exercised by making judgements that go beyond considering the impact of the neglect on the child. This occurs because physical neglect involves distinguishing between neglect and deprivation. For example, the quality of the accommodation may affect the carer's ability to provide an adequate, hygienic living environment but financial circumstances may mean the family have no alternative but to remain in the accommodation. Physical neglect also involves making judgements about adequate standards. This can be particularly difficult with practitioners reluctant to impose their own standards on families. A consequence of this reluctance can be that we accept standards of physical care that can have a significant detrimental impact on the child. In addition, as detailed in Chapter 5, practitioners can become desensitised to the effects of poor physical environments on children if they are working regularly with families living in these conditions.

When considering the impact of physical neglect on a child it is all too easy to focus on health and safety. After all, the physical health of a child is likely to be affected if they are living in a damp, cold house. Likewise, if they are living in a home with loose electric wires, no fireguard or stair gate they may injure themselves. However, physical neglect can have less obvious consequences, which affect the emotional, cognitive and social development of the child. For example, a child who is inadequately dressed and is not sent to school clean and tidy may suffer bullying at school; they may become isolated from their peers or indeed truant from school to avoid the miserable experience of not fitting in. Alternatively, children may be ashamed of their parents and home and avoid bringing friends home, living a dual existence.

Failure to Provide Supervision and Guidance

The definitions included in Box 1.1 make reference to a range of different types of behaviours which can be construed as lack of supervision. These include 'failure to protect from physical harm or danger', 'inadequate supervision or abandonment', 'desertion'. Lack of supervision is a key component in many cases of fatal child neglect (Rosenberg & Cantwell, 1993). A longitudinal research study of mothers and children, completed in Minnesota, (described in detail in Chapter 2) found that lack of supervision was prevalent amongst the six-years-olds in their sample of neglectful mothers. The children were left regularly to cope on their own in situations that they did not have the skills to manage. For example, they were left alone for lengthy periods or were placed in dangerous situations (Pianta et al., 1989). The problem for both the general public and professionals, when deciding if a lack of supervision is neglect, is determining what levels of supervision a child needs at what age. Box 1.3 describes examples of types of supervisory neglect that can occur at different ages. Ways of assessing the different types of supervisory neglect are considered in Chapter 8.

Whilst we tend to focus on lack of supervision amongst younger children, inadequate parental supervision can have a significant affect on adolescents, most notably in terms of increasingly the potential for anti-social behaviour. For example, Graham and Bowling (1995) found that 42% of young people who had low or medium levels of parental supervision had offended, whilst only 20% of those who experienced high levels of supervision had committed

---

Box 1.3   Types of Supervisory Neglect

Age	Forms of Supervisory Neglect
Infancy under 12 months	Child left unattended on a surface so can fall Sibling left to supervise baby without the knowledge and experience to recognise a dangerous situation Baby left to feed themselves Baby left alone in bath
Preschool under 5	Home is not 'child proof' and child left to explore unsupervised or without safety devices such as stair gates and fire guards Medicines, drugs toxic substances left lying around Child expected to complete task unsupervised inappropriate for age, e.g. bathing self Child allowed to play outside on road, in play area unsupervised Child left in the house alone Carer in house but not supervising child. For example, asleep or intoxicated Child left in care of an unsuitable carer
Primary school age 5–11 years	Primary school child regularly left at home after school until carer returns Older siblings expected to supervise younger ones after school and during holidays without knowledge and experience to provide appropriate care Children left to play outside in dangerous settings Children cooking meals without guidance Children staying out at night, carers unaware of their whereabouts or failed to check on quality of supervision, for example child staying at friend's house without circumstances being checked
Secondary school age 11–16 years	Carer does not distinguish between leaving older child occasionally and continually Adolescents left to own devises carers unaware of their whereabouts Adolescent staying out at night carers failed to check on quality of supervision.

(Adapted from Jones, 1997; Rosenberg & Cantwell, 1993)

crimes. This can be exacerbated if there is a poor relationship between the child and their carer. Lack of supervision can be particularly damaging when it is accompanied by lack of guidance. For example, young people who are not given clear guidance about the consequences of for example, alcohol and drug misuse, unprotected sex, etc, are particularly vulnerable when unsupervised. This has led to a significant shift in England to work, not only with young people about such issues as truancy and offending, but also with their carers. The aim being to develop parents' skills, most particularly with regard to adhering to rules and learning how to negotiate boundaries with their children (Home Office et al., 2004).

Most forms of child neglect are generally associated with socio-economically deprived parents. However as described earlier in this Chapter, supervisory neglect goes well beyond this group of parents to include middle and upper class parents who leave their children at home after school and in the holidays whilst they are at work. This group rarely come to the attention of child welfare agencies although they are placing their children in the type of vulnerable situations described in Box 1.3.

Adequate Care: Standards and Judgements

No matter how explicit we are in differentiating between the different types of neglect, identifying child neglect requires a social judgement about minimal standards of care (Garbarino & Collins, 1999). For example, do all members of a community share the same ideas as to what constitutes inadequate or dangerous housing? Do we share minimum standards of care related to the physical, emotional and psychological needs of a child? Some studies in the USA conclude that there is a commonly held minimum standard of child care (Craft & Staut, 1991; Polansky et al., 1983). However, other researchers have found that members of the lay community hold different views about child maltreatment and these vary with socio-economic status, gender, ethnicity and education (Berliner, 1994; Dubowitz et al., 1998; Giovannoni & Becerra, 1979; Ringwelt & Caye, 1989; Rose & Meezan, 1996). In addition, the values and beliefs of those interpreting the definitions of neglect have been found to influence the way in which they are operationalised (Truman, 2004; Wolock & Horowitz, 1984). Two key factors that appear to influence the interpretation of adequate care are the cultural filters and professional perspectives.

Cultural Filters

A minority of the definitions in Box 1.1 make reference to the cultural context. 'Culture is a society's common fund of beliefs and behaviours, and its concepts of how people should conduct themselves' (World Health Organisation, 2002, p. 59). This 'fund' influences cultural standards with regard to child rearing practices. Whilst Stevenson (1998) and Ward (2001) note that there is significant cross cultural agreement about the basic needs for healthy child development, Korbin and Spilsbury (1999) argue the way in which parents interpret and prioritise children's needs will depend on cultural filters. For example, there are variations amongst cultural groups regarding the level of supervision required to ensure a child's safety and well-being. This varies depending on cultural child-care practices such as sibling care-giving, and community responsibility for child supervision. However, Ferrari (2002), in the USA, explored the impact of culture on child-rearing practices and the interpretation of definitions of maltreatment. Her findings indicate that difference in child-rearing practice is related more to *views* about child-rearing practices rather than membership of a particular ethnic group. With this in mind, as considered in Chapter 4, practitioners should ask families about their views with regard to parenting rather than make presumptions based on their ethnicity and cultural heritage.

Practitioners' Attitudes towards Standards of Care

In exactly the same way that members of a community may not necessarily be in agreement about adequate standards of care, child welfare practitioners may hold differing views about adequate care. For example, social work personnel would seem to accept lower standards of care then the general public or other professionals (Birchall & Hallett, 1995; Craft & Staut, 1991; Rose & Meezan, 1997; Rose & Selwyn, 2000; Horwath, 2005). Moreover, different professionals place emphasis on different aspects of care. For example, I found in a study of child neglect (described in detail in the introduction to Part III), that social workers' concerns about an inappropriate home environment for a three-year-old were different to those of practitioners who refer cases of child neglect to social work services. These differences raise questions as to what extent referral and assessment of child neglect are affected by practitioners' interpretation of good enough, borderline and inadequate parenting. If these differences are not identified and acknowledged, when practitioners work together, they can result in the focus on the child becoming lost. (The impact of differences in perceptions amongst practitioners is a focus in Chapters 6 and 7.)

Neglect: A Working Definition

As described above, defining child neglect is no easy task. The review of the definitions included in Box 1.1, highlights some of the problems for practi-

tioners conceptualising what is meant by neglect and using the available definitions of child neglect to make sense of particular situations. In light of this
review and the problems considered above, the following working definition
will be used throughout this book.

> *Child neglect is a failure on the part of either the male and/or female care-*
> *giver or pregnant mother, to complete the parenting tasks required to ensure*
> *that the developmental needs of the child are met. This should take into*
> *account the age, gender, culture, religious beliefs and particular needs and*
> *circumstances of the individual child. This failure, may be associated with*
> *parenting issues, It has occurred despite reasonable resources being available*
> *to enable the carer/s to complete the parenting tasks satisfactorily. Whilst*
> *neglect is likely to be ongoing, one-off incidents and episodic neglect can affect*
> *the health and development of a child.*

This definition draws on the listed definitions in Box 1.1 and the available
research and literature to bring together all the key components that practitioners should consider when deciding whether a child is a victim of child
neglect. What it does not do is provide a prescriptive definition. This is intentional. The task for the practitioner is to decide what is meant by such terms as
'failure' 'reasonable resources' and 'completing parenting tasks satisfactorily' in
relation to each individual child. As will be argued throughout this book, practitioners will only stay child-focused when identifying and assessing cases of
child neglect, if they are prepared to make professional judgements about these
terms in relation to the individual child, using an evidence-based approach to
practice.

Summary

The focus of this chapter has been a review of the literature of definitions of
child neglect, in order to consider conceptual challenges, and in light of these
challenges, to develop a working definition designed to assist practitioners
identify and assess possible child neglect.

The review of definitions indicates that there is some agreement amongst
policymakers and researchers about what constitutes neglect. First, what distinguishes neglect from other forms of maltreatment is that it is an act of omission rather than commission. Second, that this act of omission is a failure on
the part of the parent or carer to provide adequate care for the child. However,
despite this agreement when exploring the implications of this conceptualisa-
tion of neglect to practice different features of neglect are given different
emphasis. These include:

- Differing attention to intentionality on the part of the carer. I argue in the chapter that it may be more constructive to focus on the affect on the child, rather than becoming over exercised with a focus on whether the carer deliberately intended to neglect the child.
- Although there is a general recognition that perpetrators of neglect are usually parents or carers, the literature and research indicates that practitioners tend to focus on neglect by mothers, marginalising the care-taking role of fathers. Moreover, few definitions consider neglect by others in a care-giving role, or the responsibility of the carer to ensure that child is always adequately cared for.
- Few definitions recognise that parenting issues, such as drug misuse and domestic violence, can in some cases be associated with child neglect.
- In addition, only a minority of definitions recognise societal or collective neglect. This exists when society or the community fails to provide the resources required enabling carers to meet the needs of their children.

Neglect is usually defined as chronic acts of omission. Yet, episodic failure to meet the needs of a child and one-off incidents can have a significant effect on a child. These episodic or isolated incidents may be indicative of developing neglectful behaviour. Alternatively, they may be an indication that the family is suffering stress or a temporary crisis as a result of parenting issues such as bereavement, separation or mental illness.

There are a range of parenting behaviours that can be classed as forms of neglect. These include:

- Medical neglect. This is a failure to seek and provide appropriate medical, dental and optical care for children. Medical neglect is most likely to be addressed if the child's health is going to be significantly affected as a result of failure to treat the medical condition. Practitioners may encounter situations where carers fail to provide medical care because of religious beliefs. In these situations, practitioners will need to balance the rights of the carers to their religious beliefs with those of the child to medical care.
- Nutritional neglect. This occurs when the carer fails to pay sufficient attention to the diet of a child and they become overweight leading to obesity. Alternatively, the carer may fail to provide adequate nourishment for the child and they fail to thrive. Whilst non-organic failure to thrive has in the past been directly linked to child neglect, research in the 1990s indicates that there is not always a direct correlation. However, cases of child neglect together with failure to thrive leave a child in a very vulnerable situation.
- Emotional neglect. The difference between emotional neglect and abuse

is intentionality. Emotional neglect occurs when the carer as a result of their neglectful behaviour fails to meet the child's emotional needs resulting in damage to the child's self-esteem, their sense of achievement and belonging and preventing healthy and happy development.

- Supervisory neglect. This form of neglect occurs when the carer fails to provide the level of guidance and supervision to ensure that the child is physically safe and protected from harm. It includes abandoning or deserting children and leaving them with inappropriate carers. Although this type of neglect is usually considered in terms of younger children with much debate as to what age it is appropriate to leave a child alone, it affects all age ranges and increasingly we are becoming aware of this as a common form of neglect amongst adolescents. It occurs when the carers fail to provide appropriate boundaries allowing a child to take alcohol under age, condoning under age sex, etc. The combination of lack of supervision and lack of guidance can place children, of all ages in particularly vulnerable situations.
- Educational neglect. This is more than not ensuring children attend school. It includes the failure on the part of the carer to provide an environment where a child is able to achieve their cognitive potential. This is likely to occur through lack of stimulation, support and encouragement.
- Physical neglect. Traditionally child neglect has been associated with physical neglect: dirty, smelly children in dirty, poorly furnished homes. Whilst practitioners recognise the health and safety issues associated with physical neglect the impact on the child's emotional, cognitive and social development is often ignored.

The way in which practitioners make decisions about the types of carer behaviour that constitute neglect is largely determined by cultural and societal standards of 'good enough parenting'. However, it is important that practitioners do not make sweeping judgements based on these standards, rather they should consider the specific developmental needs of each child and consider ways in which the parents failure to complete parenting tasks is affecting the particular child taking account of their age, gender, culture, support networks, special needs and circumstances.

This chapter concluded with a working definition of child neglect, which will be used throughout this book and should assist practitioners in remaining child focused when identifying and assessing child neglect.

2

Living with Child Neglect: The Impact on Children

Introduction

> Neglect is an insidious form of maltreatment. It starves the developing mind of stimulation. It denies the child information and interest about the self and others.
>
> (Howe, 2005, p. 111)

This statement describes, starkly and succinctly, the way in which neglect affects children. These effects will not only make the children's young lives miserable but will also influence the way in which they form relationships with others in later life and indeed parent their own children. In this Chapter, we consider the devastating effects that neglect can have on children and young people, whilst in Chapter 3 we consider the ways in which experiences of child neglect can in turn affect parenting.

Hildyard and Wolfe (2002), summarising the literature on the impact of child neglect, highlight the fact that neglect can have damaging long-term effects on a child's physical, socio-emotional, cognitive and behavioural development. In other words, it affects all the development needs of the child. Key to understanding how neglect affects this development is recognising that the environment in which a child is brought up impacts on the developing brain with long-term implications for the child's physical development, emotional and behavioural reactions and psychological health. In the Introduction to this book, the lack of research on the impact of neglect on children was noted. One area where there has been considerable development in recent years, in terms of attempting to understand how neglect affects children, has been research about the impact of neglect on the developing brain. This work will, therefore, be the focus of the first part of this chapter. We then move on to consider how this affects socio-emotional, physical, cognitive and behavioural development. However, before beginning this exploration we should ascertain the prevalence of neglect.

Prevalence of Neglect

What is particularly distressing, about child neglect, is recognising just how many children are living with neglectful carers and consequently leading unhappy lives with negative long-term consequences. In 2002–3 in the Australian states of Queensland, Western Australia and South Australia child neglect was the most common substantiated form of abuse. In Canada in 2003, neglect made up 34% of all frequently substantiated forms of maltreatment whilst exposure to domestic violence contributed to 26% of all cases. Physical neglect, which includes inadequate nutrition or clothing, and unhygienic and/or dangerous living conditions, was found in 9% of substantiated cases (Trocme et al., 2005). In England, the number of cases of child neglect rose from 13%, of all cases of confirmed maltreatment in 1988 to 39% (10,800) in 2002, to 43% (13,200) in 2005 making neglect by far the most common category for child protection registration[1] (Department for Education and Skills, 2005). The pattern is similar in the USA with child neglect increasing (Roditti, 2005). In the USA 59% of all confirmed cases of maltreatment are now described as neglect. This increase in levels of child neglect can be attributed to a number of factors. First, there may be more children being neglected than previously. Roditti (2005) argues that this increase can, in part, be attributed to the increase in substance misuse, which, as discussed in Chapter 4, means that some parents find they are unable to meet the needs of the child. This increase could also be attributed to increased professional understanding of the impact of neglect on children and a recognition that these cases should be assessed and services provided to meet the needs of the children.

It is difficult establishing the levels of neglect in developing countries, and indeed comparing any figures obtained with those from developed nations, bearing in mind the different socio-economic systems and levels of societal neglect. Nevertheless, neglect is also prevalent in developing countries. For example, in a study of maltreatment completed in Kenya, 21.9% of children reported neglect by their parents (WHO, 2002). However, what is interpreted as neglect may be different in developing countries to what we perceive to be neglect in developed countries. For example, the emphasis is likely to be on abandonment and gross physical neglect, which may well be associated to socio-economic factors such as being unable to afford to care for a child, lack of sanitation and health care.

Mortality

Clearly, the effects of neglect will vary depending on the individual child and the carer's neglectful behaviour. At the very least, neglect is likely to delay the child's development, at worst it can lead to significant long-term harm, and in a few cases, the death of a child. The extent to which child neglect is associated with death is difficult to ascertain because, as discussed in Chapter 1, many child deaths are categorised as accidental and the causes not investigated.

Turning to the actual statistics, Reder and Duncan (1999) found neglect was the cause of death in 26% of their sample of child deaths reported to the Department of Health. However, Sinclair and Bullock (2002) in their study of the child death and serious injury cases reported to the Department of Health, found that neglect was the immediate cause of death, or injury, in only 6% (n = 3) of cases. However, Sinclair and Bullock go on to consider the salient features of the other cases and found that accidental/natural causes of death, possibly resulting from neglect, were present in 25% (n = 10) of the cases. Neglect was the single leading cause of death for children who died from child abuse in 2001 in the USA with 36% of deaths being attributed to neglect and a further 22% to neglect and physical abuse (Childhelp USA, 2003). In the USA, Rosenberg and Cantwell (1993) found that mortality arising from neglect is often due to lack of supervision and to a lesser extent medical or nutritional neglect. The typical neglect fatality in the USA is a male child under three, living with his mother and two or three brothers and sisters.

The Impact of Neglect on the Brain

Before beginning the exploration of brain development it is important to note that what follows is aimed at providing an overview for non-specialist practitioners. It is impossible, within the confines of one chapter, to provide a detailed analysis. The purpose is to ensure that practitioners have an understanding of why and in what way early childhood experiences of neglect can have long-term and in some cases devastating effects on the child. As our knowledge in these areas is developing all the time and is the subject of much debate, readers are encouraged to read the following papers, which have been used to prepare the section below. These are: Greenough et al., 1987; Karr-Morse and Wiley 2000; Glaser, 2000; Schore, 2002; Davies, 2002; Perry, 2004; Schaffer, 2004; Bellis, 2005.

The parts of the child's brain that develop, and those that do not, depend significantly on the care-giving experiences in the early years (Perry & Pollard, 1997; Glaser, 2000; Armstrong, et al., 2000; Schore, 2002). Thus, experiences of abuse and neglect in infancy can have long-term effects on the way we function (National Clearinghouse on Child Abuse and Neglect, 2001). As Hildyard and Wolfe (2002) conclude from their literature review of child neglect, if neglect occurs early on in life then the consequences are most severe and can be irreversible. Why?

Brain Development

In order to understand why this is the case it is worth exploring what is known about the way in which the brain develops.

The Development of Brain Cells and Connections

Brain development begins well before birth. The development of the brain of a foetus is faster than that of all other parts of the body and this continues for the first few years of life. At birth, the baby's brain is about 25% of the weight of an adult's brain and by three months, it is about 40%. By the time the child is three years old, the brain has reached almost 90% of its adult size. The growth in the size of the brain in the foetal period is due to the production of millions of '*neurons*' or brain cells. Following birth, the increase in weight and volume of the brain is due primarily to the growth of '*synapses*' or connections between the neurons.

Experience-Expectant and Experience-Dependent Systems

A newborn baby has two neural systems that operate differently. There is the '*experience-expectant*' system. This describes those neural pathways that are pre-wired and already established at birth because they are essential for survival following birth. They are mainly linked to reflexes and functions such as heart-rate, sucking and breathing. The second neural system is dependent on inter-action and sensory input. The creation of these neural connections, their maintenance and development are '*experience-dependent*', needing external stimuli such as sight, touch, sound and movement. These neural connections require another person to interact with a baby. This interaction activates specific neuronal connections and allows for the creation of new synapses and the strengthening of existing ones – *the pathways* – or connections in the brain. The pathways that are made reflect the experiences of the child. For example, a neglected infant who is left in a pushchair or cot all day, rarely talked to, never cuddled, with no toys or other forms of stimulation will have the type of limited experiences that negatively affects the development of these pathways. When repeated experiences strengthen a neuronal pathway, the pathway becomes '*sensitised*' and a '*memory*' is created. Memories are the way in which the brain stores information for ready retrieval. For example, remembering how to walk.

Critical and Sensitive Periods

A neglectful carer may fail to respond to the specific needs of a baby or child at different times in their life. This can have serious consequences particularly for an infant for the following reasons. In the early years, different parts of the brain develop at different stages. The development begins with the brain stem. This controls the basic and essential functions for life such as heart rate, respiration and body temperature. The mid brain is the next to develop. This controls appetite and sleep. The limbic part of the brain follows, controlling emotions and impulses and finally the cortex develops, which controls cognitive functions. As each part of the brain develops it require specific experiences to stimulate the particular brain function that is developing. '*Critical periods*' is the term used to describe the time when a specific part of the brain is open to stimulation. Vision develops in such a critical period. For example, babies born with cataracts who do not receive surgery in the first few months, which is the critical period for vision development, are unable to see even when the cataracts are removed. This occurs because the brain cells that would normally process vision die from lack of stimulation.

There is much debate as to precisely which brain functions require a critical period for development. For example, early childhood is the optimal time for language development. Yet, older children can acquire linguistic skills although they are likely to find the language acquisition much harder than a young child. With this in mind, '*sensitive periods*' is used to describe the stage of development when an individual is more likely to acquire a particular function. Hence, failure to provide the correct stimulation can affect functioning but it may not be lost forever.

Pruning and Plasticity

Around the age of two years of age, a process of '*pruning*' begins to take place whereby the synapses that are not developed by the child as a consequence of their experiences are eliminated. However, the brain has a certain degree of '*plasticity*'. That is the brain has capacity to remake connections when early ones are disrupted. Undamaged parts of the brain take over functions they would not normally undertake. However, the brain's capacity for reconstruction is not limitless. It is at its greatest prenatal and in early infancy.

Castleton (personal communication with author, 2004), uses the following analogy to describe pruning and plasticity. Initially the brain is like a densely populated city with a complex web of inter-connecting roads, which enables many routes to be taken to the same destination. However, as a result of pruning the brain becomes more like a rural area with far fewer roads. The person can still get to their destination if the main route is blocked but it can be a much tougher trek.

So pre-determined by age two. Environment after that.

The Impact of Neglect on the Brain

As early brain development is influenced so directly by environmental influences neglect is one of those influences, that will impact on brain development affecting future development and functioning. The way in which neglect impacts on this development is considered below.

Prenatal Development

The period of most rapid brain growth occurs pre-birth. Environmental influences affecting prenatal development at this stage will also affect future development and functioning. The environmental influences that are most likely to affect the foetus are those transmitted by the mother. Of particular concern are the '*teratogens*', that is substances that can negatively affect prenatal development and the longer-term health and well-being of the child. Schaffer (2004, p. 55) refers to these as the 'three Ds' drugs, disease and diet. These can be associated with neglect by the carer. For example, a pregnant woman may fail to take account of the impact of continuing drug use or smoking during pregnancy on the unborn child. (The impact of drug misuse during pregnancy is considered in detail in Chapter 4.)

Neglect and the Early Years

Thinking about the impact of neglect in early childhood has been informed by research on children who have been institutionalised (See for example, Rutter et al., 1998; Rutter et al., 1999) or feral children (for an overview see Newton, 2003). Whilst this work has explored the impact of extremely neglectful environments on children, it does highlight that age and length of time in a neglectful setting are significant factors when assessing the likely impact of neglect on children. For example, Rutter and his colleagues followed the development of children adopted from Romanian orphanages. They found the children who had significant developmental delays but were adopted before they were six months old made more progress in all aspects of their development than those children placed in similar settings who were between six months and two years at the time of the placement. Perry (2002) reinforces the importance of age and type of neglectful experience. Reporting on his study of 200 abused and neglected children he found the earlier the neglect occurs and the more pervasive it is the more likely that the child will suffer persistent effects. Like Rutter et al. (1998; 1999), he found the younger the child the more likely the recovery of function if the child is removed from a neglectful environment and placed in a stable and stimulating one.

The knowledge that we now have of brain development makes one thing clear – young babies require not only food, shelter and a physically safe environment – they also need to have their cognitive, emotional and social needs met from birth and indeed considered during pregnancy (National Clearinghouse on Child Abuse and Neglect, 2001; Perry, 2004). If babies and young children are not stimulated appropriately in the first three years of life, the neuronal pathways requiring stimulation are likely to wither and children may not achieve their full developmental potential.

Childhood and Adolescence

As described above the literature on brain development and neglect tends to emphasise that the first few years of a child's life are crucial in terms of adverse brain development. Whilst this is certainly important, De Bellis (2005) notes that brain structures, involved in the development of attention, emotional regulation and memory, peak at the age of 16 years. Thus neglect amongst adolescents may affect this development.

There are also early indicators, from the very limited research on the topic, that sex differences may affect brain maturation. These suggest that boys may be less resilient to maltreatment than girls (McGloin & Widom, 2001).

Implications for Practice

If one considers the implications of these findings, it is obvious that if the carers are not meeting the needs of the baby or very young child, then the role of practitioners is to take urgent action to ensure the child is provided with a stable and stimulating environment. Delay can have devastating consequences for the child's current and future well-being. If this stimulating environment cannot be created by the family, with assistance from informal and formal support networks, then out-of-home placements and possible legal proceedings should be considered. Yet, practitioners also have a responsibility to demonstrate that they have explored all avenues before considering legal proceedings. If we take seriously the need to act quickly in the early months of a child's life, how can professionals demonstrate that they have explored all alternatives and given parents a fair opportunity to meet the needs of the child? This is one of the greatest challenges practitioners encounter when assessing child neglect. There are three factors that practitioners may wish to keep in mind when making assessments:

- *Early identification.* As neglect by carers during pregnancy, and the first few months of the baby's life, can have a significant detrimental effect on the developing brain of the child, professionals who come into contact with pregnant women and mothers with newborn babies, should be aware of the indicators of potential neglect. These indicators include lack of interest in, or understanding of, the needs of a forthcoming or newborn baby; isolation and lack of support systems; a past history of failing to meet the needs of a baby and an inability to show emotional warmth towards the baby (Hart, 2001).
- *Timescales.* Both carers and professionals should be clear, when planning interventions in cases of neglect, that particularly with infants and young children time is of the essence. Hence, plans to meet the needs of these children should include clear timescales about what should be achieved by the family and professionals within these timescales. The consequences for

the family, if expectations are not met, should be spelt out and contingency plans made. One of the most common problems, in working with child neglect is <u>allowing a case to drift</u> to the detriment of the child (Stevenson, 1998; The Bridge Child Care Consultancy Service, 1995). This can occur for two reasons. Practitioners may be uncertain about their specific concerns and consequently 'monitor' the situation rather than complete a detailed assessment. Alternatively, as described in Chapter 7, it is all too easy to see glimpses of potential for change and on this basis continually give carers another chance while the needs of the child remain unmet.

- *Child focus.* Whilst parents should be given opportunity to develop parenting skills, it is crucial that this is not at the expense of the health and development of the child. Therefore, whilst work is being undertaken with carers it is important that particularly babies and young children are provided with a stimulating, stable and secure environment. A dilemma frequently encountered by practitioners is that these resources may not be available. In this situation, practitioners may be reluctant to appear punitive to parents by removing the child. Perhaps we should consider this from the child's perspective. By leaving the child in this environment, are we punishing the child for the lack of resources?

We now move on to consider the specific ways in which neglect influences other aspects of child development. Box Table 2.1 provides a summary of the key effects that practitioners may wish to bear in mind, when assessing the impact of neglect on the health and development of a child.

Socio-Emotional Development

Our understanding of the impact of neglect on the socio-emotional development of children, has been informed by attachment theories. As described above, the development of the child is dependent on the interactions that take place between the child and their environment. Key to the interactions, particularly in the child's early years, is the relationship between the child and their carer. Underpinning this relationship is the attachment that the child forms with their primary carer. In order to understand how neglect affects the child's socio-emotional development it is crucial to understand the nature of that attachment. It is important to note that most of the research on attachment has focused on the attachment between a mother and her child. As the section below draws on this work, the focus is on the mothers. However, that does not mean that the attachment between a child and their father is not as significant (Schaffer, 2004). In Chapter 3 we pay specific attention to the role of the father in caring for neglected children.

The Function of Attachment

According to Bowlby (1969) attachment serves two functions – the biological and the psychological. The biological function of attachment is aimed at ensuring the physical survival of the child. Attachment behaviour such as crying, smiling etc, by the infant is designed to get a response from an adult to meet the child's need for food and safety. As highlighted above, a positive response is crucial for the baby's experience-dependent neural system, which is dependent on interaction and sensory input. In addition, attachment serves a psychological purpose to provide closeness, comfort, security and emotional well-being for the child.

Crittenden and Ainsworth (1987, p. 437) note that attachments operate primarily as a *'security-maintenance'* system. Attachment behaviours are most intensively activated when a person is experiencing stress that triggers anxiety or a sense of danger. As Reder and Duncan (2001, p. 411) put it:

> Attachment theory describes an innate dynamic in which an infant, when faced with stress arising internally or externally, seeks proximity to a reliable parental figure, who in turn is expected to respond sensitively to the infant's needs and provide a secure base from which the infant can explore the world.

'Proximity-seeking behaviour' on the part of the baby triggers attachment behaviours. That is the baby tries to get closer to the carer when she senses discomfort such as cold, hunger, pain or danger. The way in which the caregiver responds regulates the intensity of the child's affective state and, as described below, shapes the baby's experience of themselves and others. This is referred to as *'attunement'* (Stern, 1995). It describes the process by which the baby and primary carer begin to read each other noticing moods, affect and physical states (Howe et al., 1999).

The way in which the carer responds to the baby establishes *'internal working models'* for the baby. This is a mental representation of the child's worthiness measured by the care-giver's availability and willingness to provide care and protection (Ainsworth, et al., 1978). The internal working model forms the basis for the child's beliefs and feelings about themselves and how they will be treated, initially by the carer and then in other relationships (Davies, 2002). For example, if the child feels secure and protected by the carer they are likely to have a positive sense of self and perceive of themselves as lovable, seeing other people as available, dependable and co-operative (Howe et al., 1999).

Classifying Attachments

Ainsworth et al., (1978) categorised attachment patterns by observing the way in which young children responded to a stressful situation – the 'stranger

Box 2.1 The Possible Impact of Neglect on Children: Factors to Consider

Age	Physical Development	Cognitive Development	Socio-Emotional Development
Infants and preschool	Height, weight and head circumference below average Stunted growth and protruding abdomen Weight could be above average Thin limbs Wispy hair Dry skin Red, swollen, cold hands and feet Severe nappy rash and other skin infections Persistent or repeated infections Physical manifestation of behavioural problems such as tics, soiling, self-abuse Poor gross and finer motor development Lack of mobility, late crawling and walking	Intellectual functioning below average Language delay, difficulty using expressive and receptive language Unable to articulate feelings Poor vocabulary Issues of comprehension and expression	Anxious Behaviourally impulsive Freezing and motionless Difficulty participating in co-operative play Marginalised by peers Clingy Hyperactive Attention-seeking Shut down affect; do not respond to comings and goings of carer Undemanding and self-sufficient Non-compliant Poor self-esteem
Primary school	Growth retardation or excessively overweight Enuresis and encopresis Lethargy Vitamin deficiencies	Intellectual functioning below average Reluctant to engage in exploration of the world Poor academic	Little display of affect Less likely to seek emotional support from carers than other children Superficially appears to be more mature and independent than their peers

	Health	Education	Social presentation
	Persistent or repeated infections Suffers bouts of gastroenteritis Dental and optical problems Hearing difficulties through continual failure to obtain treatment for ear infections	performance/special educational needs Problems being task-focused, following instructions and being attentive Difficulty working independently and engaging in learning Limited attention span	Self-reliant Want to please Comfortable in environments with clear standards Isolated by and awkward with peers Co-operative and compliant Lack of intimacy, may appear gauche and awkward May exhibit hostility and anti-social behaviour Has short outbursts of anger Child may take on care-giving role *vis-à vis* carer Present as helpless, passive and vulnerable
Adolescents	Late onset of puberty Overweight or underweight Short stature Repeat infections Sight, hearing and dental problems	Poor academic performance/special educational needs Suspensions Short attention span Concentration problems	Antisocial behaviours Self-harm Conduct disorders Difficulty forming and maintaining relationships Poor sense of self-esteem and self-worth Anxiety, depression

situation'. This test was designed to activate attachment behaviours and evaluate the internal working models that children had of their relationships with their primary attachment figure. The children aged between 12–18 months experienced both brief separation from their mother and being left with a stranger. The children's responses were recorded and initially three different types of attachment behaviours were observed as shown in Box 2.2. A fourth type – disorganised attachment – was added later.

One of the problems, when discussing different types of attachment behaviours, is that there is a lack of consistency in the literature regarding terminology. Whilst there appears to be agreement when differentiating between secure and insecure attachments, problems exist because similar terms are used for different constructs and dissimilar constructs can be merged into one category (Kozlowska & Hanney, 2002). The result can be that practitioners become confused by reading different texts and may be talking at cross-purposes with other professionals. For example, whilst describing similar types of attachment behaviours to Ainsworth et al., (1978), Howe et al., (1999) and Howe (2005) refer to secure and autonomous patterns; avoidant, defended and dismissing patterns; ambivalent, dependent and preoccupied patterns and disorganised, controlling and unresolved patterns. It is also important to bear in mind that whilst a secure attachment appears to be the most common type of attachment, across all cultures, there are minor variations in the proportion of children found in the different categories depending on culture (Howe, 1995; Howe et al., 1999). In this book Ainsworth's terms will be used with reference to Howe's patterns.

Secure Attachments

Children whose primary care-giver is attuned to their needs, and experience consistency, sensitivity, love, responsiveness and acceptance are likely to make secure attachments. They develop an internal working model of themselves as lovable and psychologically intelligible and consequently gain a positive image of themselves. As they perceive themselves as lovable when they engage with others, they anticipate a positive response. Thus, they see others as available and responsive and believe other people will respond to their crises and stresses.

Neglect and Attachment

Insecure attachments between the carer and the baby can have a variety of causes – one being neglect. The neglectful behaviour on the part of carers can lead to any one of the three insecure attachment strategies described below.

Insecure Avoidant Attachment

This type of attachment is likely to occur when the baby has a primary carer who is anxious, distant or irritated by the demands of the infant. The carer is

---

Box 2.2   Classification of Types of Attachment

Type of Attachment	Attachment Behaviours of Young Child left by Carer	Attachment Behaviours of Caregiver
Secure attachment	Child is upset by the departure of carer but responds positively on return although seeking comfort and reassurance Return to play when reassured Maintain high levels of eye-contact, vocalisation and mutuality with caregiver Prefers caregiver over strangers Child confident of care-giver's availability and support in stressful situations	Care is consistent and responsive to needs of child Care-giver is alert and sensitive to the child's signals and communications
Insecure and avoidant attachments	When left by carer child not greatly upset. On carer's return the child avoids contact Does not seek physical contact Watchful and wary of carer Play is inhibited	Does not readily offer physical contact Care-giver is indifferent and insensitive to the child's signals or needs and may be rejecting
Insecure and ambivalent or resistant attachments	Infant very upset by separation from care-giver and difficult to console on return resisting attempts to pacify them Seek contact but do not settle when they receive it Demand attention but angrily resist it Nervous of new situations and people	Care is inconsistent, insensitive and unpredictable Psychologically, carer is under involved with child and therefore misses signals of distress and fails to meet needs

---

unable to provide an empathetic emotional response to the baby. This may occur because of mental health or substance misuse issues on the part of the carer, which affects their ability to engage emotionally with the baby (this is discussed in more detail in Chapters 3 and 4). The infant responds by initially protesting but if this leads to a negative response from the carer the baby 'over-regulates' and contains their emotions. In other words, the child is defending against affect on the part of the carer (Crittenden, 1999). The strong feelings remain for the infant but these feelings are inhibited. The search for comfort is sacrificed in order to achieve protection from danger. The child consequently tends to become emotionally independent, self-sufficient, self-contained and compliant. The child develops an internal working model based on the belief that they are unloved: other people are rejecting and intrusive; they can only depend on themselves (Howe et al., 1999). The result is that this group of children 'are able to make sense of what they know (cognition) but not how they feel (affect)' (Howe et al., 1999, p. 64). Crittenden argues that for these children 'human relationships become defined by performance' (ibid, p. 58). As a child and later as an adult, the person who experiences avoidant attachments depends on cognitive rules to determine their behaviour in social situations looking for signs and indicators to guide them in determining 'What am I expected to do?', 'What should I say?'. The child superficially presents as if they are coping. However, underneath there is an empty and sad child who is emotionally isolated and not equipped to form intimate relationships.

Insecure Anxious Ambivalent Attachments

Some carers are inconsistent in their response to the needs of the child. Sometimes their responses to the child are appropriate, other times they are not. The children are likely to experience a family life where the carer lacks an understanding of the child's needs. This could be related to parental learning difficulties (Howe et al., 1999). This response can also occur amongst carers who fail to put the needs of the child before their own. When it suits them to engage with the child they are happy to do so. However, at other times when the baby makes unwanted demands on the carer the carer may become irritated and even angry. Children in this situation have unpredictability to contend with; there is insufficient consistency in approach from the carer to cognitively predict the response of the carer. They consequently learn feelings and emotional displays are more likely to lead to a response and thus develop effective strategies to achieve comfort, which may sacrifice some aspects of safety. For example, the infant becomes very anxious and attempts to increase responsiveness through crying, being fractious, whining and being generally demanding and angry. When the carer does respond to the infant, the baby is ambivalent – the baby wants the contact but cannot rely on the carer's accessibility. In this situation, the baby is difficult to soothe and displays disproportionate distress at even minimal separations. This leads to further erratic responses from the carer. However, from the child's perspective the emotional outburst eventually engenders some type of response. In this way, the baby learns to rely on behaviours that are emotionally effective such as clinginess and hyperactivity. The carer in turn experiences feelings of frustration and lack of control and may complain about the child's dreadful behaviour. This is in sharp contrast to the child with an anxious/avoidant attachment who is dependent on cognitions rather than affect. Children experiencing an ambivalent attachment relationship with their carer are likely to develop an internal working model of themselves as ineffective, dependent and of little value, whilst other people are neglectful, insensitive, unpredictable and unreliable (Howe et al., 1999).

As they grow up these children use attention-seeking behaviours to obtain the interest of others and this behaviour, in turn, can trigger negative responses leading to despair and depression. For example, the young school child may be forever seeking attention from the teacher, asking questions every few minutes, offering to help at every opportunity and when this fails to get the attention required attracting attention through negative behaviours like annoying other children in the class and being disruptive. For these children negative attention is better than no attention. The coercive behavioural strategies can result in anti-social behaviours, conflict-control problems and impulsivity in adolescence. The older child or adult who has experienced an insecure ambivalent attachment may go on to try to control others unpredictable behaviour through creating crises and displaying strong emotions. This can lead to further rejection reinforcing the experience that people cannot be trusted.

Crittenden and Ainsworth (1987) found that while some neglected children showed anxious/avoidant attachments others show anxious/ambivalent attachments towards their mothers. Egeland et al., (1983) in the *Minnesota Parent-Child Project*[2]., observed three groups of maltreated children. The physically abused and physically neglected children who demonstrated predominantly anxious/ambivalent attachments and the emotionally neglected children who tended to show anxious/avoidant attachments.

Children who are severely physically neglected may develop a passive, depressed dependence and present as apathetic and listless. Their passive behaviours result in less need for their carer to engage with the child setting up a 'cycle of decreasing stimulation' (Howe et al., 1999, p. 93). These children seem to see themselves and others as helpless. However, at times they may show frenzied episodes of hyperactive behaviour designed to provoke stimulation (Crittenden, 1996; Crittenden & Ainsworth, 1987; Howe et al., 1999).

The Combination of Abuse and Neglect: Disorganised Attachments

An infant who is experiencing both abuse and neglect faces problems in developing any strategy as the baby is experiencing both hostility and inconsistent caring. The carer, who should be a potential source of comfort in times of stress, has also become the cause of stress, so the attachment strategies described above do not work. This leaves the baby unable to find an appropriate attachment style and the infant discovers that their own activity can endanger them. In this situation, the attachment behaviour becomes disorganised. What these children are trying to do is develop a 'best fit' attachment pattern based on avoidant, ambivalent and on occasion secure attachment behaviours

(Howe et al., 1999 p128). The baby shows confusion and distress and a lack of confidence in the carer's ability to meet their needs. This is demonstrated through frozen watchfulness, confused behaviours, such as continual turning around in circles, head banging, rocking etc. The baby develops an internal working model of themselves as confused and bad and other people as frightening and unavailable (Howe et al., 1999). Disorganised attachments can be found amongst children who experience hostile and inconsistent caring because their carers are heavy alcohol and drug mis-users, chronically depressed, severely neglectful, sexually or physically abusive or disturbed because of unresolved loss or trauma, or any combination of these (Howe, 2003).

Children who experience a disorganised attachment learn that they can trust no one other than themselves. They often become controlling, showing no sense of fear or emotion being bossy and aggressive. Alternatively, they become 'compulsive compliant' suppressing their emotional and attachment needs to become independent, self-sufficient and self-contained. For example, Crittenden (1992) found children who were both abused and neglected were difficult or compliant in interaction with their mothers. These children can become compulsive care-givers or demonstrate 'parentified behaviours', and show aggression towards siblings.

What is clear, from the above, is that any assessment of the impact of neglect on the socio-emotional development of the child has to take into account 'children's states of mind, mental representations and behaviours in terms of their particular attempts to adapt, to make sense of and survive in a particular care-giving environment' (Howe, 2003, p. 380). According to Howe (2003), in order to do this it is important to gather information from observation, case files and discussion with the family, and other practitioners from different disciplines, about the child and their carer/s. This information should include:

- knowledge about the carer's own behavioural and relationship history;
- the quality and nature of the current and past care-giving environment;
- the child's behaviour and relationship style, both past and present and in different social contexts.

By making sense of this information, using our knowledge of attachment strategies, it is possible to begin to hypothesis about the type of care-giving environment the child is experiencing and the child's adaptive strategies.

(The following works provide a useful resource for the reader and were used in preparation of this section Bowlby, 1951, 1979; Crittenden, 1996; Crittenden, 1992, 1999; Crittenden & Ainsworth, 1987; Goldberg, 1999; Howe, 2003; Howe, 2005; Howe et al., 1999; Howe et al., 2000; Rosenberg & Cantwell, 1993.)

Cognitive and Behavioural Development

What is beginning to become clear is that the effects of child neglect are all-encompassing, affecting every aspect of the health and development of the child. Erickson and Egeland (2002, p. 3) summarise it well when they note that the lack of human contact and love can erode a child's spirits until they lose the desire to relate to others and explore the world. In this section, we consider how this erosion of the child's spirit affects their cognitive and behavioural development.

Infants and Preschool

Bearing in mind the way in which neglected, insecurely attached children are likely to engage with their carers it is not surprising that Egeland et al., (1983), who completed the Minnesota Study of Risk and Adaptation, found that physically neglected children, at two years of age, when completing problem-solving tasks with their mothers, were non-compliant and displayed considerable amounts of anger. At 42 months of age they lacked impulse and ego control. They demonstrate behaviours designed to gain attention. Their moods are extreme and swing from happy to sad; from love to hate (Howe, 2005). The physically neglected children at 24 months and 42 months displayed anger, non-compliance and minimal positive affect.

At 42 months, Egeland et al., (1983) found these children's performance, on standardised tests of intellectual functioning, were the lowest of the maltreated groups of physically abused, physically neglected and emotionally neglected (Erickson et al., 1989). In addition, preschool children with a history of neglect have problems in the use of expressive and respective language (Gaudin, 1999; Hildyard & Wolfe, 2002; Howe et al., 1999; 2000). Whilst those who have suffered severe physical neglect, may have very poor speech and may be developmentally delayed (Howe et al., 1999). Not only do these children have problems articulating emotion, they are often confused by and have difficulty distinguishing between the emotions shown by others. They do not know what to expect or how to respond (Pollack et al., 2000).

Emotionally neglected children 'appeared to lack the self-esteem and agency necessary to cope effectively with the environment' (Egeland et al., 1983 p468). They go on to describe them, based on the Minnesota cohort, as an unhappy group of children who were the least positive and had the most negative affect of all the groups of maltreated children. These children tend to be listless, blank and vacant; they do not scream or bawl, rather they whine or whinge (Howe, 2005). They tend to be loners, isolated from their peers, finding it difficult engaging in activities and with a poor sense of humour. These behaviours are not surprising if one considers that the unresponsive and inconsistent approach of the carer has given the child an internal working model of themselves as unworthy of love and attention.

A striking finding, from the Minnesota Study, was that between the age of nine months and two years the emotionally neglected children had the most dramatic decline in scores on standardised tests used to assess cognitive and motor development. And at 54 months these children presented with a range of serious behaviour problems. For example, they were prone to soiling, tics and self-abuse.

Primary School

Emotionally neglected children, in the Minnesota Study, continued to have problems when they went to school. These children appear to internalise their problems having difficulty relating to others, remaining withdrawn and isolated and generally lacking in social skills (Erickson & Egeland, 2002; Hildyard & Wolfe, 2002). Their levels of self-esteem remain low. Iwaniec (1995, p. 57) notes they show 'longing and desire to belong and be wanted but lack social skills to get themselves into a circle of peers'. In addition, problems of poor hygiene, and encopresis and enuresis, associated with developmental delay, exacerbate isolation. To compensate for this, some children may try to get close to the teacher and ancillary staff at school, following them around and volunteering for everything. The children tend to crave physical contact. They experience 'touch hunger' and will seek contact from anyone who shows an interest in them. This makes them vulnerable targets for perpetrators of sexual abuse. Not surprisingly, educationally, their performance is poorer than non-maltreated children and children suffering other forms of child maltreatment (Erickson et al., 1989).

The physically neglected children, in the Minnesota Study, missed more school than the control group and children suffering from other forms of maltreatment. When at school they had problems managing the social and educational demands of school. Socially, acceptance by peers is low (Erickson & Egeland, 1996; 2002). In addition, their academic performance was poor and their attention-span limited. Indeed 18 of the cohort of 19 physically neglected children were receiving special education services three years into primary education.

This group of children are easily distracted. They have problems remaining task-focused, following instructions and being attentive. They also tend to leave tasks uncompleted, having a limited concentration span. They find it difficult working independently and engaging in learning and seek the attention of the teacher in whatever way they can – usually in ways that irritate the teacher and their class mates. Their behaviour is often labelled as immature, annoying or silly (Kendall-Tackett & Eckenrode, 1996; Kurtz et al., 1993; National

Clearing House on Child Abuse and Neglect, 2001; Howe, 2005). These children are as desperate for attention from their peers as they are for adult attention. They often have a poor understanding of such emotions as anger and sadness. Indeed they do not appear to understand the causes and consequences of different emotional situations. Their lack of understanding means that they do not respond appropriately to others or they misinterpret comments and actions. This confusion may result in them avoiding displays of emotion in themselves or others (Shipman et al., 2005). Alternatively, they may manage relationships through extreme demonstrations of emotion. For example, one minute they love a class mate who they describe as their best friend; the next they are offended; the friend is hateful and their worst enemy.

Adolescence

Findings from the Minnesota Study indicate that by the time these neglected children had reached adolescence they were experiencing a range of problems. The physically neglected children were not achieving academically. They were more likely to be involved in heavy alcohol use and to drop out of school than the other groups of maltreated children (Erickson & Egeland, 2002). The immaturity and impulsivity of the physically neglected children is likely to have got them into trouble to the point where carers, and indeed the school, consider they are beyond the control of parents or school. This can lead to rejection of the child by the carer (Howe, 2005). It is often in these circumstances that parents end up physically abusing the child, ringing up social work services demanding the child is taken into care, or being driven to leaving the child in a social work office, refusing to take the child home.

The emotionally neglected children also displayed a number of behaviour problems. They remain isolated and alone with few social skills, often the subject of bullying. It is not surprising therefore that these children are significantly more likely to attempt suicide compared with other maltreated children (Barnes & Farrell, 1992; Cullingford & Morrison, 1997; Salmelainen, 1996).

If one considers these problems, alongside the children's difficulty in developing and sustaining relationships, it is not surprising that there are links between neglect and the development of anti-social behaviour. Lack of active interest by carers, demonstrated through lack of parental support and monitoring, is highly predictive of delinquent and criminal activity, drug taking and school misconduct in young people (Koenig et al., 2004). Neglected children were found to engage in significantly more cheating behaviours and less rule compatible behaviours, compared to non-maltreated children (Kendall-Tackett & Eckenrode, 1996). This group of children also received more suspensions and more disciplinary referrals within schools than non-maltreated peers (Johnson-Reid & Barth, 2000). Summarising the consequences of neglect in adolescence Smith et al., (2005) conclude that it is associated with both short- and longer-term negative behavioural outcomes, with an increased risk of general and violent offending behaviour in late adolescence and risk of arrest and drug use in early adulthood. Moreover, Rosenberg and Cantwell (1993) found that children reported to child welfare services for neglect were more likely to be incarcerated as adolescents than those reported for physical or sexual abuse. They hypothesise that this may be the case because neglected children move from passive to aggressive behaviour as they grow up. Second, because of their behaviour and family situation, they may not have opportunities to obtain benefits from school and social activities, which can mitigate the effects of maltreatment. Most significantly, therapy services for this group of children are not always readily available.

The experiences of neglect in childhood and adolescence can affect these children's ability to maintain healthy relationships as adults. For example, in a study of attachment styles amongst undergraduates Gauthier et al., (1996) found that adults who perceived themselves as neglected as children had difficulty maintaining relationships with others and were more likely to report psychological problems such as anxiety, depression, somatisation, paranoia and hostility than those who reported only physical abuse. In addition, neglected children have little opportunity to develop empathy (Perez & Widom, 1994). As empathy is necessary for sustaining relationships and parenting, Rosenberg and Cantwell (1993) warn that those who grow up without empathy are at high risk of becoming abusive and neglectful themselves. This is supported by Straus and Savage (2005) who found that the more a child experienced neglect the greater the probability of assaulting and injuring a dating partner. Neglected children, as described above, also have low levels of self-esteem. Herrenkohl et al., (1998) found a relationship exists between low self-esteem, early maltreatment and teenage parenthood amongst both males and females.

It is not surprising that the cognitive problems experienced by the neglected child appear to continue into adulthood, with adults who were abused and neglected having lower scores on intelligence and reading tests than adults who have not experienced abuse (Perez & Widom, 1994; Rosenberg & Cantwell, 1993). The impact of child neglect and maltreatment on adults' ability to care for children is considered in detail in Chapter 3.

Physical Development and Child Neglect

The classic image of a neglected child is of a small, skinny child with sparse hair and pale complexion. Whilst child neglect can be associated with lack of nutrition leading to weight and growth problems, as outlined in Chapter 1 neglected children may also present as obese as a result of the carer's failure to provide them with an adequate diet. Within the same family, some children may be obese whilst others are undernourished. This is well illustrated by the case of 'Paul' who died from neglect and malnourishment whilst earlier concerns about his siblings had centred on them being overweight (The Bridge Child Care Consultancy Service, 1995).

Severe and chronic malnutrition can impede brain growth. For example, the head circumference of a malnourished child is less than that of a child receiving an appropriate diet (Dubowitz et al., 2000). A lack of adequate nutrition can also result in delayed bone development and growth retardation. Gross motor language and personal-social development are most likely to be effected by failure to thrive (Rosenberg & Cantwell, 1993), whilst childhood obesity can have a long-term detrimental impact on a child's health. This includes Type II diabetes, cardiovascular disease, respiratory problems and sleeping disorders and gastro-intestinal problems (Sabin et al., 2004).

Nutritional deficits can also have a significant impact on a child's behavioural development. Mackner and Starr (1997), in a summary of research findings on nutritional deficits and human behavioural development, found that malnutrition affects cognitive functioning, academic performance and levels of activity in both pre- and school age children. Mineral and vitamin deficiencies also have a negative impact on cognitive performance. Children who have been diagnosed as suffering from both neglect and failure to thrive are more likely to show significant deficits in cognitive functioning than children who experience only neglect or only failure to thrive (Kerr et al., 2000). Kerr et al. (2000) found children with a history of failure to thrive and maltreatment (defined as at least one report to the child protection service for neglect) had more behavioural problems, worse cognitive functioning and poorer school performance than children who just had problems associated with failure to thrive. (The challenges associated with assessing neglect and failure to thrive are considered in Chapter 8.)

A child's physical development will depend not only on the child receiving appropriate nourishment but also on the right stimulation to develop gross and motor skills. Young children need opportunities to learn to walk and run, to explore the world and to develop physical skills. Some neglected children do not get these opportunities. For example, a toddler may be kept immobilised in their pushchair or left in a cot all day. If the child is deprived of opportunities to develop these motor skills, they become frustrated and can respond in one of two ways. First, they may become withdrawn, apathetic and give up attempting to explore the world around them. Other children demonstrate their frustration through head or fist banging, out of control play and restlessness. Children also need opportunities to develop fine motor skills such as hand to eye coordination. Neglected children who are deprived of opportunities to use toys, crayons, etc, may experience delays in developing these skills, which will impact on their progress at school (Wachs, 2000).

Children Particularly Vulnerable to Child Neglect

Whilst all children who are brought up by physically or emotionally neglecting carers are likely to suffer as described above, there are groups of children who are especially vulnerable to neglect. These are children who are considered to be particularly difficult to care for by their carers (Dunn et al., 2002). These vulnerable groups of children include:

- Children born to mothers who use drugs during pregnancy.
- Low birth weight babies.
- Children with disabilities.
- The child perceived to be difficult-to-parent.

Children Born to Mothers who use Drugs during Pregnancy

Research, primarily from the USA, indicates that infants exposed to substances in utero, such as opiates, stimulants and benzodiazepines, may suffer withdrawal symptoms often referred to as Neonatal Abstinence Syndrome. Infants suffering from this syndrome can exhibit distressed behaviour, which in turn parents find difficult to manage (Jaudes et al., 1995; Kelley, 1992). Infant drug withdrawal can also result in stiffness, agitation, over-activity and restlessness with unpredicted variations in the baby's behaviour (Alison, 2000). These responses mean that the carer cannot easily comfort the child. Indeed, Kelley (1992) found that foster-carers had difficulty with these babies, finding them hyperactive and less adaptable to their surrounding than other infants. This in turn can affect the interactions between baby and carer. Parents, who are unsure about their ability to parent and may already lack both motivation and support possibly through their own drug use, are likely to find these children a particular challenge. (Drug and alcohol misuse and child neglect is discussed in more detail in Chapter 5.)

Low Birth Weight Babies

Low birth weight babies are vulnerable to neglect for a number of reasons (Watson 2005). First, parents of these babies are under considerable stress. They have to manage daily life, which may include coping with other children at home, while at the same time coping with the baby who is on a special care baby unit and subject to life-threatening crises. Second, parents of preterm babies have had less time to prepare for parenthood then other parents. Third, the physical environment in a high dependency unit, can have a negative influence on the ability of carer and baby to form attachments. In addition, the circumstances surrounding the birth and the ongoing care may result in reduced psychological and physical proximity and poor parent–child interaction (Fahlberg, 1994).

The physical, cognitive and emotional consequences of very low birth weight make caring for these children very stressful. For example, these children are more likely to have feeding difficulties, chronic disease, neurological, behavioural and cognitive disabilities than other children. In situations where parenting is already borderline these additional stresses can lead to a failure on the part of the carer to meet the needs of the child.

Watson (2005) also found, in a ten-year overview of small babies in Scotland, that these babies are most commonly born to mothers under 15 years of age and over 40 years. If the first birth is a low birth weight, the risk increases significantly for the second child. In addition, she found the inter-pregnancy interval is low, often with a six-month gap between delivery and conception of the next pregnancy. Mothers of very low birth weight babies, according to Watson, are also more likely, than mothers who go to full term, to suffer from such socio-economic disadvantages as financial insecurities, poor and over-crowded home conditions, unsupportive relationships, feelings of helplessness, anxiety and depression. It is not surprising therefore, that she concludes that these babies are subject to a 'double whammy' (ibid, p. 189). Their characteristics and the consequences of very low birth weight may increase their vulnerability to possible neglect whilst the pre-existing parental and socio-economic circumstances not only contribute to preterm birth but are also antecedents of child neglect.

Children with Disabilities

Disabled babies maybe vulnerable to neglect for all the reasons outlined above, as well as the stress experienced by the carers coming to terms with the disability and learning how to meet the needs of the disabled baby. However, the stresses associated with caring for a disabled child are ongoing and may lead to child neglect. For example, parents may not be receiving the services and support they require to meet the needs of the child. This places the carer in a stressful situation attempting to care for a child with complex needs, without appropriate support and resources. This can result in poor or negligent care for the disabled child who becomes the perceived or real source of frustration to the carer (Goldson, 1998; Kennedy & Wonnacott, 2005). Alternatively, the family may be receiving adequate services but there are adverse family conditions such as parental mental health problems, substance misuse, domestic violence or problematic relationships, which affect the carer. In this situation, these stresses may be projected onto the disabled child resulting in scapegoating and/or abuse and neglect of the child (Kennedy & Wonnacott, 2005). The situation can be exacerbated when the professional network also focuses on the disabled child rather than the adverse family conditions. Finally, practitioners should also recognise that carers may maintain low stress levels by dissociating themselves from the children to the point of neglect (Benedict et al., 1992). *Why are they having them then?*

It is also important to bear in mind that the child's disability maybe the result of child maltreatment. Garbarino (1987) argues children who are disabled as a result of maltreatment have already been victimised by their carers and are therefore even more vulnerable to abuse and neglect as a result of the disability – a double jeopardy. The carers clearly had problems meeting the needs of the non-disabled child, now the additional needs associated with the disability, mean that additional care demands are being placed on carers who were already struggling to cope. *Why did they have an additional child then?*

The Child Perceived to be Difficult-to-Parent

Another form of neglect that can occur is when one or more children are singled out and neglected whilst others are adequately parented or may be particularly favoured – a Cinderella situation. These children engender feelings in the carers that influence the way the carer relates to the child (Brayden et al., 1992; Reder & Lucey, 2000). These feelings can be associated with incidents around the birth of the child, such as death of a partner or parent or a change in lifestyle. The negative feelings about the situation are projected onto the child. Alternatively, the child may be unplanned or a step-child and the parent may resent having to care for this unwanted child. *✗*

Reder and Lucey also recognise that there are some children whose temperament contributes to them being more difficult to parent than other children. For example, a child who is fractious, irritable and continually crying without any apparent cause. It is worth noting that neglectful carers may have lower tolerance levels than non-neglecting carers and may perceive their children to be more difficult than non-neglecting carers.

✗ If you are a step parent you think before you leap and if you are a biological parent you think before you fuck.

Resilience and the Neglected Child

As described above, the effects of neglect can be life-long and have a serious impact on a person's quality of life. Not least it can leave children and adults, who have been neglected, feeling unloved and unlovable. Yet, not all children who have been neglected will respond in the same way to seemingly similar adverse conditions. Some children cope with, and overcome, the socio-emotional effects of child neglect. Increasingly, we are becoming aware of the protective factors within children and families that appear to reduce the effects of neglect and foster the resilience of the child. Resilience allows a child to manage stresses and bounce back when faced with adversities (Hall & Pearson, 2003). This is likely to occur if the protective factors – the sources of resilience outweigh the sources of vulnerability (Gilligan, 2001).

Bifulco and Moran (1998) hypothesise that at each life stage risk factors increase the likelihood of further risk factors which cumulate to lead to poor outcomes for children. For example, the neglected young child may be irritable and difficult to settle. The carer finds the behaviour hard to manage and responds by hitting the child or ignoring the needs of the child. This in turn exacerbates the child's response, provoking a more abusive or neglectful response from the carer. At each stage it is possible to reduce risk of harm to a child, if sufficient protective factors are there to promote resilience. Bifulco and Moran (1998, p. 154) conclude, 'the search is not on for a single factor which promotes resilience: instead it involves the identification of a variety of factors arising at various life stages, with each factor reducing or protecting against risk combinations, thus breaking the chain of linked disadvantage'. Drawing on their interviews of women who had suffered neglect as children, they identify three protective factors that appear to promote the resilience of neglected children. These are support, coping strategies and meaningful rewards.

Support

Someone who is able to develop a child's sense of self-worth, enable the child to feel they are loveable and assist in opening up opportunities for the child, appears to have a beneficial effect (Gilligan, 2001). Support provided by a relative, teacher, family friend or even a peer is particularly helpful if it:

- Provides the child with a person they can go to for help.
- Offers a confident when a child has problems.
- Supplies a good role model.   (Bifulco & Moran, 1998)

When considering possible sources of support, practitioners should not only consider the informal contacts and networks but also the local resources available, to the child within the community (Jack & Gill, 2003). For example a positive school environment where teachers and support staff recognise and meet the emotional and social needs of the child can be the salvation for many children living in neglectful environments. Moreover, positive friendships with peers are also important to children as they provide opportunities to develop inter-personal skills and self-knowledge, provide fun and companionship and offer emotional support in times of stress (Dowling et al., 2006).

Coping Strategies

Coping behaviours found to be helpful to children in stressful situations, such as neglect, include:

- Self-efficacy and competence in managing life crises and dealing with and adapt to change.
- Having a sense of positive self-esteem and confidence.
- Taking initiative.
- Planning ahead.
- Practical problem-solving using a range of approaches.
- Taking responsibility for a problem.
- Being optimistic.

(Bifulco and Moran, 1998; Rutter, 1985)

This in its own right did not appear to counteract the effects of abuse, in Bifulco and Moran's study. However, it appeared to reduce the level of abuse. These behaviours were often associated, in the study, with a sense of responsibility and protectiveness for others, with children reversing roles and taking responsibility for caring for their parents. In addition, the resilient children found strategies for preventing problems from developing. For example, one respondent, in the study, rang the police when her parents began fighting. Others stood up to their abuser. In adolescence these copers had the confidence and ability to make significant life-changes, such as leaving home.

Meaningful and or Rewarding Roles

These provide a child with a sense of self-worth and self-esteem and they may act as a source of pleasure and hope. These are usually associated with activities such as sport and provide opportunities for a child to develop a sense of achievement. However, as noted in this chapter and confirmed by Bifulco and Moran (1998) in their study, neglected children are less likely than non-abused children to achieve well academically and obtain a sense of reward from academic study. They found parental lack of interest, which can be associated with non-school attendance and little encouragement to do home work, hampers children educationally as well as emotionally and socially.

Bifulco and Moran (1998) conclude that the protective factors tend to cluster and reinforce each other. That is those with good support tended to be better copers and also managed to find meaningful roles for themselves.

When assessing the resilience of neglected children practitioners may wish to consider the following questions:

- Does the child have any interests and hobbies?
- Do they have good relationships with siblings, peers, extended family and significant others in their life?
- Can the child identify a person they can go to for comfort, discuss feelings and confide in?
- What is their personality? (consider, temperament, disposition, coping style, sense of self-esteem, social skills, problem-solving behaviours, ability to balance help seeking with autonomy).
- What is the level of extended family support and involvement, including care-giving help?
- Are there supportive adults outside of the family who serve as role models/mentors to the child modelling pro-social behaviours and providing a supportive relationship?

(U.S. Department of Health and Human Services, 2003)

Summary

Key to our understanding of the way in which neglect affects the health and development of a child is an understanding of the long-term negative effects of neglect on brain growth and development. If babies and young children are not stimulated appropriately in the first three years of life, children may not achieve their full developmental potential. Neglect and brain development is a developing area of research. However, based on the research to date, it appears that the age of onset, intensity and length of neglect determine the likely effects on the child. For example, children removed from a very neglectful environment before the age of six months and placed with stable, secure and stimulating care-givers achieved a higher level of overall functioning than children aged between six months and two years placed in similar environments.

Neglect affects every aspect of a child's development socio-emotional, cognitive, behavioural and physical. The socio-emotional development of the child is dependent on the interactions that take place between the child and their environment. Key to these interactions is the initial attachment between the child and their primary carer. A child experiencing emotional or physical neglect by their carer is likely to develop an insecure attachment strategy designed to assist them in coping with and surviving the neglectful behaviour of the care-giver. A consequence of developing this type of strategy is that whilst it assists the child in functioning in the family it is likely to affect cognitive and behavioural development and the child's ability to form effective relationships.

Some children are particularly vulnerable to child neglect. These include children born to mothers who use drugs during pregnancy; low birth weight babies; children with disabilities and children perceived to be difficult-to-parent.

A neglectful environment clearly does not provide the child with the secure base from which to develop into a healthy well-balanced adult. These neglectful experiences and the strategies the neglected child uses to manage their world mean that they are likely to have physical and ongoing cognitive and socio-emotional development problems throughout childhood. These problems can persist into adulthood and, as will be discussed in Chapter 3, can lead to the children themselves becoming maltreating carers. However, not all children who are neglected go on to become maltreating carers or indeed suffer long-term effects of neglect. Increasingly, we are becoming aware of the protective factors that appear to reduce the effects of neglect and foster the resilience of the child. These include providing the child with support, coping strategies and meaningful rewards.

Notes

1 Registration is a system used in England to identify children where there are concerns that the child is suffering or likely to suffer harm as a result of maltreatment and requires a multidisciplinary child protection plan to safeguard and promote their welfare.
2 This is a longitudinal study of risk and adaptation which has been ongoing since the mid-1970s, using a sample of 267 first born children in the USA.

Part II

Assessing the Care-Giver and the Care-Giving Context

The majority of carers provide parenting that is 'good enough'. That is they provide a 'facilitating environment' (Winnicott 1965, p. 223) that puts the child's needs first and enables a child to develop into a healthy, well-balanced adult. In this part of the book, we consider the reasons why some care-givers fail to do this and are unable 'to complete the parenting tasks required to ensure that the developmental needs of the child are met' (working definition in the Introduction).

To provide this 'facilitating environment' the carer must have the parenting capacity to meet the needs of the child. The capacity of the carer to respond to the needs of the child depends on their *ability* and *motivation* (Horwath & Morrison, 2001). Moreover, the carer needs the *opportunity* or right socio-economic conditions in which to raise their child (Dubowitz, 1999b; Jack, 2001; Lacharite et al., 1996). Good enough parenting is most likely to occur if all three components are in place. A child is vulnerable to neglect or deprivation if any of these components are missing or minimal. For example, a carer who has a learning disability may be highly motivated to meet the needs of their child and may be receiving a great deal of support from family and professionals. However, despite their motivation and support they may be unable to develop the skills or absorb the knowledge required to care for the child.

In the following 3 chapters, we consider the care-giver and the care-giving context and consider ways in which lack of ability, motivation and care-giving opportunities can result in a failure on the part of the care-giver to meet the needs of the child. In Chapter 3 we pay particular attention to carers' own negative life experiences and how these may affect carers' ability and motivation to meet the needs of the child. We also consider the knowledge and understanding a carer requires in order to meet the needs of the child and the role of both the mother and the father in meeting these needs. In Chapter 4 we recognise that carers have problems of their own and consider a range of parenting issues that may influence a carer's ability and motivation to provide the facilitating environment a child requires. In the final chapter in this section of the book, we consider parenting opportunities and ways in which a range of socio-economic factors such as poverty and lack of support can affect a carer's ability and motivation to meet the needs of the child.

3

Carer Behaviours: The Past Influencing the Present?

Introduction

In the introduction to this section of the book, we considered how parenting capacity is influenced not only by parenting opportunities but also by the ability and motivation of the carer to meet the needs of the child. In this chapter, we think about what it is that the carer should be able to do if they are to meet the needs of the child. Having established the parenting tasks, we go on to consider reasons why carers lack the ability and motivation to complete these tasks. Understanding the nature of the interaction and relationship between the child and their carer is crucial if we are to understand child neglect (Macdonald, 2001; Schumacher et al., 2001; Turney, 2005). Therefore, particular attention is given to the way in which the carer's own child-rearing experiences and their relationship with their own carer can in turn affect their ability and motivation to interact with their own child and meet their needs. We also consider the antecedents associated with child neglect. The chapter concludes with a discussion of the particular role of the male carer and the complexity associated with establishing their ability and motivation to meet the needs of the child are discussed. We also consider the particular role that maternal grandmothers appear to play in neglectful families.

The Development Needs of the Child and the Parenting Tasks

The *Framework for the Assessment of Children in Need and their Families* (Department of Health et al., 2000, p. 21) specifies both the needs of the child and the parenting tasks required of the carer to meet those needs. However, if carers are to complete these tasks satisfactorily they should have particular knowledge and skills. Pugh et al., (1994) have specified the knowledge and

71

skills required of confident, competent parents. Box 3.1 draws on the knowledge and skills identified by Pugh et al., and links this to the parenting tasks outlined in the Assessment Framework. The table provides an overview of what a carer needs to know about a child's needs and the skills required of carers in order to successfully complete the parenting tasks.

Parenting Ability and Motivation

Detailed in this way, one realises that parenting is complex: it is not something we do naturally but something that we learn through observation, our own experiences and for some through parenting classes. Moreover, Box 3.1 highlights that successful parents require a rudimentary knowledge of child development as well as a wide range of parenting skills.

Parents who neglect their children may not possess this knowledge and skills and this can result in a lack of ability to meet a child's needs. This failure to acquire the knowledge and skills required to be a good enough parent can occur for a number of reasons. First, the carer may have a learning disability, which limits their ability to gain the required knowledge and skills (this is discussed in more detail in Chapter 4). Second, the carer may never have been given the opportunity to look after a child or learn how to do so. Once these carers have been shown how to parent, through, for example, the support of midwives and health visitors and activities such as parenting classes, they are likely to become effective parents. Third, some carers may lack the motivation to meet the needs of the child. In these cases they may possess the knowledge and skills but other factors such as drug misuse, depression or their feelings towards the child, mean that they do not apply their knowledge and skills to parenting the child (this is discussed in further detail in Chapter 4). Finally, some carers may have had poor parenting role models. For example, Polansky et al., (1981) found that parents who go on to neglect have often experienced a background of maltreatment and neglect themselves. While Pianta et al., (1989) found that carers who had been neglected as children have less understanding of the complexity of care-giving and also demonstrate less ability to respond to the needs of another person than did carers who had not been neglected. In the next section we consider in more detail how carers' past experiences can influence care-giving ability and motivation.

The Impact of Carers' Past Experiences on Care-Giving Ability and Motivation

All carers bring with them a history of being cared for. Their attitude towards caring for their own children will be shaped by this history and by their

Box 3.1   Knowledge, Skills and the Parenting Task

Parenting Tasks	Knowledge, Skills and Attributes
Basic care Meeting child's physical needs Providing appropriate health care and medical attention Ensuring child has nutritious diet, warmth, shelter Giving clean and appropriate clothing and ensuring adequate personal hygiene	Knowledge of: • healthy diet and the food and drink requirements of a child at different ages • a comfortable temperature for a baby and small child • toileting requirements of baby or child • how to bath a baby and hygiene requirements of child • common ailments and how to cope with accidents • how to access GP, dentist, optician, etc • particular medical requirements of the child Skill in being able to: • provide a diet that enables child to thrive • recognise if a child is uncomfortable because they are too cold or hot • identify and respond to child's toileting needs • keep a young child clean and teach a child to take increasing responsibility for their own hygiene • identify and respond to child's health care needs • meet the particular needs of the child related to their disability or health issues
Ensuring safety Ensuring child is adequately protected from harm and danger Protecting child from possible significant harm Avoiding contact with unsafe adults/ children Protecting child from self-harm Recognising hazards and dangers both at home and elsewhere	Knowledge of: • sources of potential harm such as hazards in home, need for supervision, risk posed by unsafe adults and other children • ways in which child can become involved in anti-social behaviours and indicators of this involvement • particular vulnerabilities of a disabled child.

⊃

Skills in being able to:
- provide a safe environment for the child both within the home and elsewhere
- identify the signs and indicators that the child is at possible risk of harm

Stimulation
Promoting child's learning and intellectual development
Encouraging, stimulating cognitive development
Providing social opportunities
Talking and responding to the child
Encouraging and joining in play
Enabling the child to experience success
Ensuring school/play school attendance
Facilitating child to meet the challenges of life

Knowledge of:
- the education system and resources available to promote child's intellectual development within the community
- the way in which a child develops cognitive and language skills
- impact of child's disability on their cognitive development

Skills in being able to:
- engage with the child in play activities
- stimulate the child through verbal communication or child's particular communication method, reading, play materials, etc
- access and use educational resources in the community
- prepare child for preschool and school activities and support child enabling them to maximise the opportunities provided by these activities
- have appropriate expectations of child when encouraging them to take on the challenges of life

Emotional warmth
Ensuring the child's emotional needs are met
Giving the child a sense of being valued and a positive sense of own race and cultural identity
Ensuring the child has secure, stable and affectionate relationships with significant others
Demonstrating sensitivity and responsiveness to the child's emotional needs

Knowledge of:
- the child's cultural background
- the emotional needs of children

Skills in being able to:
- offer child love and acceptance and being able to respond sensitively to their needs
- foster a sense of identity
- have confidence in the child's worth and abilities
- provide appropriate physical contact in light of age and ability

Providing appropriate physical contact, comfort and cuddling sufficient to demonstrate warm regard, praise and encouragement

Guidance and boundaries
Enabling the child to regulate their own emotions and behaviours
Demonstrating and modelling appropriate behaviour and control of emotions and interactions with others
Providing guidance involving the setting of boundaries enabling child to develop values, a conscience and appropriate social behaviours
Enabling the child to grow into an autonomous adult acting appropriately with others
Allowing child to explore and learn
Enabling child to manager anger, consider others
Use effective methods of discipline to shape behaviour

Stability
Provide a sufficiently stable family environment to enable the child to develop and maintain a secure attachment to the primary care-giver
Ensure secure attachments are not disrupted
Provide consistent emotional warmth
Respond in a similar way to the same behaviour
Recognise and respond to child's changing needs
Ensure child keeps in contact with family members and significant others

• demonstrate consistency, reliability and dependability, providing a stable environment

Knowledge of:
• appropriate behaviour for age and ability
• effective methods for disciplining child
Skills in being able to:
• understand how their values and attitudes impact on others
• be authoritative, rather than over protective, permissive or authoritarian
• offer a secure environment where rules are clear and consistent
• set appropriate boundaries, providing adequate supervision and encouraging children to set their own boundaries
• avoid harsh punishments but reinforce good behaviour
• model effective methods of dealing with conflict, demonstration of emotions and interactions with others
• have confidence in child
• have appropriate expectations of child

Knowledge of:
• what a child needs to develop a secure relationship with a care giver
• their own upbringing and its effect on their ability to parent
Skills in being able to:
• maintain relationships with significant people in the child's life
• recognise the changing needs of the child as they mature and develop
• create a stable home environment

attachments to their own care-givers (Howe, 1995; Macdonald, 2001). In other words the 'ghosts from the nursery' come back to haunt the next generation (Karr-Morse & Wiley, 2000). In Chapter 2 the effect of secure and insecure attachment strategies on children was explored in detail. It was noted that adults who have experienced insecure attachments are likely to have unresolved interpersonal problems regarding trust, dependency and autonomy (Pianta et al., 1989). These experiences will affect their approach towards parenting in a number of ways. For example, they may not notice the signals from the child about its needs, or recognise that the signal requires a response from the carer. Alternatively, they may recognise the signals and understand that a response is needed, but do not know how to respond or do not provide what is required by the child (Crittenden, 1992).

Crittenden (1999) argues that the response of a carer, to a child, is determined by the way in which the carer processes information about signals of danger and protection. Their response will be determined by the interplay between information with regard to cognition and affect. *Cognition,* is defined as the effects of one's behaviour. It requires an understanding of what actions cause what outcomes. *Affect,* is information about feeling states that motivate protective and affectionate behaviours. A good enough parent is one who is attuned to the needs of the child both cognitively and emotionally. Neglectful behaviours by care-givers are likely to occur if the care-giver is not attuned either cognitively or emotionally and, in the most damaging cases, both cognitively and emotionally. Crittenden describes different types of neglect reflecting the different combinations. These are:

- Disorganised neglect.
- Emotional neglect.
- Depressed neglect.

What follows is a detailed discussion of the ways in which these different forms of parental neglect may present to practitioners and what the research tells us as to why parents act in these ways. However, when categorising neglect we need to be careful that we do not stereotype families or try and fit them into neat categories. Rather, these descriptions are offered to provide some guidance to practitioners as to *possible* reasons why families may be acting in particular ways.

Disorganised Neglect

This type of family will be familiar to most practitioners. They are the families that are known to everyone in the office and indeed the multi-agency network. The files are thick and may go back a generation or more. When one knocks on the door of the house it is difficult to predict what to expect when the door is opened. Who will be there? What mood they will be in? What problems will greet you? The first impression, when entering the home, is one of chaos and noise. Animals, children, extended family and friends are likely to be milling about, with the carer sitting in the middle of the room shouting orders to all and sundry. The burning problem last time one visited is no longer a cause for concern: there is another more immediate crisis that needs resolving. The child that was 'as good as gold' last week is out of control and 'needs sorting or I will kick them out'. The partner who was never going to be allowed back into the home because of their behaviour is now back and is the love of the carer's life. Wedding bells are in the air.

These carers tended to have experienced childhoods where they felt emotionally deprived and undervalued. They work on the basis, 'to be noticed is to be loved: to be ignored is to be unloved' (Howe, 2005, p. 120). The result is that the course of the day is governed by their feelings. If all is well, and they feel loved and valued, then all is well with the world. The carers mental processing is dominated by affect rather than cognitions. This is likely to lead to caregiving, which is volatile, disorganised and chaotic as described above.

These carers are likely to have experienced an insecure, anxious and ambivalent attachment with their primary care-giver (see Chapter 2 for detail). They may be both over-involved and irritated by their children: one minute they are hugging and kissing the child. Something happens to upset the carer and the next minute they are shouting and swearing at the child. The child, in turn, does not understand why the mood of the carer has altered so suddenly: the child learns that the emotional response of the carer is unpredictable. Crittenden and Ainsworth (1987) note, in this situation, the carer's own attachment behaviour is in conflict with the child's. For example, the carer may find the needs of the baby over-demanding – they are tired and want to sleep but the child wants attention. They put their feelings first and may delay or avoid responding, or may become angry and irritated by the demands of the infant. This leaves the child unsure what behaviours produce what response from the carer. As the baby grows up and develops an identity of their own, the child's emotional needs are likely to conflict with those of the carer. The carer wants to be loved and the centre of attention but the child has learnt the only way to gain attention is through attention-seeking behaviours. These may initially be aimed at positively engaging the carer, but if they do not work the child may exhibit negative behaviours towards the carer who will, in turn, experience these behaviours as rejection by the child. The carer then feels out of control, devalued and unloved and shouts, screams and makes threats to try and achieve some form of control.

These families pose a particular challenge to practitioners: when is enough, enough? Carers lurch from crisis to crisis; nothing is planned; promises to do things amount to nothing. As children, these carers did not learn how to engage effectively with others, so they depend on affect and emotion to guide.

Therefore, as adults they find by creating crises they can ensure the necessary attention they need from the helping network. The carers can be endearing, frustrating and exhausting. Professionals can easily become absorbed into these families believing that they will change, as the commitment appears to be there. However, unintended crises always get in the way of change. This can result in professionals working with the family for years being over-optimistic, feeling positive about minimal evidence of change when in actual fact there is no significant change to the quality of life for the children in the family: their needs remain unmet.

Emotional Neglect

Professionals are often kept at bay by emotionally neglecting parents. If they do become involved with the family, it may mean visiting at an agreed time. When entering a home, where emotional neglect is occurring, the practitioner may feel confused. The home may be clean and tidy, everything has a place and everything is in its place. The carer can be clear and articulate, discussing the needs of the child in a distant, intellectualised manner. The practitioner often gets a sense that under the superficial politeness there is underlying hostility. The carer is tense and there is a sense of emotional brittleness. Any problems or concerns are firmly focused on the child and their behaviour. The carer has unrealistic expectations of the child and can be punitive and belittling towards the child, as the child consistently fails to live up to the carer's unrealistic expectations. Any discussion about the child occurs in a vacuum. There is no warmth or passion, no anger or frustration. Everything is flat.

In complete contrast to the disorganised, neglectful carer, these carers are living in an emotional desert. Carers, who are emotionally neglectful, are likely to have experienced an insecure and avoidant attachment, with their own carer and consequently feel overwhelmed by the emotional demands of their child and therefore want to keep them at a distance. They are likely to demonstrate emotional unavailability, being isolated and distant from each other, they are vague when expressing feelings and show little emotional warmth and empathy to the child (Crittenden, 1999; Gaudin et al., 1996; Iwaniec, 1995). Their mental processing is dominated by cognition. As the carers have difficulty expressing emotion in a healthy manner, there is much unresolved emotional conflict, which can be expressed though arguments, intimidation and violence (Howe, 2005). As carers they can often provide adequately for the child materially, and education and stimulation may be valued. However, as affect is low, alongside the criticism and belittling the child will experience little emotional warmth and empathy. This high criticism, low warmth environment can be the most damaging family environment for a child (Gibbons et al., 1995).

These families may not come to the attention of child welfare professionals until emotional neglect has led to severe problems for the child, which brings them to the attention of child and adolescent mental health teams. At one level, the carers appear to be providing adequate care. The child may be fed and dressed, there is likely to be structure at home, homework is completed, the child attends school and may do well academically as academic performance and success are encouraged but the child is not happy. Alternatively, in some cases of emotional neglect the carer may isolate themselves and the family from professionals and the outside world. The child is kept at home, the family are never in when practitioners visit, and if practitioners do visit, excuses are made so that practitioners do not see the child (Howe, 2005). As described in Chapter 2, children brought up in this environment are loners, vulnerable to bullying and unable to express emotion or form meaningful relationships.

Iwaniec (1995) describes the features of the carer–child relationship which are likely to exist in this type of family. These include:

- Little or hostile physical contact and the lack of appropriate touching.
- Limited verbal contact – communication tends to be commands, shouting and criticising.
- Ignoring the child's presence or avoiding the child.
- Rejecting.
- Inflicting psychological pain through threatening, provoking anxiety, inducing fear and deprivation of love.

This type of neglectful family is difficult to work with. How can the carer understand the child's needs for emotional warmth when the carer themselves does not know what this means and has never experienced it? If the child is removed from the home the child's feelings of rejection and worthlessness are likely to be reinforced. Ideally the child needs to be well supported by a non-abusing carer or family member (Doyle, 2003).

Depressed Neglect

These carers are the ones that make the practitioner's heart sink into their boots. Before one enters the house a sense of neglect and depression is in the air. The house, or flat, stands out from the rest. The outside of the house is littered with broken toys, cars and bikes, dogs and cats run amok, the door is patched up with hardboard, torn and tattered curtains hang from broken windows. As one enters the house there is no greeting other than the smell that makes one retch. There is a sense of apathy amongst both the carers and children. The family are unkempt and dirty. Soiled nappies and animal faeces litter the floor. A baby may be sitting amongst the remains of takeaway meals, instant snacks, beer cans and cigarette stubs. The baby may be whimpering from hunger or out of pain, because of severe nappy rash or untreated ailments, but no-one takes any notice. There is not a clean or clear surface to be seen, the sparse furniture is broken, the rooms badly in need of redecoration, bedding is inadequate and the soiled kitchen and bathroom a health hazard. The TV is on continually but as a background noise, as everyone is too apathetic to even engage with a TV programme. Children are either whimpering or they sit listlessly with blank expressions on their pale faces.

This is the bleakest parenting environment for children as both cognition and affect are missing from the carer's mental processing. The behaviours reflect 'a deep profound lack of caring, either about oneself, loved ones or the world at large' (Wilson & Horner, 2005, p. 473). For the carer, relationships with others are a source of confusion and the adult becomes 'emotionally neutral' (Howe, 1995, p. 203). This means that they remain flat: they do not demonstrate warmth, neither do they demonstrate anger: everything washes over them leaving them unmoved. The carer is unavailable to the child and is likely to be unaware of and unresponsive to the child's attachment signals (Howe, 2005). There is a general lack of supervision and basic physical care is frequently ignored. Hence, the children are vulnerable to accidents from exposure to hazards inside and outside the home, nutritional and medical neglect. If the children remain in the home, they may end up caring for their carers, who are unable to cope with the demands of life, let alone parenting. Depressed neglect may be linked to drug misuse and mental health problems. These types of issues may lead to a lack of cognition and affect. However, the carers do not recognise or are unable to address, these contributing factors (Wilson & Horner, 2005)

These are the cases where practitioners have to be realistic about the level of change that can be achieved. These families, because of their emotional state, can be difficult to engage in work to improve life for their children. However, it is important that practitioners do not prejudge and are not overwhelmed by the feelings of hopelessness that emanate from the carers (Wilson & Horner, 2005). A thorough Core Assessment should provide an opportunity to identify carer engagement, quality of parenting and the impact on the children. It is crucial that the assessment focuses on both ability and motivation to change. It is also important to recognise that in some cases the carers are unable to make changes at a pace that will ensure the changing needs of the child are going to be met. In these situations, practitioners should consider what support services are available to ensure a good enough parenting environment for the children if the children remain in the home. If these services are not available or the parents will not co-operate, then out-of-home placements may be required.

Assessing Care-Giving Styles

Crittenden (1999) believes practitioners can only work effectively with the carers described above if, as part of the assessment, practitioners take account of the different ways in which affect and cognition are present or absent in interactions in the family. This requires knowledge about the way in which the parent or carer responds to the child. Maccoby (1980) considers the type of responses that should be central to an assessment of care-giving styles. These include:

- Sensitivity to the child's signals and communication of their needs.
- The carer's acceptance of their responsibility to meet the needs of the child.
- The way in which the carer co-operates with the child, recognising them as an autonomous individual.
- The carer's accessibility and openness to meeting the needs of the child.

In Box 3.2 the interactions identified by Maccoby are linked to questions that the practitioner may wish to consider when assessing care-giving style.

In order to answer these questions about care-giving styles, practitioners will need to undertake direct observation of the interactions between carer and child, as well as discussing the interactions with the carer and where possible obtain the child's perceptions of what occurs. A one-off observation is unlikely to provide practitioners with a sound understanding of routine interactions. Hence, staff in family centres and family support workers, who work with the child and carer within the home, are well placed to make these assessments.

Establishing a nurturing relationship with carers is crucial, when practitioners assess and meet the needs of these neglectful families (Crittenden, 1999). Crittenden cautions that these relationships will take a considerable time to develop, as the carers have been hurt in the past by all the key people in their lives and will therefore take time to begin to trust and engage meaningfully with professionals. For example, as a social worker I was involved in undertaking an assessment of a family that had the characteristics of a disorganised neglectful family. The mother was abusive or ignored me for the first few times I visited. When she realised I was going to persist she acknowledged my presence but would not engage in any meaningful discussion. The breakthrough came after six weeks of regular visiting when I was offered a cup of tea. At this point she was prepared to open up and discuss concerns about her parenting. We worked together for a number of weeks until on one visit I made the mistake of refusing a cup of tea. She interpreted this as rejection of her and withdrew. I was never able to engage her in a meaningful way again. Having an opportunity to develop meaningful relationships with these carers is a real challenge in the current child welfare world. As described in Chapter 7, staff turnover, staff shortages, set timescales and performance indicators militate against long-term consistent involvement with families. However, Crittenden (1999) warns that short-term professional involvement in these families does

---

Box 3.2   Assessing Parenting Interaction

Parenting Approach	Factors to Consider
Sensitivity to the child's signals and communications regarding their needs	Does the carer notice the signals from the child such as different types of crying, distress, desire for comfort, interaction and attention?
	How does the carer respond to these signals – do they ignore the child, respond inconsistently, critically or positively?
	Is there reciprocity between child and carer? Do both child and carer initiate positive exchanges and respond to each other?
	Does the carer provide a variety of interactions with the child that involve all the senses, for example, smiling, cooing, hugging?
Acceptance of their responsibility to meet the needs of the child	What is the attitude of the carer to the child – do they see the child as a burden or a source of joy and pleasure?
	How does the carer communicate their responsibility to meet the needs of the child? Do they only respond when the child's distress becomes an irritant to the carer? Are they hostile and aggressive in their response? Does their attitude to the child's needs depend on their mood?
	Does the carer initiate interactions with the child?
	Do they have realistic expectations of the child in terms of needs and behaviours?
	Are their disciplinary techniques appropriate?
Co-operation with the child, recognising them as an autonomous being	Whose wishes and feelings dominate – those of the carer or the child?
	Does the carer respect the wishes and feelings of the child?
	Are they aware of and able to respond to the varying moods of the child?
	Are they aware of the child as a separate person?
Accessibility recognising and being available to meet the needs of the child	Is the carer preoccupied with their own needs and thus fails to notice the signals from the child?
	Do the needs of the child come first distracting the carer from other activities, etc?
	Is the carer able to identify and respond to the child's communications about their needs before the child becomes distressed?
	Can the carer make plans that prioritise the needs of the child?

little more than reinforce the carers' past negative relationship experiences and makes the carers more resistant to subsequent involvement with professionals. This raises serious questions about our current approach towards assessment. As described in more detail in Chapter 7, these cases of chronic neglect are often patched up and dispatched by child welfare services. Workload pressures mean that practitioners do no more than a superficial assessment of current need, aware that a more in-depth assessment is not worthwhile as the services may not be there to address the multi-faceted problems presented by these families (Cleaver & Walker, 2004).

One can be left despairing about the possibility of bringing about change amongst chronic neglecting families, presuming that the problems of the care-givers will inevitably lead to problems for their children. However, Crittenden and Ainsworth (1987) and Fongey et al., (1994) found that carers' insecure childhood attachments do not necessarily always lead to interpersonal problems and insecure attachments with their own children. If the adult can acknowledge and accept the reality of their problematic childhood and 'forgive' their primary carer, they can alleviate the effects of an insecure attachment and establish a secure attachment with their own child. The development of a secure attach-ment with another person in adulthood and successful counselling, can assist this process.

Parental Antecedents of Child Neglect

As an inexperienced social worker I wanted the answers. I wanted to know exactly what it was that I should be considering when assessing child neglect and I was keen to find lists of antecedents that could be used to predict the like-lihood of neglect. However, I learnt very quickly that no list of antecedents was going to make the task straightforward. Research findings, with regard to antecedents, can do no more then alert practitioners to the kind of parenting behaviours that *appear* to be associated with child neglect. As yet the evidence base is not available to be specific about what *causes* child neglect. For example, we do not know why only certain carers who have insecure attachments will go on to neglect their children. Moreover, the research regarding the antecedents or potential risk factors, associated with parenting capacity and child neglect, is limited and confusing. The studies, are often small scale or as noted in the Introduction, fail to distinguish child neglect from other forms of maltreatment. In addition, the identification of risk factors is based on studies of mothers and so little is known about risk factors associated with neglectful fathers. However, Macdonald (2001) makes the case that the findings from the studies that focus on mothers should not be ignored on the basis that male carers were not included (unless their exclusion invalidates the findings). She takes a pragmatic line recognising that whether it is right or wrong women continue to be the primary care-giver for the majority of children. In addition, many of the findings in principle could apply equally to men and women. Another factor that should be taken into account when considering the work on antecedents is that the majority of studies were completed in the USA. Whilst the findings would seem to be relevant and strike cords with European and Austral-Asian practitioners the setting of the studies needs to be borne in mind.

Despite the reservations, outlined above, research into antecedents can give the practitioner an indication of the areas that should be explored with carers and other practitioners when assessing factors that could lead to neglectful parenting. This can be particularly useful when identifying children that may be vulnerable to neglect and the types of preventative interventions that could support both child and carer. Based on research and literature reviews, the antecedents in Box 3.3 appear to be associated with neglectful behaviours.

Some key themes emerge from the literature on antecedents in cases of child neglect. Neglectful parents appear to have poorer parenting and problem-solving skills than other parents (Brayden, 1992; Coohey, 1998). This manifests itself in a number of ways. For example, Coohey found in a study of 37 mothers who did not provide adequate supervision for their children, the mothers were less able than non-neglectful mothers to make realistic plans for the family and to see the plans through. A particular area of difficulty found amongst neglectful parents, is their lack of ability in dealing with children's behaviour in relation to limit setting and gaining the co-operation of the child (Hansen et al., 1989; Lacharite et al., 1996). Neglectful parents appear to find social interactions with their children difficult and consequently fail to provide verbal and social stimulation (Garbarino, 1999; Wilson et al., 2005). The parents also seem to lack social skills, finding it hard to show warmth in their relationships and be curious about others (Coohey, 1998).

Parental educational levels also appear to influence neglectful parenting. Although the studies focus on mothering, the research indicates that the less education the mother received the greater the risk of child neglect (Salmelainen, 1996; Connell-Carrick, 2003). Not only do neglectful parents lack the knowledge and skills to meet the needs of the child, but as described above they can also lack motivation. Coohey (1998) found in her study of mothers who did not provide adequate supervision to their children, that they were less motivated than the control group. She found that the mothers who lacked motivation also had poorer problem-solving and social skills and more problems with their children than the control group.

The most vulnerable children appear to be those who are living with carers who have limited capacity as care-givers and, in addition, have parenting issues which influence their parenting capacity. These parenting issues include learning disability, depression, suicide attempts, substance misuse, and not surprisingly,

---

Box 3.3 Antecedents of Child Neglect

The carers (remember the research studies are predominantly about mothers) are likely to:

- Have less positive and fewer interactions with the child than mothers who provide adequate care.
- Be immature.
- Have poor knowledge of a child's needs.
- Find difficulty meeting the dependency needs of the child.
- Become upset or angry easily and have difficulty controlling impulses.
- Function at a lower intellectual level than other mothers.
- Are less confident and outgoing than other mothers.
- Have less socially skills than non-neglecting mothers.
- Have a poor sense of self-esteem.
- Suffer persistent but small stresses (acute major stresses may not be a factor).
- Have a history of child neglect.
- Have a large number of children.
- Feel social isolated with few support networks. socially maybe?
- Have problematic relationships with partners and own mothers.
- Live in poor socio-economic circumstances.

Sources: Coohey, 2003; Dubowitz, 1999a; Erickson and Egeland, 2002; Gaudin et al., 1996; Iwaniec, 1995; Schumacher et al., 2001; Stevenson, 1998; Wilson et al., 2005.

bearing in mind the consequences of neglect as described in Chapter 2, a history of maltreatment as a child (Cleaver et al., 1999; Scannapieco & Connell-Carrick, 2005; Wilson & Horner, 2005).

The Role of Male Care-Givers in Cases of Child Neglect

Fathers as care-givers

While there is an emphasis in the research on mothers and women as care-givers, fathers also have a significant part to play in bringing up children. For example, Milligan and Dowie (1998), based on interviews with children, conclude that children look to their fathers to provide them with physical contact and love. The children want them to act as a role model, be supportive and give them quality time. While the exact influence a father has on the development of the child is difficult to establish, fathers do seem to have an important role in children's psycho-social development and their academic performance and attitude to school. In addition, the absence of an engaged father reduces the emotional and material resources available to the child (Daniel & Taylor, 2001).

Schaffer (2004), summarising the research on attachments between fathers and their children, observes that fathers can act as attachment figures. Moreover, there is frequently consistency between the attachment formed between the child and their mother and the child and their father. He believes this may reflect consistency of treatment by both parents. However, different attachment strategies between the child and parent may develop, for the reasons described earlier in this chapter. This can have positive benefits for a vulnerable child. For example, if the attachment between a child and their mother is insecure the father may have formed a more secure attachment to the child, which may act as a buffer for the child against the negative effects of the poor attachment with the mother

Fathers appear to be significant throughout a child's life. For example, Flouri and Buchanan (2003) studied the role of father and mother involvement in relation to the psychological well-being of adults. They found, irrespective of the gender of the child, that whilst both parents contributed to offspring happiness, father involvement had the stronger effect. Moreover, family disruption and low involvement of the mother does not appear to weaken the significance of the association with the father.

Child Neglect and the Role of Fathers

Clearly, fathers have a significant role to play in child-rearing. However, if the research studies focus on mothers does this mean that fathers, or male care-givers, are not involved in child neglect? The answer, not surprisingly, is no. Guterman and Lee (2005, p. 144) reviewed the role of fathers in studies of physical child abuse and neglect. They found specific father factors associated with the risk of physical child abuse and neglect. There was direct correlational evidence to indicate that the following were associated with maltreatment:

- Absence from the family home.
- Unemployment.
- Substance misuse.
- Lack of support and undermining the mother.
- Violence towards the mother.
- Lack of direct provision of childcare.

They also found indirect evidence that the following contributed to increased risk of maltreatment:

- Low income.

- Job or major financial loss.
- Young age.
- Family of origin maltreatment.

We will explore some of these factors in more detail.

Lone Mothers and the Role of Fathers

There is a strong correlation between single-parenthood by mothers and child neglect (Connell-Carrick, 2003). This could lead one to assume that in these situations there are no male care-givers involved with the child. This is not the case and depends on our interpretation of 'single-parenthood'. For example, Coohey (1995) in a study of 69 neglectful mothers found 75 per cent of the mothers did actually have a 'partner', albeit not living with them full-time. However, these mothers had less contact with their partners, knew their partners for less time and were less likely to be living with them then non-neglecting mothers. The men worked fewer hours than men living with women who had not neglected their children, were more likely to receive government aid and were less likely to be the father of one of the mother's children. In contrast, Lacharite et al., (1996, p. 19) noted a large proportion of the lone parents had a male 'figure' in the family at the time the maltreatment began. They found that compared to men in non-maltreating families the men in the neglectful families were perceived by the mothers as being less adequate *marital* partners, less supportive and more violent. However, the mothers did see these men as being adequate *paternal* figures to their children as did the non-maltreating mothers. Yet Coohey (1995), in her study, found that neglectful mothers both received and also provided emotional support to their partners. For example, they listened to each other, and make decisions together. The mothers however, did not perceive their partners as someone to do things with, or someone who could provide practical support, such as baby-sitting or helping with housework. These studies indicate that when assessing neglect in these situations it is worth discussing the nature of the support the mother believes she is or is not receiving from her partner

Although initially it is easy enough for practitioners to assume that a lone mother is just that, what is evident is that she may have complex parenting relationships with male carers. This can make it difficult for practitioners to determine who is caring for the child and who should be included in the assessment. For example, the children in the family may have different fathers. Whilst some partners may take responsibility for all the children, irrespective of the birth father, others may be shadowy figures in the household (Daniel & Baldwin 2002). However, these men and their behaviour may have a significant impact on the life of the child. For example, Daniel and Taylor (2001) describe the risks posed by such men in terms of sexual and physical abuse. In addition, they may be exacerbating existing neglect or increasing the risk of neglect by under-mining the mother's already limited sense of self-esteem, using family income for their own needs or bringing friends into the home who pose a risk to the child. Moreover, the coming and goings of a diverse range of men in single-mother homes may lead to instability. With this in mind, it is important that practitioners take into account how all men in the child's life are influencing the way in which the needs of the child are being met.

It is important to note that while fathers who are not living in the home with their child may still play an active part in their upbringing, there are fathers who may be physically present in the home but they play such a minimal part in the care of the children and are so little involved in family life that they are to all intent and purposes absent fathers (Guterman & Lee, 2005).

Vulnerable Fathers

Guterman and Lee (2005) identified a range of factors, highlighted in the liter-ature, that could increase the risk of the father physically abusing or neglecting a child. They note men who become fathers at a young age can find fatherhood particularly stressful. For example, a young man recently described, how becoming a father felt 'like someone had just parked a lorry on my chest' (BBC, 2005). Young single fathers in a study by Speak et al., (1997) described the issues which impacted on their ability to develop and maintain relationships with their children. The problems often began before the birth of the child when they were made to feel unimportant during pregnancy and after the birth of the baby, with little encouragement to engage and maintain involvement with the child. The degree to which they developed a relationship with the baby was strongly influenced by the attitudes of the paternal and maternal grandparents. These men were frequently unemployed, they lacked money but did contribute to supporting the child. Lack of finance meant they were unable to establish and maintain an independent home, which prevented them from becoming involved with their children. They also lacked knowledge and under-standing of what fatherhood meant. Although they considered it was important that they were there for their children, they received very little professional support with parenting. Against this backcloth it is easy to see how these fathers are almost set up to fail to meet the needs of their children.

Another factor which may be associated with child neglect by fathers is their own upbringing. As described earlier in this chapter, children who have formed insecure attachments with their carers are not best equipped to meet the needs of their own child.

Guterman and Lee (2005) also draw attention to the significance of the interactions between the father, mother and child in both increasing the risk of physical abuse and neglect and acting as protection from it. Domestic violence and a negative relationship between the carers, as we will see in Chapter 4, can have a detrimental effect on children. However, the father can play a positive role in supporting the child and protecting them from negative outcomes, for example, when the mother is suffering from mental health issues, drug or alcohol misuse, which is affecting her ability to meet the needs of the child. In a rare study of father figure involvement in the family life of neglectful families, Dubowitz et al., (2000) found that the nature of the father's involvement influenced the degree of neglect. A long duration of involvement, a strong sense of parenting efficacy, involvement in household tasks and *less* involvement with child-care were associated with less neglect. Dubowitz et al., commenting on this last, somewhat surprising finding, hypothesise that fathers involved in child-care may reflect that the father was forced to take on child-care responsibilities because the mother was not available to the child. Hence less child-care may mean better interaction between the child and mother. why?!

Professionals' Perceptions of Fathers

Men may be marginalised by practitioners when assessing child neglect because of practitioners own attitudes towards the fathers. For example, Scourfield (2003 cited in Daniel & Taylor, 2005) found that social work practitioners held a range of views about men in the families. These included perceiving the men as a threat, of little use when it came to caring or indeed irrelevant. Some practitioners did not consider finding out about their involvement, if they were absent from the home. In a study of child neglect which I completed in Ireland (For more details see the introduction to Part 3 of this book) workers tended to ignore the contributions that fathers played in creating a neglectful environment for children. The respondents to the study were asked to list their concerns about a case of chronic neglect involving four children. The father was described as 'unemployed, drinks heavily and is believed to be violent towards May (his depressed wife). He takes no responsibility for child-care and refuses to have contact with staff from the Board (health and social work services)' (Horwath and Bishop, 2001, p. 147). Of the 40 social work respondents, only 3 expressed concern about the father's lack of co-operation with the Board; the lack of support for the mother was considered a concern by a further 3 respondents and only 5 perceived a lack of interest in the parenting role as an issue. The focus, in terms of the workers concerns and possible interventions, was on the mother who was perceived to be responsible for the care and protection of the children.

The Role of Maternal Grandmothers

Another family member who appears to play a significant role in neglectful families is the maternal grandmother. Despite often experiencing poor parenting from their own mothers, mothers who neglect their child appear to maintain relationships with their mothers. Coohey (1995) explored the nature of these relationships. She found that the mothers tended to live in proximity to their own mothers and had high levels of interaction with them. However, the quality of the relationship differed to that of non-neglecting mothers. The neglectful mothers tended to have a less positive relationship with their own mothers and rated them as having more undesirable attributes. For example, they considered they lacked warmth, were not caring and were unable to control their anger. The daughters appeared to be less interested in receiving emotional support from their mothers than the non-neglecting mothers and instrumental support focused on baby-sitting. Although they *received* fewer supports from their mothers, they also *gave* significantly less support to their mothers. Coohey (1995) postulates that the low level of reciprocation may be associated with the lack of positive feelings the daughter has for her mother. If, as described above, neglectful carers are more likely than other carers to have experienced maltreatment in childhood and insecure attachment patterns, it is not surprising that the emotional connection with their mothers developed in childhood continues to dominate the relationships once they become adults.

Maternal grandmothers can play a significant part in the lives of neglected children. However, in my experience, it is all too easy to presume that the grandmother can act as a support for the carer and her children or indeed as the primary carer, if the children cannot remain with their parents. Practitioners should bear in mind that the maternal grandmother may well have maltreated her own children and may have poor parenting skills. With this in mind practitioners may wish to consider the following questions when assessing the capacity of grandparents and other extended family members to meet the needs of the children:

- How does the grandmother respond to questions about parenting knowledge and skills as outlined in Box 3.1?
- How does the carer and her siblings describe their own childhood?
- How aware is the grandmother of her behaviour towards her own children?
- How does she relate to her grandchildren and meet their needs?
- What supports are available to the grandmother that may enhance her parenting ability, for example, a supportive partner?

Summary

Both mothers and fathers have a crucial role to play in meeting the needs of the child. However, in cases of child neglect, the focus, in terms of both research and practice, tends to be on the mother. It is important that practitioners recognise the important contribution that fathers, whether living in or outside the child's home, can make to meeting the needs of the child.

Unfortunately, the information available about parenting and the antecedents for neglect is from research studies that sampled mothers. The research does however highlight the likelihood that these mothers have poor cognitive and social skills with a low sense of self-worth and are often isolated, finding it difficult to form relationships. The limited research on fathers indicates that absence, unemployment, substance misuse, and a negative relationship with the mother appear to directly correlated to physical abuse and neglect.

Assessing parenting capacity in cases of child neglect requires practitioners to consider the carer's ability and motivation as well as the opportunities available to meet the needs of the child. If these three are not present the child is likely to be neglected. Parenting ability and motivation are influenced by a number of factors. These include first, the carer's knowledge and understanding of the parenting task and ways in which they should respond to the needs of the child. Second, the parent's own negative life experiences, most significantly their attachment to their primary care-giver. Insecure attachments appear to lead to three different forms of neglect: disorganised, emotional and depressed. The type of neglect will be influenced by the mental processing of the carer about cognitive and affective information with regard to danger and protection.

In this chapter the focus has been on the factors that influence the carer's ability and motivation to meet the needs of their child. In the next chapter consideration is given to the parenting issues and parenting opportunities that influence both ability and motivation.

4

Parenting Issues and Child
Neglect: What Do We Know?

Introduction

In the previous chapter we considered how the childhood experiences of the carer can have a negative influence on their ability to meet the needs of the child, which in turn can result in neglect. In this chapter, we move on to consider how carers' current problems and issues can, usually unintentionally, result in neglect of their children's needs.

A range of parenting problems are associated with child maltreatment. This includes mental health issues, drug misuse and learning disability (Cleaver & Freeman, 1995; 1999; Farmer & Owen, 1995; Horwath & Bishop, 2001). Although professionals are increasingly recognising the links between parenting issues and maltreatment, it is all too easy to focus on these issues in relation to specific incidents, such as a drunken father hitting their child, or a drug misusing carer leaving a syringe lying around within reach of a toddler. What becomes marginalised is the way in which parents' problems impinge on the daily life of the child. For example, I can vividly remember being involved in a case where a mother was involuntarily admitted to hospital just before Christmas because of mental health issues. I presumed her 13-year-old son would be distressed that his mother would be away for Christmas. Instead he was joyous. He explained that for the last ten years his mother had destroyed the Christmas tree his father brought home each year. She always smashed any decorations and threw away presents, convinced they came from the devil. She refused to allow the family to eat Christmas dinner as she thought the food was poisoned. The boy went on to say birthdays had been ruined in the same way and he welcomed the opportunity to share, with his father, for the first time in his memory, a traditional Christmas. What is clear from this example is that unless we ask children we do not know how parenting issues are affecting their life. They are the ones who are best placed to describe the way it impacts on their life. The words of a 15-year-old young woman, who was living with domestic violence, illustrates what I mean:

child

> I'd think about my mum being hit and then I just would walk out of school and come home ... I didn't like the thought of her being on her own , so I stayed at home all the time. (McGee, 2000, p. 81)

The purpose of this chapter is to explore ways in which carers' issues do impact on the daily life of the child and to consider how this can result in child neglect. Particular attention is given to ways in which professionals can assess the impact. Although a range of parenting issues, such as physical disability, parental separation and divorce, may impact on a carer's ability to meet the needs of a child, four particular parenting problems known to be associated with neglect, are considered in detail. These are: mental health issues, drug and alcohol misuse, domestic violence and learning disabilities.

Mental Health Issues

There are wide variations in the quality of the parent–child relationship when one or both carers are experiencing mental health issues (Royal College of Psychiatrists, 2002). Whilst many carers with mental health problems are able to successfully bring up their children, a percentage struggle. It is difficult to estimate the extent of the problem as most studies use specific samples where mental illness and maltreatment are already linked (Aldridge & Becker, 2003; Stanley, et al., 2003). Nevertheless Gibbons, Conroy and Bell, (1995) found mental health issues present in 13% of cases referred to social services department for child protection concerns. While a link is made in the literature between emotional abuse, child sexual abuse and mental health issues, this link is not so apparent in studies of neglect and physical abuse (Cleaver et al., 1999; Hunt et al., 1999). Yet, parental mental illness can have a significant impact on the carer's ability to meet the ongoing developmental needs of their child with different forms of illness giving rise to different concerns about parenting capacity. Box 4.1 summarises the common types of mental health problems, the possible impact on parenting ability and motivation and the factors practitioners may wish to consider when assessing the needs of children living with these carers.

Mental Health Issues and Assessment Practice

As can be seen from Box 4.1, mental health problems can affect parenting capacity in a variety of ways. However, irrespective of the nature of the mental illness there are some common key factors that should be considered as part of an assessment (Louis et al., 1997). These include:

Box 4.1   Impact of Mental Illness on Parenting Capacity and the Assessment Task

Types of Mental Illness	Impact on Parenting Capacity	The Assessment Task
Schizophrenia	Experiences episodic problems of functioning may neglect personal hygiene, lose contact with reality, have strange thoughts and become preoccupied with inner world May demonstrate incongruence of affect which can confuse child who cannot make sense of or process signals from carer which can affect attachment between carer and child Chronic schizophrenics may display lack of motivation, withdrawal, apathy and lethargy exacerbated by neuroleptic medication, which can also affect attachment May experience florid psychosis behaving unpredictably and chaotically leading to poor lack of judgement resulting in severe neglect or safety issues Disengaged and emotionally inaccessible and unresponsive to child affecting child's cognitive and psycho-social development Child may become part of paranoia and delusions which could be fatal	Consider: • History of illness and carer's behaviours • History of the relationship between child and carer • Carer's responsiveness to the needs of the child • Their understanding of the needs of the child • Their recognition of the impact of their illness on their ability to meet the needs of the child • The interaction between child and carer • The content of the psychotic ideation • History of the carer's ability to manage their anger during illness • The presence of another responsible adult who will take a caring role • Whether the child is achieving milestones • Child's support network
Affective disorders	Characterised by misery, irritability, agitation, social isolation, failure to cope and guilt Includes both depression and bipolar affective disorder. During manic episodes carer may be overwhelmed by surge of physical and mental energy leading to restlessness, excitability, over-talkative or argumentative states Feelings of hopelessness and lack of energy resulting in insensitivity and unavailability can lead to insecure avoidant attachment strategy	Consider: • Attachment between child and carer • Level of engagement with child • Carer's sensitivity to the needs of the child • Emotional availability ability to cope with the child when the child is distressed • Strategies for managing the child's behaviours • Impact of carer's behaviour on child • Support available to child and carer

	Depressed mothers may show more verbal and physical hostility in interactions with children Feeding may be irregular and erratic	Consider: • The pre-occupation of the carer and the way in which this affects their functioning • Establish parenting tasks carer finds difficult to manage and strategies if any used to manage the situation • The expectations the carer has of the child • The child's experience • Supports available to child and carer • Impact of the carer's behaviour on the child
Anxiety disorders	Includes phobic states e.g. agoraphobia, obsessive-compulsive disorders and panic attacks Person experiences range of fear responses Pre-occupation with disorder can result in carer being detached, unresponsive or inconsistent towards child Parent may not be able to manage such tasks as taking child to school, shopping, etc. Child may be deprived of age-appropriate opportunities for socialisation Children can become drawn into the obsession and lose sense of appropriate behaviour	
Eating disorders	Carers who are anorexic or bulimic Carers can have distorted ideas about a healthy weight and shape for a child May dilute formula or restrict child's food intake Can distort child's image of their own body	Consider: • These problems are often concealed so practitioners may not always be aware of the possible risks to the child • Exploration of past history of carer in relation to eating disorders • Relationship with child and carer • Carer's attitude towards the child • Carer's and child's attitude towards food, feeding regimes and body shape • Perceptions of other family members • Support available from the family particularly at mealtimes ensuring the child is fed regularly and appropriately • Monitoring of weight and general progress

(handwritten annotation) emot and abuse → child sexual abuse →
mental health issues
? → neglect and physical abuse

Sources: Bifulco and Moran, 1998; Cassell and Coleman, 1995; Cleaver et al., 1999; Cox, 1988; Cox et al., 1987; Fellow-Smith, 2000; Panaccione and Wahler, 1986

The ability to 'parent proper' (ibid, p. 591)

This includes the carer's ability to meet the physical and safety needs of the child as well as emotional responsiveness and parenting style. If the carer has little understanding of the needs of a child, before the onset of mental illness, then the preoccupation with self associated with many of the disorders described above, is likely to exacerbate the situation. If however, the carer already appreciates and recognises the needs of the child and knows how to respond, this may assist the carer, when ill, to develop strategies to ensure that the needs of the child are met.

The child's characteristics

As parenting involves interactions between children and their carers, practitioners should take into account characteristics of the child such as temperament, particular needs and the carer's opinion of the child, which are likely to influence the carer's approach to the child (see Chapter 2 for more detail about the difficult-to-parent child). For example, a child with a difficult temperament or special needs, may challenge a carer whose ability to respond appropriately to the needs of a child is already compromised through depression (Cassell & Coleman, 1995; Fellow-Smith, 2000; Rutter & Quinton, 1984). One can see that certain children will be particularly vulnerable if support is not available to the child and their carer. For example, a baby with a disability or complex health needs whose mother is suffering from post-natal depression.

The nature of the mental illness

The carer's mental state, the impact of the illness on the carer and diagnostic uncertainty will all influence ability and motivation to parent. Consideration should also be given to the carer's engagement with any treatment regime, the side effects of drugs and the services provided to and used by the carer to address the mental health concerns (Foss et al., 1999). Practitioners should also consider the impact that the mental illness and any treatment, has on the carer's cognitive state, most particularly their ability to make judgements about the child, and their emotional availability to the child. For example, some medication may make the carer lethargic and slow to respond to the child.

Support with caring for the child

The resilience of the child, the support systems available to the child and carer and the living and economic conditions can play a considerable part

| | in ensuring the needs of the child are met despite mental health problems (Cleaver et al., 1999; Stanley et al., 2003). Particular attention should be given to the level of insight and understanding that partners and supporting family members have of the mental health problems and the strategies developed to support the child and carer.

Carer's past history

The carer's own experiences of childhood trauma, consistency of caring, as well as a past history of overdose and self-harm should also be considered. In addition, the carer's personality pre-existing and/or exacerbated by the illness such as irritability and hostility may influence parenting capacity. Finally, problematic relationships with professionals and violent, unstable, conflictual relationships with partners and family may also affect parenting capacity and the ability to work with others to meet the needs of the child (Royal College of Psychiatrists, 2002).

Mental health practitioners who are working with carers on their mental health issues, are the ones who are best placed to identify the possible impact of the issues on the carer's ability to meet the needs of the child. For example, professionals may become aware that the carer is negative, emotionally unavailable or unresponsive to the needs of the child or indeed, does not recognise the needs of the child. They may also discover that the carers have inconsistent or inappropriate expectations of the child or they may observe distorted, confusing or misleading communication with the child (Royal College of Psychiatrists, 2002). Because of their knowledge and understanding of the impact of mental illness on carer's cognitions and affects professionals within psychiatric services can contribute to the assessment of the needs of the child in a variety of ways. This includes providing information about the:

- History of contact with psychiatric services, and knowledge about the parent and family.
- The psychiatric diagnosis and information about illness morbidity.
- The possible impact of the illness on parenting capacity.
- Previous psychiatric history and the impact on parenting.
- Emotional availability and stability.
- Observed interactions with the child/ren.
- Treatment progress.
- Compliance regarding treatment.
- Attendance at appointments.
- Availability and take up of services by carer.

(Buckley et al., 2005b)

Drug and Alcohol Misuse

Between 200,000 and 300,000 children in England and Wales are living with parents who have serious drug problems. This is about 2–3% of children under the age of 16. In Scotland the situation is worse with 4–6% of all children under the age of 16 having a parent with a serious drug problem (Advisory Council on the Misuse of Drugs, 2003). While in the USA as far back as 1991 40% of substantiated child maltreatment cases involved drug misuse by the carer (Murphy et al., 1991). Around a quarter of cases of children on the English child protection register[1] feature a parental drug or alcohol problem (Advisory Council on the Misuse of Drugs, 2003). And children from drug-misusing families, in England, are twice as likely as others to be subject to care proceedings (Forrester, 2000).

It is apparent from the numbers of children on the child protection register that drug misuse can have a significant impact on a carer's ability to meet the needs of their child. Consideration has already been given in Chapter 2 to the impact of drug misuse on a baby in utero and following birth. Yet, it is not only these infants who are affected by the carer's drug or alcohol misuse. Children of parents who misuse drugs and alcohol are not as well adjusted socially and perform less well academically than other children (Keen & Alison, 2001; West & Prinz, 1987). Developmental problems such as lack of adaptability, insecure attachments, poor language development and conduct disorders have been reported (Sheridan, 1995; Ammerman et al., 1999; Dube et al., 2001; Dunn et al., 2002). The children themselves describe feelings of hurt, rejection, sadness and anger regarding their parents' drug problems and 'expressed a deep sense of absence and isolation … their parents were not 'there for them'' (Advisory Council on the Misuse of Drugs, 2003, p. 11). These children are also affected by the social consequences of drug and alcohol use. Walker and Glasgow (2005) argue that these social consequences can be more detrimental to children than the drug use itself. For example, the stigma associated with drug use may isolate the child within their school and community. Children may be ashamed of their parent's behaviour and may carry the burden of keeping these illegal activities secret.

The relationship between substance use and neglectful behaviour in parents is not a simple cause – effect relationship (Sheridan, 1995). The studies indicate that many adults, who misuse drugs, like those who neglect their children, are likely to have suffered adverse childhood experiences (Ammerman et al., 1999; Dunn et al., 2002; Nair et al., 1997). Dunn et al., (2002, p. 1072) put it well:

> It appears that the developmental pathway to neglectful parenting in SUD (substance misuse disorder) begins with childhood experiences of maltreatment,

leading to socio-emotional maladjustment in their own development, which, in conjunction with social support deficits and difficult-child characteristics, exert direct and cumulative effect on deficient parenting outcomes.

Alcohol Misuse

Despite the high levels of drug misuse associated with child neglect it is important to recognise that much greater numbers of children are living in families affected by alcohol misuse (Tunnard, 2002). Dube et al., (2001) make a detailed examination of the association between parental alcohol abuse and multiple forms of child abuse and neglect. From a questionnaire of 8629 individuals, those respondents who indicated that their parents did abuse alcohol were between 2 and 13 times more likely to indicate experiences of abuse, neglect or adversity in childhood than those whose carers did not abuse alcohol. Moreover, the NSPCC (1997) found maternal drinking was the most frequent form of alcohol misuse associated with child neglect. In a study completed by the author (for more detail see the introduction to Part III of this book), alcohol misuse was identified by social work practitioners as a major cause for concern in 31% (n = 23) of child neglect cases (Horwath & Bishop, 2001). Social workers, who responded to the questionnaire included in the study, described a range of problems associated with alcohol use. The most frequently mentioned problem was concerns about supervision and safety to the children (18%) followed by the emotional impact on the child of the parents' drinking (10%).

Ten of the respondents described difficulty in assessing the impact of alcohol misuse on parenting capacity when the carers are binge drinkers. They recognised that carers could provide good enough parenting in-between periods of binge drinking and found it was all too easy to minimise the impact of this binge drinking on the children in the family.

Impact of Drug and Alcohol Use on Parenting Capacity

As with various mental health issues described above, certain drugs can have a specific impact on a user's behaviour, which can in turn impact on parenting capacity. The effects on the users are shown in Box 4.2 and the impact considered below.

Substance and alcohol misuse do not automatically lead to child neglect or other forms of maltreatment. As Murphy and Harbin (2003, p. 355) conclude 'substance abuse in families is not tantamount to child abuse. Substance misuse *will* have an impact on the individual adult, which *may* have an impact on their parenting capacity, which in turn *might* effect the development of the individual child'. There are a variety of ways in which drug and alcohol use may impact

Box 4.2   Likely Impact of Specific Drugs on User's Behaviour

Type of Drug	Effect on User
Opiates such as heroin	Users experience a sudden rush of pleasure that lasts for seconds followed by a dreamlike unreal state
	The effects of the drugs are to reduce emotional responsiveness anxiety and discomfort
	As tolerance develops the user needs to increase the dose to obtain the euphoria that accompanies use
	At some stage, the positive effects of the drug cannot be obtained through increased dosage and the drug is used to feel normal. This can create a strong psychological dependency
	The withdrawal reactions can be unpleasant
	Carers on prescribed methadone are usually able to function well, maintaining a stable lifestyle
Stimulants such as amphetamines, cocaine and crack	The user presents as confident and happy. Also likely to consider themselves to be competent however, their concentration is often impaired
	After drug has worn off they may feel depressed and hopeless
Depressants such as sedatives, alcohol and tranquillisers	Depress the functioning of the nervous system. This affects memory, concentration and psychomotor functioning
	The body becomes tolerant to depressants and higher doses are required to obtain the same effects
	Dependency is likely to develop and withdrawal is accompanied by irritability, over-arousal and sleeping problems
Stimulants such as ecstasy cocaine and crack	Increases the wakefulness of the user
	The user considers performance is enhanced and mood elated.
	Withdrawal can be accompanied by anxiety and depression.
	Excessive use can lead to paranoia and psychotic illness
Hallucinogenic drugs include cannabis and LSD	Cannabis user experiences a sense of heightened awareness and feeling relaxed
	LSD causes visual and other hallucinations and sensual experiences are likely to be enhanced
	Withdrawal can lead to sleeping problems, anxiety and 'flashbacks'

Sources: Coleman and Cassell, 1995; Cleaver et al., 1999; Harbin and Murphy, 2000

on parenting capacity and the development of the child (Advisory Council on the Misuse of Drugs, 2003; Alison, 2000; Ammerman et al., 1999; Cleaver et al., 1999; Donohue, 2004; Dunn et al., 2002; Harbin & Murphy, 2000; Mounteney, 1998). These include:

Failure to attend to the health needs of the child
The parent may lack awareness of the child's health problems because they are so pre-occupied with their own needs. In addition, the carer may be reluctant to take the child for medical checks and treatment as they fear medical professionals will criticise their parenting and they could ulti-mately lose the child. Some drug users lead a chaotic lifestyle and have more accommodation moves than other groups. As a result of this they may not always register with a GP, the child may not be taken for health checks and the child's health records may be incomplete.

Failure to meet the child's physical needs
Carers who use drugs and alcohol may have difficulty organising their own lives, let alone the lives of their child. Basic standards of hygiene may be neglected and the carer may fail to establish routines for the child such as mealtimes, bedtimes and regular school attendance. Nutritional neglect may also occur if drugs or alcohol suppress the carer's own appetite and they fail to recognise the child's need for food. Moreover, money spent on alcohol and drugs may mean that little is left over to cloth and feed the child.

Failure to meet the child's emotional needs
Carers who use drugs may be emotionally unavailable to the child. This can result in the carer finding it difficult atuning into, interpreting and responding to the needs of the baby or child. This can affect the forma-tion of a secure attachment between the child and primary care-giver. Drug and alcohol use can result in dramatic mood swings and an incon-sistent approach towards the child leaving the child unsure how to respond to the carer's unpredictable behaviour.

Failure to protect the child from physical danger
Children can be in danger if drugs and needles are left around the home leading to accidental poisoning, drug ingestion or sources of HIV infec-tion. The children may be left home alone while the carer obtains their drug supplies or remain unsupervised in the house while the carer is in an alcohol or drug induced state and unable to care for the child. The child may also be in danger of physical abuse as substance misuse can dis-inhibit aggressive impulses and lower tolerance levels, meaning the carer can become both verbally and physically aggressive towards the child.

Failure to protect the child from unsuitable carers and adults
This may occur if the house is used for drug dealing or drink binging. The child may be left with carers who are unable to meet their needs. Alternatively, the child is open to abuse by other people visiting the home. Finding the funds to support a drug habit may lead the carer into criminal activity or prostitution, which the child may witness, be aware of or actively involved in. For example, the child may be involved in the procurement of drugs or money, or the child may be expected to act as a courier for the carer.

Alison (2000, p. 17) has identified the factors associated with risk of maltreatment to children by drug misusing parents. These include:

- addicted carer being a mother, under 18 or over 30
- The carer having poor parenting skills and history of prior maltreatment.
- A pattern of long-term drug use, which affects life style.
- Taking methadone and other additional drugs.
- Using drugs through pregnancy.
- Parenting issues such as domestic violence.
- Poverty and poor social support.
- Infant exhibiting drug withdrawal symptoms.

Positive outcomes for children appear to be related to a number of factors. These include the more obvious factors such as carer's voluntary participation in treatment programmes and effective treatment. However, positive outcomes are also linked to the extent to which the carer is able to provide a stable home, adequate financial resources and maintain family routines and activities. Stability and routine are more likely to be achieved if there is another consistent adult present, or the child and carer are living with family members who are not using drugs (Advisory Council on the Misuse of Drugs, 2003; Alison, 2000). The child's regular attendance at a supportive school has also been found to promote positive outcomes for children living with drug misusing carers (Advisory Council on the Misuse of Drugs, 2003).

Assessing the Impact of Drug and Alcohol Misuse

As with the assessment of mental health issues, a multi-disciplinary assessment is crucial when assessing the impact of alcohol and drug misuse on parenting capacity (SCODA (Standing Conference on Drug Abuse), 1997). Murphy and Harbin (2003, p. 358) believe the assessment should include three key components. First, establishing the pattern of substance misuse. For example, the drugs or alcohol used, pattern of use and lifestyle implications. Second, identifying how the substance or alcohol misuse is impacting on parenting capacity and exploring ways in which the needs of the child are or are not being met (Box 4.2 can be used for this purpose). Finally, considering support available from partners, extended family and community to provide alternative parenting resources and establish the parents/carers understanding of the need to change and what change might be acceptable and attainable.

Domestic Violence

Witnessing domestic violence is known to have a negative effect on the health and development of a child (Hester et al., 1999; Humphreys & Mullender, 2003; Mullender, 1996). Domestic violence includes seeing a carer being physically abused; hearing the violence and being told negative things about the non-abusing carer; seeing the aftermath of a violent incident; being used as a human shield by a carer; witnessing the carer being arrested; witnessing the distress of the non-abusing carer (Kantor & Little, 2003).

In England Wilding and Thoburn (1997) found 17% of child protection referrals for child neglect were associated with extreme abuse by a spouse, while in the author's neglect study (see introduction to Part III for further details) domestic violence was an issue in 21.6% (n = 16) of neglect cases (Horwath & Bishop, 2001). Indeed, the negative effects of witnessing domestic violence have been acknowledged by policymakers. Through the Adoption and Children Act 2002, which came into force in December 2005, the Children's Act 1989 has been amended and the definition of 'significant harm' broadened to include 'impairment suffered from seeing or hearing the ill-treatment of another'.

Carers themselves may be unaware of the ways in which living with domestic violence can impact on the child's health and development. For example, they may believe if the child does not actually witness violent acts they will not be affected by the situation (Kantor & Little, 2003). However, living with domestic violence is likely to affect children emotionally and cognitively. They can become isolated from peers, bullied at school and the effects of witnessing domestic violence can have a lasting influence on their ability to build relationships (Cleaver et al., 1999; Hester et al., 1999; Mullender et al., 2003). Their experiences may also result in adolescent boys in turn becoming aggressive and engaging in anti-social behaviours, whilst girls are more likely to internalise the problems and show signs of depression (Edleston, 1999). Children in domestic violent situations may also take on inappropriate roles, which can impact on their health and development. As one boy in Buckley et al.'s (2006) study put it:

I was doing so much ... I was trying to take care of my sister, I was trying to stop my mam and her boy friend from fighting. I had barely any time for study and it was just horrible.

Cleaver et al., (1999, p. 34) argue that the impact of domestic violence on children is likely to be aggravated if the domestic violence is combined with any of the following: problem drinking or drug use; the child witnessing the parent's sexual or physical abuse; the child being drawn into participating in the abuse of a carer or the child colluding in the secrecy and concealment of the assaults.

Children who witness domestic violence are experiencing a world which is confusing and for which they are ill prepared:

You're like spinning the whole time. If it's not happening, you're waiting for it to happen. When it's happening it's almost a relief because, here it is, what I'm waiting for. And then when it's not happening you're waiting for it again.

(Buckley et al., 2006, p. 38)

Good enough carers usually filter daily life experiences for children enabling the child to understand and make sense of these experiences. However, in cases of domestic violence the perpetrator is likely to have detached themselves from the experience of the family, whilst the victim may dissociate from the aggression or normalise the situation. In these cases, the carers may become so occupied with their own needs that they lack empathy with the child's experience and consequently fail to protect them or support them through these experiences (McIntosh, 2002). Indeed witnessing domestic violence is regarded as child neglect through 'failure to protect' in many American states (Kantor & Little, 2003; Lyon, 1999).

Parenting and Domestic Violence

Being subject to domestic violence affects women in a number of ways, which in turn impacts on their ability to meet the needs of their children. For example, as the main perpetrator of domestic violence is usually the male this leaves the mother as the person who is placed in the position of not only protecting herself but also her children from the violence (Cleaver et al., 1999; Hester et al., 1999; Jouriles, 1998). This pre-occupation with safety for themselves and their children can become all consuming, meaning that other aspects of parenting are given less attention. The emotional and psychological abuse that, together with physical abuse, makes up domestic violence is likely to have a negative impact on the woman's self-worth and confidence and her sense of trust and security. The abuse may also lead to the mother being pre-occupied, irritable, exhausted and depressed. In these circumstances she may find it difficult exerting any authority or control over her children (Cleaver et al., 1999; Levendosky & Graham-Bermann, 2001; Mullender et al., 2003) These effects impact on the interactions between the mother and the child. For example, the child may experience the mother as someone who is not emotionally available and consistently fails to meet their needs. Lack of authority and control can lead to children who have witnessed their father abusing their mother following suit, challenging their mother and becoming physically aggressive towards her (Jackson, 2003). The negative impact on parenting in situations of domestic violence, is further compounded by depression, alcohol and substance misuse, poverty, unemployment and social isolation (Cleaver et al., 1999). These factors can contribute to tensions between couples resulting in situations that escalate into violence.

Buckley et al., (2006) completed a review of the very limited literature on the father–child relationship in cases of domestic violence. They conclude that abusive fathers are less likely to be involved with child rearing than those who are not abusive. When they do interact with their children these interactions tend to be negative. These include being controlling and authoritarian towards the child and using the children to meet their own needs. For example, using them to undermine or manipulate their mother.

The Assessment 'Traps'

Each child's experience of witnessing domestic violence will be different, even if they are living with siblings within the same family. Hence, practitioners, assessing the impact of domestic violence on children, need to identify exactly what the child is witnessing, the way in which the child is drawn into the interaction between the carers, the child's role and the child's feelings about their situation. Consideration should also be given to factors that assist the child in managing the situation.

Humphreys and Mullender (2003) describe a number of traps that professionals can fall into when assessing the impact of domestic violence on family members. These traps result in a failure to identify the needs of the child. They include:

> *Minimising the effect on women and children of domestic violence or paying more attention to other factors*
> Practitioners working with adults may fail to consider domestic violence when assessing for routine services. Alternatively, the perpetrator's behaviour may be minimised by the carers or obscured by other issues. Effective assessment means being alert to possible domestic violence in every case, engaging the man in the assessment process and drawing attention to any aggressive behaviour, naming the behaviour and being explicit about its consequences.

Colluding with the perpetrator
The perpetrator may appear plausible and confident and blame his partner for his behaviour. This can be avoided if the practitioner attempts to gain information from a range of sources including, evidence on case files, the opinions of other professionals who know the family and the individual members of the family themselves. In this way practitioners can identify not only the patterns of behaviour but the consequences for different family members.

Assessment becomes the action or intervention
In this situation, the focus is on identifying needs but no services are provided to meet the needs of the family.

Inappropriate or delayed responses to black service users
For example, practitioners may not appreciate the consequences for an Asian woman of discussing the abuse in a situation where she runs the risk of being shunned by her family and community. Delayed assessments for women and children in this situation may occur because of lack of availability of appropriate interpreting services.

Learning Disabilities

It is all too easy for professionals to believe that parents with learning disabilities who fail to meet the needs of their child constitute a more extensive problem than is actually the case. This can occur for two reasons. First, whilst there are increasing numbers of parents with a learning disability those coping with children rarely come to the attention of professionals. Hence, practitioners are only likely to meet parents who have problems (Booth & Booth, 1994; Dowdney & Skuse, 1993; Woodhouse et al., 2001). Second, the research on the topic tends to use samples of mothers and young children where problems have already been identified so, as with mental health issues, it is difficult to gauge how many carers with learning disabilities are managing successfully to meet the needs of their children (Dowdney & Skuse, 1993; Tymchuk & Andron, 1994).

Although it is important to recognise that many learning disabled parents manage to meet the developmental needs of their children, it is as important to recognise that a group of parents are struggling and their children are suffering. Amongst this group of carers, neglect is the most common form of maltreatment and is usually an unintentional result of the carer not realising what they should be doing (Newman, 2003). Where the parents are unable to meet the needs of their children 'there is a higher incidence of developmental delay in younger children, and learning difficulties and challenging behaviours in primary school aged children' (McConnell & Llewellyn, 2002, p. 304). Cleaver and Nicholson (2005) identified that half the children in their study, living with a learning disabled parent and known to social workers, had severe developmental needs in comparison to a quarter of cases where the carer did not have a learning disability. In situations where learning disabled carers neglect their children, the studies indicate intrusive interventions by professionals take place with around half the children being removed from their carers (Dowdney & Skuse, 1993; McConnell & Llewellyn, 2002; Tymchuk & Andron, 1994).

Factors Influencing the Parenting Capacity of Learning Disabled Carers

The challenge for practitioners, assessing the impact of a learning disability on parenting capacity, is that successful parenting, when the carer has a learning disability, is a complex interaction between the carer's intellectual impairment and the support provided to develop and sustain their parenting skills (McGaha, 2002). In addition the context in which parenting occurs plays a significant part. With this in mind, when undertaking an assessment practitioners should consider the interaction between the following factors.

Cognitive Functioning

There is general consensus that unless a person's IQ is below 60 an IQ score is not a good predictor of parenting capacity (Dowdney & Skuse, 1993; Tymchuk & Andron, 1990, 1994). What is important is cognitive functioning, that is the ability of the parent to *learn* parenting skills and make use of support services. For example, the carer's ability to understand the importance of and to actually manage household and child-care routines. Tymchuk and Andron (1994) found learning disabled mothers who did well caring for children had reading and comprehension skills sufficient to make use of traditional information sources such as reading labels on products and following written instructions.

Low cognitive functioning, on the part of the carer, can affect the child in a number of ways. For example, learning disabled carers tend to use fewer descriptive statements and do not praise or use verbal labels as often as other parents (McGaw & Sturmey, 1994; Peterson et al., 1983). Therefore, parents with a learning disability may have difficulty providing children with appropriate stimulation for language development. Carers with learning disabilities may also have problems with logical reasoning, in terms of thinking through the consequences of particular actions. This can be a particular issue when carers do not know how to keep themselves and their children safe. These can, for example, make them vulnerable to targeting by sex offenders (Jackson, 1998).

Co-Morbidity

For children of parents who are already struggling as a result of a learning disability the combination of the disability and parenting issues compounds the difficulties experienced by carers attempting to meet the needs of their children (McConnell & Llewellyn, 2002; Tymchuk & Andron, 1990). Cleaver and Nicholson (2005) found that many of the learning disabled parents, in their study, were experiencing one or more of the following: poor physical or mental health; domestic violence; alcohol or drug misuse; a history of abuse and experience of the care system. As described earlier in this chapter, each of these issues in their own right make parenting difficult and the combination can place the child in a very vulnerable situation. This can be exacerbated if the child is themselves disabled (see Chapter 2), which Cleaver and Nicholson (ibid) found was the case in some of the families they studied.

Poor Self-Esteem

Learning disabled parents may well have experienced negative childhood experiences, both within the home and within the community, such as bullying and ridicule (Westcott, 1993). These experiences are likely to lead to a negative self-image and undermine the parent's confidence in their ability to meet the needs of their own child. This can be a particular problem in terms of the parent knowing how to praise the child (Tymchuk & Andron, 1990). Other learning disabled carers may have been brought up in an environment where others have told them what to do as adults. As a result of this they may depend on an external locus of control waiting for others to tell them what to do (McGaha, 2002). This can result in the carer being passive and feeling impotent when encountering and addressing problems in their own right.

Lack of Positive Parenting Role Models

Adults who have a learning disability are more likely to have experienced maltreatment than other adults (McConnell & Llewellyn, 2002; McGaha, 2002; Westcott, 1993; Westcott & Cross, 1996). This means that they may not have had positive models of parenting. Indeed they may well have learnt neglectful parenting behaviours from their own carers. In addition, learning disabled adults are likely to have had less preparation for parenthood than other adults (McGaha, 2002). For example, many adolescents learn about babies and young children through baby-sitting for friends and neighbours. A teenager who has a learning disability may not be considered an appropriate baby-sitter and is therefore deprived of this learning experience. The impact of lack of positive parenting models and experience of being with babies and children needs to be explored as part of the assessment. It is all too easy to presume that these parents have been shown what to do and cannot do it rather than recognising that they may never have had an opportunity to learn how to care for children.

Support

Many learning disabled parents are often isolated and unsupported (Llewellyn et al., 1998; Tymchuk & Andron, 1994). Booth and Booth (1994; 1997) found that 'good enough' parenting by people with learning disabilities is related to the amount of support available to the parents and their children via family and social networks. When assessing support networks practitioners should consider two factors. First, the level of support required by the carer. Some carers will require minimum support because the carer is able to live on their own with the child. Other carers will need someone else to take primary responsibility for the child. The quality of the support is also important. Support that is inconsistent or undermines the role of the parent, is unlikely to lead to positive outcomes for the child (James, 2004).

Adverse Social Conditions

Learning disabled parents are more likely to experience adverse social circumstances such as unemployment, poor housing and harassment than other groups of parents – factors which increase levels of stress and depression. This in turn can impact on parental motivation and ability to meet the needs of the children (Feldman et al., 1997).

How did they manage to overcome adverse social conditions in order do have sex which produced the child/rey?

Assessing the Parenting Skills of a Parent with a Learning Disability

When it came to assessing the needs of families where carers have learning disabilities, Cleaver and Nicholson (2005) found that social workers were very committed to working in partnership with parents with learning disabilities. The workers spent a considerable time explaining and involving the carers in the assessment purpose and process. However, they were often unsure how much the parents actually understood. For example, parents would often say 'yes' but it was not clear whether they had fully appreciated what they were agreeing to. Practitioners require specialist skills to undertake these assessments and members of children and family teams may not have and indeed, one can question whether they should be expected to have these skills. Although the practitioners in Cleaver and Nicholson's study did try to draw on learning disability specialists they experienced difficulties because with the majority of assessments workers from adult services did not contribute to the assessment. This seems to occur because the carers do not meet the threshold for adult services, so no adult worker is involved or the child and family workers do not, in many cases, consider approaching adult services. The practitioners in the Cleaver and Nicholson study (ibid) did however make effective use of family centres, but again the staff did not necessarily have the specialist assessment and intervention skills and the carers themselves often felt out of place at these centres.

One of the key questions professionals need to ask as part of the assessment is 'If the parent is not currently parenting adequately can they be taught to do so?' (Dowdney & Skuse, 1993). In order to answer this question, the parent should be given the appropriate opportunities to learn about and demonstrate their ability to undertake the parenting task. These opportunities to learn about parenting should be:

- Tailored to the parent's learning needs.
- Geared to motivating the parent by initially addressing topics of interest to the parents.
- Based in the parent's home so they can learn and apply in the same setting.
- Concrete and systematic.
- Based on modelling, allowing opportunities for practice with feedback and positive reinforcement.
- Reinforced through maintenance training.

(McConnell & Llewellyn, 2002)

One of the dilemmas, encountered by practitioners, in these cases, is balancing the needs of the child against those of the carer. The pace at which the parent is able to learn new skills must be such that the needs of the child are met. It is all too easy to see minimal indicators of change and be over-optimistic about the outcome for children in these families. Moreover, as the child develops, the parent must have the ability to understand the changing needs of the child, at different developmental stages, and be able to adjust their parenting accordingly. This involves the carer being able to apply abstract thinking and understand the world from the child's perspective. This may be an issue for some carers. For example, they may struggle managing behavioural problems such as understanding why a child is being defiant. Alternatively, they may find it difficult making decisions about safety issues, such as whether the child is able to cross the road unaccompanied (James, 2004). When working with other types of parenting issues one hopes that the issues will be resolved and the carer will be able to meet the needs of their children. Working with parents with learning disabilities, as described above, is different. This means that assessing parenting capacity is an ongoing, long-term process that needs to centre on identifying and meeting the changing needs of the child.

Summary

The carer's ability and motivation to meet the needs of their child can be negatively affected by a diverse range of parenting issues. Four common issues associated with child neglect have been explored in this chapter. They are: mental health issues, domestic violence, drug and alcohol misuse and learning disability. Whilst each of these issues is likely to impact on the carer's behaviour in different ways there are some common themes that should be considered when assessing child neglect.

Carers may be unaware of the impact of their own problems on their children. For example, the alcohol-misusing carer may believe they are hiding their alcohol use from their child. Moreover, whilst the carer may not intend to provide poor parenting their pre-occupation with their own issues can result in a lack of responsiveness and failure to consider the needs of their children.

The impact of parenting issues have on children goes beyond the emotional and cognitive problems, often highlighted in the literature. These are children who, as they grow up, are ashamed of their family, may isolate themselves from their peers and are vulnerable to bullying. In addition, these children may take on considerable caring responsibilities in relation to both their carers and their siblings. Certain groups of children are particularly vulnerable to neglect when parenting issues exist. These include the difficult-to-parent child and disabled children.

The impact that parenting issues has on children will be influenced by the formal and informal support available to both carers and the children. If the needs of the child are met by others, or the child is supported in ways that reduce their vulnerability, the parenting issues may not necessarily have a negative impact on the child.

When undertaking assessments in these situations, a multi-disciplinary assessment is crucial. Workers from adult services are the best equipped to make an assessment of the parenting issue and the way in which it can affect parenting capacity, whilst workers from children's services are able to assess the impact on children. Assessing the needs of children and families where there are parenting issues can be very complex, particularly when there are a number of parenting issues within the family. For example, learning disability and depression. In these cases a diverse range of professionals should be involved in the assessment to ensure that the impact of all the parenting issues is taken into account. A final, but perhaps the most important theme in this chapter, is that it is only when practitioners work together with the child and family that the true impact of parenting issues on family life becomes apparent and possible interventions that meet the specific needs of the child can be identified. Most particularly, it is the child who is experiencing the impact of the parenting issues and their feelings about the situation must be considered.

Note

1 A local English register of all children in who are considered to be suffering from or likely to suffer from significant harm and require a multi-disciplinary child protection plan

5

The Care-Giving Context

Introduction

Having considered the way in which carer ability and motivation influences parenting capacity, in this chapter we move beyond the individual. We consider the socio-economic factors that can influence parenting: that is the context in which carers bring up their children. In Chapter 1, we made a distinction between carers who fail to meet the needs of the child because the resources are not available and those who neglect their children, despite resources being available. The first is described as societal or collective neglect the second neglect by the carer. Although, in theory, it is possible to draw a distinction between the two, practitioners identifying and assessing neglect when the socio-economic circumstances are not conducive to child-rearing face a difficult task. For example, how does one distinguish between deprivation and neglect? How do we know the difference between self-imposed social isolation and exclusion? It is these complexities which are the focus of this chapter.

We begin by discussing the topic which in my experience practitioners often find most difficult to assess: the impact of poverty and poor housing on child-rearing. We move on to consider the influence of faith and culture on a parent's approach to parenting and how membership of a faith community or ethnic group, may inform both family and practitioners' perceptions of good enough parenting. The chapter concludes by exploring an area which is often considered to be significant in terms of reducing both the likelihood and the impact of neglect: social support. We consider extended family and informal community support networks, exploring the type of support that is most likely to meet the needs of neglectful carers. (Support from professionals and child welfare services is discussed in Chapter 8.)

Neglect, Poverty and Poor Housing

> Living on a low income in a rundown neighbourhood does not make it impossible to be the affectionate, authoritative parent of healthy, sociable children. But it does, undeniably, make it more difficult. (Utting, 1995, p. 40)

When working with cases of child neglect, the question practitioners should ask, in light of Utting's comment, is '*How much more difficult and what allowances should I make?*' Distinguishing between low standards of care resulting from deprivation and low standards because of the ability and motivation of the carer, is a dilemma for most practitioners. Clearly, carers who are struggling to meet the needs of their child are going to find it far more difficult if the parenting opportunities are limited. Thus it is not surprising that poor carers find it difficult meeting the needs of their children and that child neglect is frequently associated with poverty (Drake & Pandey, 1996; Gaudin et al., 1996; Nelson et al., 1993). For example, Thoburn et al., (2000), in their study of 555 English families referred because of neglect or emotional abuse, to child and family social work teams, noted that almost all the families were living in socially deprived communities or in pockets of deprivation in more prosperous communities. Of the families, 3% had more than five children; 59% lived in crowded accommodation (more than one person per room); 57% had no wage-earner in the household and 10% lacked three or more basic utilities such as a cooker with oven, a bath or shower, running hot water, an indoor flushing toilet, fridge, washing machine, etc. They found that a large proportion of those referred for neglect were concerned parents who wanted to do the best for their children and had a 'strong work ethic' (ibid, p. 60). The carers were, however, trying to bring up their children in very difficult circumstances and needed practical services such as better housing, transport and pre and after-school care to enable them to do this.

Why did they have children in one first place?

The Impact of Poverty and Poor Housing on Child-Rearing

So how does poverty and poor housing affect child-rearing? Flaherty et al., (2004), collated information about poverty from a variety of English sources, such as the *Households below Average Income* statistics (Department for Work and Pensions, 2004), to demonstrate how many children in the United Kingdom are living in poverty. They found in 2002–3:

- 3.6 million (28%) of all children are living in poverty (defined as 60% median income after housing costs).
- 34% lacked more than one essential item. For example, adequate clothing, a healthy diet, a holiday or social activities – 18% lacked two or more.

- Families with children and larger families are more likely to be poor.
- Children and women are also more likely to be poor.
- 51% of lone-parent families were poor.
- 69% of Pakistani and Bangladeshi, 46% of black non-Caribbean and 32% of black Caribbean people are poor compared with 17% of white people.
- 29% of working disabled people are poor.*
- Children are twice as likely to die within their first year if their parents are from unskilled manual rather than professional classes.
- One in 20 mothers sometimes goes without food to meet the needs of their children.

The reality of the above, for the daily experiences of children, is that the resources are not available to provide adequate basic care within a safe, comfortable home environment. For example, as described in Chapter 1, low-income families are likely to have poor diets and are more likely to suffer from ill-health than better off families. There is little money to undertake family activities. Poverty can also isolate children from their peers, particularly in a society where young people place such importance on designer labels and being seen to wear the right label. Children who do not have access to such clothing are vulnerable to bullying and ridicule. Children may be ashamed of their home and are therefore reluctant to bring others home. Moreover, resources may not be available for peer-based activities such as swimming etc. isolating them even further (Jack & Gill, 2003).

Looking specifically at housing, the charity Shelter highlights the impact that poor housing can have on a child's health and development (Shelter, 2004; 2005). They found 1 million children are living in poor housing. This includes homeless children living in emergency accommodation. Poor housing means overcrowded, damp, cold, infested conditions, often with landlords who neglect repairs and threaten eviction. This can affect children in a number of ways. The children are particularly vulnerable to bronchitis, TB and asthma. Children who are living in bed and breakfast accommodation are twice as likely as other children to be admitted to accident and emergency departments with burns and scalds. And 11% of childhood accidents are a result of badly designed housing and dangerous fittings. Turning to education, homeless children are missing 25% of their schooling: they move schools frequently and can wait for weeks for a school place. If they do attend school and want to do well, those in poor housing often have nowhere to do homework with 100,000 children having no bedroom, sleeping in a living room or kitchen. It is not surprising that these children are more likely to feel insecure and stigmatised, leading to behaviour problems and bullying (Shelter, 2004; 2005).

This situation is exacerbated for a group of children who, as described in Chapter 2, are particularly vulnerable to neglect: disabled children. Families with disabled children are more likely to be living in poor housing than other families (Beresford & Oldman, 2000). As we have seen trying to bring up children in poverty is no easy task. To try and do this when the child has additional needs that the carer is unable to meet through lack of resources, places additional stresses on the carer and increases the child's vulnerability to neglect.

Family Resilience

Many families living in disadvantaged areas of high levels of poverty and poor housing are able to promote their child's well-being and safeguard them from the harm associated with living in such an environment. For example, Seaman et al., (2006), in a study of four deprived areas of Glasgow, highlight a range of factors which are associated with positive child-rearing, in environments where there were not only high levels of poverty and poor housing but also unemployment, drug and alcohol misuse and youth gangs. These included both parents and young people being aware of risks in the community and having a network of family, friends and neighbours who look out for the children; parents promoting organised and supervised activities; carers engaging in an open and democratic style of parenting, which involves listening to the children and respecting their views. Parents setting clear boundaries about where the children are going and what they are doing is also important. This enables them to assess and monitor levels of risk. Finally, parents trying to protect their children from the effects of poverty through creative and skilled budget management is effective. In addition the young people, as they grow up, need to learn to take responsibility for keeping themselves and their friends safe by staying together in a group and looking after each other. However, as they grow older, whilst the young people value parents' interest and rules, they are likely to subvert or ignore them to develop a sense of independence.

Reading this list of protective factors, what is striking is that parenting in a disadvantaged community requires very skilled interactions between the carer, the child and other members of the community. If one considers the different types of neglectful parenting styles described in Chapter 3, one can appreciate that for depressed carers or those with limited ability, to parent consistently at this level may be too difficult. And in these cicumstances borderline parenting can become inadequate.

Poverty and Neglect: the Assessment Task

> I've had letters from school telling me the kids smelt really bad. The teachers thought the kids had wet themselves but it was their clothes that stank from being in the flat. I'd washed them and everything, but it doesn't help, everything stinks.
>
> (Shelter, 2005, p. 13)

It is all too easy for practitioners, faced with smelly children, to jump to the conclusion this is due to parental neglect, rather than poverty or poor housing. It is therefore useful to consider that 'poverty is not a predictor of neglect: it is a correlate of neglect' (DiLenonardi, 1993, p. 562). Parents, with borderline parenting skills are far more likely, as described above, to be placed in situations where parenting becomes inadequate. For example, Lee and George (1999) found that teen pregnancy, combined with poverty, is a contributory factor to child neglect. They studied a multicultural cohort in the USA of 59,062 children and found that children born to mothers aged 17 and under, who live in high-poverty communities, are over 17 times more likely to become an indicated case of neglect than are children born to mothers aged 22 and over living in low-poverty areas. They also found that later born children are at more risk of neglect than first born. They argue that the impact of economic hardship becomes more apparent the larger the family. These findings are commensurate with Chaffin et al. (1996) who noted a similar correlation between age, number in the household, socio-economic status and child neglect.

Income Assessment

When assessing the link between neglect and deprivation it can be useful to assess whether the family's income is sufficient to meet their needs, taking account of family membership, housing, level of debts, geographical location and specific needs resulting from disability or ill-health. Consideration should also be given to financial support from extended family, friends and neighbours. It is also important to recognise that expenditure is likely to vary over time. For example, costs of clothing, shoes, etc, need to be taken into account when calculating weekly income and expenditure. Moreover, income may alter over time. For example, the current situation may be short-term, as a result of unemployment or more long-term through ill-health. If it is a transitory experience it is likely to have a different impact on the children and their carers than if it is an ongoing long-term experience (Jack & Gill, 2003). Jack and Gill (ibid) also identify the importance of assessing individual family members' response to living on a low income. Some members may be resilient to the effects of poverty, whilst others may become demoralised and lose their sense of self-worth.

Living in Rural Communities

Poverty, as described above, is usually associated with inner city deprivation. However, a key finding from the neglect study I completed in the Republic of Ireland (see introduction to Part III for details), was the prevalence of poverty and neglect in rural settings. In this context, the impact of poverty on the carer's ability to meet the needs of the child is exacerbated by lack of access to public services such as child-care, health, housing and leisure services. Poverty in small affluent rural communities can have two consequences. It can raise the family's awareness of their comparative disadvantage. Alternatively, the lower population density and isolation of rural homes and farms, means that poverty and its impact on the child and family, may be invisible (Pugh, 2000).

Neglect, Culture and Religious Beliefs

Thoburn et al. (2000), in their study of family support in cases of emotional maltreatment and child neglect, found referrals regarding concerns about maltreatment amongst children from ethnic minority groups were more likely to be non-specific, expressing generalised concerns, than for other children. However, the cases were often complex and the extent of material deprivation, particularly amongst asylum seekers, was higher than for other families. In addition, communication problems, resulting from linguistic barriers; trauma; mental health problems and lack of understanding of the child welfare system added to lack of clarity regarding the nature of the concerns. The parents, themselves, were less likely to be in touch with family members and had fewer sources of support than the white families in the study. In addition, the parents were also more likely to report problems with parenting and higher levels of emotional stress than white parents. The families from minority groups were more likely to have problems that could be categorised as acute stress (an overwhelming issue or series of events triggering concerns) or a specific issue, whilst the white families were more likely to be categorised as having multiple and long-standing problems.

In response to these referrals, Thoburn et al., (2000) found black and Asian families were more likely than white families to be provided with a general assessment of need or to be assessed for a specific service. The children referred for concerns of maltreatment and neglect, were less likely to be subject of inquiries under section 47 of the Children Act 1989 and more likely to be provided with an assessment of need than white children. The researchers found this was most likely to be the case when the referral was linked to child safety and home alone issues. In these cases, practical help such as day care, or assistance with benefits, or finding more appropriate accommodation was required to alleviate the situation. Finally, emotional neglect, resulting from the carer's stress, trauma or mental health issues, was often categorised as emotional abuse, implying that there was intent, rather than an inability to meet the emotional needs of the child.

Assessing the Needs of Children from Ethnic Minority Groups

The task for practitioners, assessing child neglect in these situations is complex. Parents may have a variety of problems in their own right, such as depression and coping with loss, as a result of immigration. In addition, the family may not understand English and have little knowledge of the dominant cultural norms. This can inhibit them from participating in community activities, such as parent-toddler groups, reinforcing their sense of isolation. Added to this, the families as described above, are more likely than white families to be living in poverty in deprived communities and may also be experiencing harassment (Department of Health, 2000; Webb et al., 2002). In this context, parenting ability and motivation are likely to be affected and meeting the needs of the child can be particularly difficult (Dwivedi & Varma, 1996).

The quality of assessment that children and families from ethnic minority groups receive appears to be a lottery depending on the knowledge, skills and tenacity of individual workers. O'Neale (2000) reporting on a Social Services Inspection of services to ethnic minority families, found workers did not take a holistic approach towards the assessment, often failing to identify issues of maltreatment and special health needs for fear of offending cultural norms. Individual workers often carry the burden of attempting to find and deliver ethnically sensitive services when appropriate services are not available. However, workers often failed to recognise that culture and its significance varies from family to family and do not consult with families about their specific needs. This can leave families feeling practitioners have not worked in partnership or engaged them in planning interventions. One group who fair particularly badly, are black children who are disabled. Issues of personal care, the impact of culture and religion and special dietary requirements are often not considered by practitioners.

Practitioner judgements, about neglect and cultural norms, are influenced by the dominant values of the society and the personal beliefs of practitioners completing the assessment. For example, Cemlyn (2000) found professionals lack an understanding of Traveller culture and receive mixed messages from society, at large, about its importance in the context of assimilation policies across Europe. This creates problems for professionals in deciding how to identify and meet the needs of Travellers and their children who wish to maintain their ethnic and cultural identity without conforming to the dominant norms of the society. The interaction of these structural factors and the family's individual circumstances mean that some Traveller children are vulnerable in terms of needs remaining unidentified. For example, Traveller children have a poor level of attendance at school (Hawes & Perez, 1995). A commonly held view amongst the general public is that this occurs because Travellers do not value education. However, as Fisher (2004) argues there are other reasons why attendance may be low. First, the education system is designed for a settled community, Travellers who are not on permanent sites move around. This has been exacerbated by the removal of the duty of local authorities to provide sites for Travellers in the Criminal Justice and Public Order Act 1994, which has resulted in Travellers staying on unofficial sites, constantly facing the risk of eviction. Second, Traveller children who attend school are excluded from school in disproportionate numbers. This may well result from a failure to appreciate cultural norms on both sides. However, the child is caught in the middle, isolated from mainstream society, often bullied and ridiculed when they attend school and fails to receive a formal education.

Gill (2005), in an unpublished report of a study which involved consulting various minority ethnic community and faith groups who are living in England, found there can be differences in perceptions of what constitutes neglect that need to be explored and addressed. For example, the African participants, in her albeit small-scale study, believed that Africans do not neglect their children. They considered neglect to be a Western phenomenon arguing that Western families do not love or look after their children in the same way as African carers. Some respondents did, however, concede that if children were ever neglected by African carers it was due to mental illness. They also believed that children accuse parents of neglect if they do not give them the money they want. These groups also discussed parenting practices. They considered that four-year-olds were responsible and could be left alone and look after other children. In addition, some thought it was acceptable to tie a child to a table either as a form of punishment or to ensure safety if the carer wants to leave the child alone. Many of the participants also thought it was acceptable to withhold food as a form of punishment. The participants were furious that child welfare professionals could consider these practices to be indicators of neglect. Interestingly, the Southern Asian participants thought children nowadays were children for longer and this needed to be recognised. So for example, one mother said children could have been left alone at four years of age in the past, but that now it is not sensible to leave them until they are about ten. Interestingly the young Asian participants thought that neglect was not possible in their communities, believing it only occurred in broken homes and amongst carers who use drugs.

What is striking about these findings is that stereotyping works both ways. White dominant groups in society may have stereotypical perceptions of parenting practices amongst ethnic minority groups while members of these groups hold stereotypical images of white Western families and poor parenting practices. Moreover, it is difficult to know to what extent the Asian carers' perceptions of what is acceptable for children have been influenced by living in England and taking on the norms of the dominant culture.

However, caution must be exercised in drawing any conclusions from these findings. They represent the views of a limited numer of participants in one study. They are included here to make the point that it is all too easy to stereotype. What we should do is check out the views of each family and establish the basis for these opinions. Webb et al., (2002, p. 405) summarise the dilemma for professionals providing services for people from cultures other than their own, stating that they have 'a delicate path to tread in attempting to be culturally sensitive without tipping the scales on the one hand toward colour blindness ... or on the other towards cultural deficit – accepting a lower or different standard through cultural stereotyping'.

Religious Beliefs and their Impact on Parenting

This 'delicate path' also needs to be taken into account when considering the impact of religious beliefs on parenting practices and perceptions of neglect. For example, Lord Laming, in his inquiry into the death of Victoria Climbié, indicated that the religious beliefs of professionals, members of the faith community and Victoria's carers influenced the perception of Victoria's needs and the ways in which those needs were met. In Victoria's case, the religious beliefs of her carer, and the members of the church which she attended, resulted in the perception of Victoria as someone possessed by an evil spirit. This perception influenced the way her carer viewed and responded to Victoria's problem of incontinence. The situation was exacerbated by the social work supervisor also interpreting abuse and neglect from a particular faith perspective. Whilst there is danger of losing focus of the needs of the child when interpreting neglect from a particular faith perspective a more common reaction is to ignore the influence of faith on perceptions of parenting and the needs of the child and family. For example, the Southern Asian carers in Gill's study (2005) complained that social services did not take into account their faith or culture when they were being assessed or in plans for interventions. This is not surprising if one considers that Cleaver and Walker (2004) found that practitioners frequently failed to indicate religious beliefs when completing assessment forms.

Members of faith communities frequently see their beliefs as providing a 'world-view', that offers the conceptual underpinning for how they live their life. The religious beliefs of carers influence family life, including methods of raising and disciplining children, medical interventions, educational provision, dress codes, and much else (Barnes et al., 2000; Duriez & Soenens, 2004; Hill & Pargamount, 2003).

It can be difficult distinguishing between the impact of religious beliefs and practices and cultural influences. The world-views of faiths, represented in the UK, may have come to fruition in countries with cultures significantly different from the contemporary British context. As well as the basic tenets of the faith itself, other aspects of culture, history and ethnicity can play a crucial role in the development of world-views. However, aspects of religious belief will be part of the cultural environment of all communities, and as such may have significant influence on approaches to parenting.

Informal Support Systems within the Community

The British newspapers recently reported a story about a three-year-old boy who was left in a high rise flat for six weeks with his dead mother's decomposing body. He was eventually found by police severely dehydrated, and very weak. This case is a stark example of the consequences of poor support networks. Neighbours had complained about the smell in the high rise block of flats but failed to notice the child and his mother were not out and about. Family and friends had not considered unusual the lack of contact from mother and child. The nursery school eventually raised the alarm.

Support from social networks not only prevents this kind of incident occurring but also can act as a 'stress-buffering factor' by providing help and support and boosting carer's self-esteem and sense of efficacy thereby enhancing parenting (Ghate & Hazel, 2002, p. 17). A carer without support is therefore going to be more vulnerable to maltreating their children (Pianta et al., 1989).

'Social networks' is a term used to describe the relationships that exist between the individual and the wider family, friends, neighbours and professionals (Jack, 2000). These social networks can be supportive of the carer, both emotionally and instrumentally. However, not all social networks equate to supportive networks: they can also be a source of stress. For example, when a family suffers racial harassment from neighbours or is isolated from neighbours because of difference, such as religious beliefs. The child neglect research highlights three potential areas of support for neglectful carers: the partner, the carer's mother and the community (Coohey, 1995; Dubowitz, 1999b; Stevenson, 1998). The role of partners and the maternal grandmother have been considered in Chapter 3. However, in this chapter, the focus is on informal support from the community.

Informal Community Support Networks

Carers' Perceptions of Social Support

Support covers a range of different activities, including emotional support or comfort; advice; offering and providing information and practical help and resources such as borrowing and lending (Quinton, 2004; Roditti, 2005). These may be accessible through neighbours, friends and extended family or drop-in and neighbourhood groups. When assessing the needs of children using the *Framework for the Assessment of Children in Need and their Families* (Department of Health et al., 2000), practitioners are expected to consider family social integration or put another way, the level of social isolation. Throughout this book reference has been made to neglectful carers frequently lacking social support and experiencing social isolation. The term social isolation is one that is used by practitioners to 'incorporate everything from the restricted network of social contacts of an impoverished, lonely, single parent through to social isolation due to antisocial, hostile, argumentative behavior, which has led to relative isolation' (Jones, 1996, p. 239). However, assessing levels of social support and isolation does not appear to be straightforward. It is not about just identifying who is available to support the carer and their family rather, the research indicates that it is the carers' perception of the quality of relationships with this network that is crucial for example, both Coohey (1996) and Roditti (2005) found neglectful mothers identified at least eight important network members. What is significant is that the mothers felt *less* supportive and positive about the nature of the contacts than non-maltreating mothers. They reported fewer contacts who really listened, who helped them make decisions or who provided companionship or practical help such as baby-sitting (Coohey, 1996). In contrast, Thoburn et al., (2000) found that the sample families in their English study of emotional maltreatment and neglect, had very few people available for support and listed approximately one to two people in whom they could intimately confide. Therefore, it appears although neglectful mothers may have access to a social network they have less access to emotionally satisfying relationships, which in turn leads to a sense of loneliness (Jones, 1996). One group of carers who seem to be particularly isolated are carers who have issues associated with substance misuse and domestic violence. These carers may be deliberately avoiding old networks but failing to develop new support networks, contributing to increased stresses and the possibility of relapse (Roditti, 2005).

Negative Interactions

Not surprisingly, negative interactions with members of social networks can be an additional stress for neglectful families. For example, Polansky et al., (1985) found that neglectful mothers were more likely than other mothers to perceive their communities as less friendly and more unsupportive. In addition, they did not enter into social exchange in the same way as other members of the community. The researchers concluded that neglectful families stand out from the rest of the community, who perceive them as deviant, and consequently keep a distance. Not only were these families not supported, they were also not approached by other families in need of help. That is the neglected families were excluded from the reciprocal helping arrangements that operate in many neighbourhoods.

Gaudin and Polansky (1986) explored the way in which members of the community relate to neglectful families. They found that the respondents considered that the *majority* of members of the community would keep their distance from a neglectful family; however the respondents would *personally* be prepared to help these families. As this study used vignettes, rather than actual experiences, one can only speculate about the double standards operating amongst the respondents.

These studies demonstrate that neglectful families are caught in a viscious circle. The families are marginalised in communities because they stand out and do not operate to community standards, which in turn increase the family's sense of isolation. This isolation acts as a further stress exacerbating the possibility of neglect, in an already vulnerable family, thereby reinforcing the community's feelings about a deviant family and increasing the social distancing. Moreover, social disorganisation and lack of social coherence is highest in neighbourhoods with high maltreatment rates (Garbarino & Kostlny, 1992; Vinson et al., 1996). Thompson (1995, cited in Jack & Gill, 2003) noted in these communities there is high mobility, families tend to disengage from the community, there is less sharing of resources, little awareness of local services, limited social capital and limited social networks for children. In conclusion, the very families that need community support are the ones least likely to receive it.

Whilst recognising that the focus of this chapter is on parenting capacity, it is worth acknowledging the importance of support networks for children who are vulnerable to or suffering from child neglect (this is discussed in more detail in Chapter 2). Gilligan (1999) highlights the importance of utilising appropriate family and community networks to support the child. He also notes how social isolation contributes to the child's vulnerability it 'cuts off potential support and removes the child from easy view and unobtrusive surveillance' (Gilligan, 2001, p. 183).

Assessing Informal Support Networks

'Support even as a good piece of ordinary social action, is complex to assess, to get right and to deliver' (Quinton, 2004, p. 22). First, it is difficult to get the balance between ignoring family problems and seeming to be intrusive. Second, differences in perceptions of what is appropriate parenting, as described in Chapter 1, vary and will determine perceptions of what support is required. Moreover, members of a community may not know what kind of support is most appropriate for families who have multiple problems, as is often the case with neglectful families.

Quinton (2004) notes that when assessing the impact of community support on parenting capacity practitioners should consider how the support could make a difference to parenting. He notes three ways of making this difference:

1   Support to make parenting more enjoyable. For example, informal friendship groups of parents, reciprocal baby-sitting arrangements.
2   Assist the child's development. For example, parent and toddler groups, parenting classes.

3   Work on issues and problems associated with parenting behaviour. For example, networks to assist a carer with a specific problem such as neighbourhood rota to take children to school when a carer is ill.

When assessing the impact of social and community networks on parenting capacity Jack and Gill (2003) suggest that practitioners consider the following:

- The nature of the relationships in the community. Do people help each other or keep themselves to themselves?
- What are the rates of mobility in and out of the community?
- What is the nature of the relationship with immediate neighbours?
- What level of environmental stress is the family experiencing? For example, poor housing.
- Is the structure of the community balanced? For example, age, ethnicity.
- Do the parents and children perceive the community to be safe? For example, people's safety, crime and drugs, physical safety, harassment.
- What are the community norms around child-care practice and values?
- What are the parents' personal level of knowledge and skills enabling them to access available resources?
- What are their perceptions of the community and available resources? Are they perceived as a source of support or stress?

   The nature of these questions highlights that the effects of support are influenced by the receiver of the support as much as the giver (Quinton, 2004), informal support usually being dependent on reciprocity, for example, reciprocal baby-sitting arrangements. If, as described above, members of a community are reluctant to enter a reciprocated relationship with a neglectful family then this will affect the relationship and can result in the family becoming isolated and unsupported. Moreover, support does not just magically appear: the carer needs to make some effort to seek and maintain support. Quinton (2004, p. 29) poses a number of questions that can be used for assessing the family's perception of what they want from social networks:

- What does the carer want from support?
- How do they view the support they currently receive?
- Are there any issues associated with receiving this support?
- Does the support assist the carer to meet the needs of the child?
- What is the relationship between formal and informal support – do they complement each other?
- Does one make up for the gaps in the other?
- Can informal support be mobilised to improve parenting?

Assessing Multiple Caring Arrangements

Roditti (2005) found that multiple care-giving was dominant amongst the neglectful families in her study. The average number of care-givers was five. This care-giving involved family members, friends and neighbours, supporting the carer by taking and picking up children from school and day care, and providing occasional weekend and evening care. The mothers, in Roditti's study, felt close to these carers but found they could be more critical than others in their support network. When assessing the quality of multiple caring arrangements practitioners should consider the extent to which these carers meet the needs of the children. For example, I can remember supervising a student who was really enthusiastic about the support offered to a mother by her sister. However, when the student made enquires about the actual nature of the care-giving she discovered the sister had children on the child protection register, for child neglect, and was keeping the children in a house where workers had expressed concerns about health and safety issues, and the lack of supervision.

Summary

This chapter has focused on the context in which parenting takes place. We have considered the issues that can influence the ability and motivation of the carer to meet the needs of the child such as low income, poor quality housing and limited social networks. Whilst these factors do not necessarily lead to child neglect they can be a correlate and result in borderline parenting become inadequate parenting. Assessing the needs of the child and their family, in these types of situation, can be particularly challenging for practitioners. They may well over-empathise with the carers, sympathising with the situation they find themselves in, all too aware of the difficulties of parenting in an inadequate environment. However, throughout this chapter the negative influence of factors such as poverty and poor housing on the child's health and development has been discussed. If we are to promote the well-being of children then interventions are necessary to address these issues.

There are groups of children and families whose needs appear to be inappropriately assessed in terms of assessing the parenting environment and that includes children of ethnic and faith communities. The research would seem to indicate that these are areas where practitioners fear to tread, scared of being perceived to be oppressive and judgemental.

This chapter finishes with a discussion about the nature of informal support networks. Although neglectful carers often describe feeling socially isolated what appears to be the case is that the carers may have links in the community but do not find these links emotionally satisfying, leading to a sense of loneliness and isolation. Social interactions can be both positive and negative. Families may be isolated and labelled within the community because they stand out and do not operate to accepted community standards. In communities with reported high rates of maltreatment there may be high mobility, social disorganisation and a lack of social cohesion leading to a limited ongoing, consistent support.

Part III

Referral and Assessment: Practice Reality

The first two parts of this book have focused on the assessment task. Particular attention has been given to both ways in which neglect can present amongst children and young people and also the reasons why parenting may be compromised, resulting in neglectful practices. In other words, we have focused on *what* practitioners should consider when assessing neglected children. In this part we move on to consider the *how*: the referral and assessment process.

Assessment frameworks and tools designed to assist with this process, place emphasis on the use of evidence-based practice, including empirical research, developmental theories and guidance (Adcock, 2001; Macdonald, 2001; Munro, 2000). These are all forms of technical-rational activity. However, practice-moral activity, which recognises that individuals do not fit neatly into boxes, and that personal and professional values and beliefs influence judgements, is often minimised or ignored by both practitioners and managers (Taylor & White 2001). Yet, inquires into child deaths indicate anxiety associated to the assessment task, personal and professional values, feelings about the child and family, perceptions of professional role, the working context and culture and the practitioner's own situation, influence the way in which professionals make judgements about a case (Morrison, 1996; Munro, 2000; Reder & Duncan, 1999; Reder et al., 1993; Woodhouse & Pengelly, 1991). For example, in my experience, most practitioners can recognise the 'Friday afternoon' scenario. A professional, such as a teacher or a health visitor, may have concerns about the vulnerability of a child. Come Friday afternoon their concerns are such that they have doubts about leaving the child in the home over the weekend. They know they will spend the whole weekend worrying about the child and consequently make a referral to social work services. The social worker, keen to go home for the weekend, may respond to the referral in a different way to the way they would respond if they received the referral first thing on a Monday morning. While this commonly recognised situation can have a significant impact on the assessment process, resulting in a loss of focus on the child, rarely are these types of influence acknowledged in assessment reports as affecting decision-making.

This part of the book draws on the findings of a study I completed in the Republic of Ireland, which showed that the effective identification and assessment of child neglect is a combination of both technical-rational and practice-moral activity. Whilst recognising that the study took place in just one country, it appears that the lessons learnt are transferable as they are supported by findings from other studies and are, arguably, relevant to practice irrespective of jurisdiction.

At the time of the study, which was completed between 2000–3, child maltreatment services in Ireland were managed on a regional basis by ten health boards (the boards have subsequently been subject to restructuring and are now part of the Health Service Executive). Each health board region was divided into community care areas. The Board that commissioned this study was responsible for three community care areas covering urban and rural populations. Each area had two child-care social work teams who worked with children and families in the community. The teams consisted of a team leader, between six to eight professionally qualified social workers, a child-care worker (workers qualified to work directly with children) and one or two unqualified family support workers. In addition, the Board was responsible for hospital services and employed public health nurses (undertaking similar duties to health visitors in the United Kingdom), speech and language therapists, clinical psychologists, area medical officers (known as community paediatricians in the UK) and general practitioners (GPs) who all work in the community and have a role in identifying child neglect.

The study was undertaken in two phases. The first phase centred on assessment in cases of child neglect, following referral to social work services. And the second phase explored referral practice. Details of the aims, sample size, research methods and analysis are included below in Boxes III.1 and III.2, whilst Box III.3 shows the diverse range of professionals who participated in Phase Two of the study.

Drawing on the findings from the study and the literature in the field, the two chapters included in this section explore guidance, frameworks and tools designed to provide an evidence-base for assessment practice. In addition, we consider the personal, professional and organisational factors that influenced the identification and assessment of child neglect. Chapter 6 focuses on identification and referral practice and in Chapter 7 we discuss assessment practice in cases of child neglect. In Chapter 6 we consider referral from a diverse range of professional perspectives and in Chapter 7 we pay particular attention to social work practice.

Box III.1   Summary of Phase One a Study of Social Work Practice in Cases of Child Neglect

Aims
The study sought to:
- identify practitioners and managers understanding of neglect
- increase understanding of the factors which inform decisions when assessing and intervening in cases of child neglect

with a view to improving practice within the Health Board.

The Sample and Research Methods
All members of the child-care social work teams, the team leaders and the child-care managers were provided with opportunities to participate in this study. Although 75 staff were employed by the Board at the time of the study staff sickness and vacancies meant the potential sample size was reduced.

Three methods for data collection were used:

An analysis of case files. 57 cases, designated as cases of child neglect, were qualitatively analysed by the researcher. 20 files were originally selected from each of the three social work teams providing an opportunity to compare and contrast practice. (3 of the sample files were not available because of ongoing work with the family).

An anonymous postal questionnaire. 40 members of staff responded to the questionnaire which included questions designed to obtain a profile of age and experience of staff, open-ended questions, questions using a Likert scale (statements with graded responses from strongly agree to strongly disagree) included to identify approaches to different aspects of neglect and multi-disciplinary work and two case vignettes that required respondents to decide on causes of concern and possible interventions in a case of an 8 year-old-boy left home alone and a chronic case of neglect of four children by parents with a number of parenting issues.

Focus groups. Three for practitioners and two for managers. 25 practitioners and nine managers attended the focus groups. These were designed to explore, amplify and extend the themes generated from the study of case records and responses to the questionnaire.

Analysis
The information obtained from the case files was analysed using a standardised content analysis framework. An analysis of themes and sub-themes was undertaken. The framework was developed based on a literature review and knowledge of file content, obtained from reading a randomly selected sample of cases.

The quantitative data from the questionnaire was analysed using Statistical Package for Social Scientists (SPSS) and content analysis was used to identify themes and sub-themes from the qualitative data.

Content analysis was also used for the focus group data.

Box III.2   Summary of Phase Two a Study of Multidisciplinary Practice in Cases of Child Neglect

This phase was designed to build on the findings from Phase One, and the relevant literature, to explore the perceptions of child neglect held by a range of professionals within and outside the Board who come into contact with children and families.

Aims
The study sought to:
• identify professionals[1] understanding of neglect
• increase understanding of factors which currently inform decisions made by professionals to notify the statutory social work services of potential cases of child neglect with a view to improve practice within the region covered by the Board.

Sample and Research Methods
A purposive sample was used for this part of the study. Professionals who are in contact with children and families and therefore have a role in identifying and referring cases of child neglect were selected.

Two research methods were used:
   Anonymous postal questionnaire. The questionnaire in this study included a variety of open-ended and multiple-choice questions. In addition, there were statements that used Likert scales and two case scenarios. The questions and scenarios were adapted from the questionnaire used in Phase One to enable a comparison of responses between social workers and other professionals. 794 questionnaires were distributed, 405 were returned, however only 390 were used in the data set: a response rate of 49% (the remaining 15 contained insufficient data or were returned months after the agreed return date). Item completion rates varied. For the majority of the questions there was a 96% response rate. However, the non-response rate to open-ended questions was around 90% and for the final qualitative questions that required a written response regarding ideas for changing policy and practice the response rate was 83%. Box III.3 provides a breakdown of respondents by professional group. The steering group had negotiated with GPs that they would complete a shortened version of the questionnaire that did not include the two case scenarios.
   Focus groups. These were used in Phase Two to give professionals an opportunity to comment on and interpret the findings from Phase One and the Phase Two questionnaire. In addition, the focus groups provided opportunities to test out some of the hypotheses made by the researchers and steering group based on a preliminary analysis of the questionnaire data. Ten focus groups were held. Where possible this was done by professional group. In total 85 professionals attended the focus groups including 12 managers.

Analysis
The data from the questionnaires was analysed using SPSS for closed questions and content analysis by themes was used for the open-ended questions. Qualitative methods were used to extract meaningful themes from the data generated by the focus groups.

Note: [1] The term professionals is used throughout to refer to practitioners and managers who come into contact with children and families.

Box III.3   Breakdown of Respondents to Phase Two Questionnaire by Profession

Profession	Number of Questionnaires Returned	Number of Questionnaires Sent	Percentage Response Rate
General practitioners	59	141	41.8%
Public health nurses (health visitors)	56	119	47.1%
Primary schools	56	115	48.7%
Preschools	42	80	52%
Post primary schools	33	57	57.9%
Mental health workers	15	45	33.3%
Clinical psychologists	11	29	37.9%
Child psychiatry	11	22	50%
Garda Síochána (police)	50	80	62.5%
Speech and language therapists	24	34	70.6%
Accident and emergency nurses	10	39	25.6%
Paediatricians	8	13	61.5%
Drug outreach workers	6	6	100%
Disability workers	5	10	50%
Area medical officers (community paediatricians)	4	4	100%
Total	**390**	**794**	

6

Identifying and Referring Cases of Child Neglect: The Theory and the Practice

Introduction

Child neglect, as discussed in Chapter 2, has both short- and long-term negative effects on the health and well-being of children. Therefore, it is important that all professionals who come into contact with possible cases of child neglect, are not only aware of the indicators of neglect but understand the systems and process for referring these cases to other agencies. Moreover, they must be confident that the system will operate to meet the needs of the child.

At one level, reporting cases of child neglect would seem to be a relatively straightforward procedure. For example, the English guidance *What To Do If You're Worried a Child Is Being Abused* (Department for Education and Skills, et al., 2003) states if a practitioner has concerns about a child's welfare they should:

- Discuss these concerns with their manager or named designated health professional or teacher[1].
- Consider whether the child and family would benefit from services and consider which agency could provide these services.
- Refer to social services if they believe a child is or may be a child in need (a child in need is defined under s17 of the Children Act 1989 as a child unlikely to achieve or maintain a reasonable standard of health and development without the provision of services, or whose health and development will be significantly impaired without services or a child who is disabled).

(Department of Health et al., 2003, p. 7 11.1–3)

Although this type of procedure is standard practice in most developed countries, identifying cases of possible child neglect is not clear-cut. Practitioners have to make professional assessments and reach conclusions as to whether their concerns warrant referral to other professionals. For example, a teacher may have concerns about a child in her class. What are these concerns? What evidence has she got to support her worries about the child? If she then goes on to discuss the child with the designated teacher what does she decide to tell her colleague? How does she describe the child and their situation? What subjective factors, such as past experiences of referral, influence the school's decision to refer to social services or other agencies? Irrespective of setting and legal framework professionals need to answer these questions.

The aim of this chapter is to explore the complexities associated with identifying and referring cases of child neglect to appropriate agencies, drawing primarily on the findings from the Health Board Study (the study is described in the Introduction to this part of the book). In total 430 professionals participated in the study. The respondents divided into 390 'case finders' (Wattenberg & Boisen, no date, p. 1); that is professionals who are in a position to identify child neglect and either work with the case or refer it on to other professionals, and 40 'gatekeepers': that is social workers who are responsible for responding to requests for assessments and services.

We begin by considering the particular contributions that professionals who are in contact with children and their families can make to identifying and assessing possible cases of child neglect. This discussion also explores the struggles experienced by different professionals when making decisions about the types of concern that warrant a discussion with other professionals, or a referral to social work services. The second part of the chapter focuses on making referrals to social work services. More specifically, how decisions to refer are influenced, not only by the needs of the child and their family, but also by the practitioner's perception of social work services, the thresholds they believe are in operation and their own personal and professional fears and anxieties about referring particular cases.

Identifying Neglect: Professional Contributions and Struggles

As described above, practitioners who come into contact with children and families have a responsibility to identify and, where appropriate, refer their concerns to social work services. In England this goes further, as all organisations that work with children have a duty under s11 of the Children Act 2004 to ensure that their functions are discharged with regard to the need to safeguard and promote the welfare of children (HM Government, 2006, p. 10,

2.3). The functions discharged by particular organisations mean that certain professionals are particularly well placed to identify possible cases of child neglect. These include General Practitioners (GPs), health visitors; paediatricians; educational professionals and the police. Below, we explore the particular contribution these groups of professionals can make to identifying, referring and assessing possible child neglect in line with their roles, responsibilities and statutory duties. However, irrespective of the expectations placed on these professionals, the very task of identifying and referring neglect poses different challenges to different professional groups, which will influence their practice. These challenges are also considered in relation to each professional group.

General Practitioners

Members of primary care teams, notably GPs, have a crucial role to play in both identifying and working with cases of maltreatment including child neglect (Department of Health et al., 1999). The Royal College of General Practitioners, in a position paper on child maltreatment, describes the common clinical features of child neglect that professionals in primary care are likely to come across. These include:

- Untreated medical conditions.
- Inadequate compliance with health surveillance and immunisation programmes.
- Poor hygiene.
- Failure to thrive.
- Developmental delay.

(Carter & Bannon, 2003, p. 13)

Not only are these practitioners in a position to identify possible indicators of child neglect, they have unique knowledge about the development of the individual child; the family and family issues which may impact on parenting capacity (see Chapter 4). Indeed, Sinclair and Bullock (2002) found, of the 40 children in their review of child deaths, GPs and health visitors were more likely to be involved with the children than any other professional group. Thorn and Bannon (2003) believe GPs can also make a significant contribution to both assessing child maltreatment and to service provision. They also emphasise that GPs are well placed to become actively involved in the child protection plan and, through participation in the child protection process, can further their own knowledge and understanding of the family.

However, whilst recognising the crucial role GPs can play in identifying and assessing child neglect, their general lack of engagement in child protection work has been well documented (see for example, Hallett & Birchall, 1992;

Lord Laming, 2003; Sinclair & Bullock, 2002). More specifically with regard to child neglect, of the 59 GPs included in the Health Board Study, 98% recognised they had a role in referring cases of child neglect to child welfare services. However, only 19 (32%) believed they should be involved in assessing neglect and only 16 (27%) believed that they should provide services to neglected children.

The GPs, who participated in the Health Board Study, identified a number of factors that acted as barriers to their participation in the child protection process, in cases of child neglect. These barriers are similar to those found in other studies. They can be divided into three categories: 'bad for me'; 'I can do better than the system'; and 'not reportable' (Zellman, 1990 cited in Haeringen et al., 1998).

Bad for Me

This category includes both practical and personal reasons for not engaging in work with neglectful families. Practical reasons, cited in the Health Board and other studies, include heavy workloads and a belief that child neglect forms a very small part of this workload. In addition, practical reasons are frequently cited by GPs for not attending case conferences such as timing, inadequate notice and location prevent them attending conferences (Birchall & Hallett, 1995; Horwath, 2006; Lea-Cox & Hall, 1991; Polnay, 2000).

Various personal reasons were given by the GPs, in the Health Board Study, for not engaging in work with child neglect. These included fear of litigation, if the case went wrong, and worry about the impact of reporting child neglect on their ongoing relationships with the family. This would seem to reflect an inherent tension between the principles underpinning primary care, which focuses on the family and those underpinning child protection, which focus on the child (Bannon et al., 2003). In addition, a number of the GPs were anxious about their skill in identifying and working with child neglect. They recognised that a diagnosis of child abuse does not have the same level of certainty as a diagnosis in other clinical situations (Bannon et al., 2003). Indeed, Coles (2003) questions whether doctors see child abuse as real medicine and therefore outside their areas of expertise.

I Can Do Better than the System

One of the most striking findings from the Health Board Study, in relation to GPs, is their lack of confidence in social work services. Difficulty accessing social workers; previous lack of response and poor relationships with social workers were factors that influenced GPs decisions as to whether to refer cases of child neglect. A striking example of this was shared by a GP in a seminar I ran. She described how she received a message during surgery to ring the duty officer at social work services about a family where there were concerns of child neglect. She rang to be greeted with 'How do? Kev here'. She described how immediately she lost all faith in Kev, and was reluctant to share any information with him. She explained that she had no idea in what capacity he was ringing her and had no confidence in a professional who introduced himself in this way being able to assist the family. Indeed, 51% (n=30) of GPs in the study stated that their decision to refer cases of child neglect to social work services is also influenced by the perceived consequences for the child and family. If GPs do not think a referral will lead to service provision, or improve the situation for the child and family, they tended not refer (Polnay, 2000; Haeringen et al., 1998; Burton, 1996).

However, the GPs in the Health Board Study recognised that their negative perceptions of social work services were associated with a lack of knowledge and understanding about the services. One GP summarised the barriers to referring cases of child neglect as:

> No direct contact with social work team, no knowledge of its structure, function-ing or work practices, no feedback at all from social workers.
>
> (Horwath & Saunders (2004b, p. 22))

Not Reportable

Haeringen et al., (1998) found that both general practitioners and paediatri-cians struggle with identifying neglect. They consider it to be a grey area where their standards and expectations may be higher than those accepted by society. The Health Board Study, in line with other studies (Bannon et al., 2003; Birchall & Hallett, 1995; Burton, 1996; Hendry, 1997), finds that GPs do not routinely receive the training necessary to enable them to make informed deci-sions about when to report possible cases of child neglect to the police or child welfare services. For example, in the study of GP registrars, completed by Bannon et al. (2001), only 27 respondents (24%) considered themselves to be adequately prepared for child protection work.

Health Visitors (known as Public Health Nurses in Ireland)

> Health visitors provide a universal service in addition they have expertise in assess-ing and monitoring child health and development which means they have an important role to play in all stages of family support and child protection.
>
> (HM Government, 2006 p. 27 para 2.77)

As health visitors have a mandatory responsibility, in both the United Kingdom and Ireland, to visit new babies in their home, they are well positioned to iden-tify possible indicators of child neglect. Indeed, the public health nurses (n = 56) in the Health Board Study recognised they have a role in not only identifying (95%) and assessing child neglect (89%) but in working with parents on neglect issues (73%). However, active involvement in child neglect can create problems for health visitors. The individual health visitor has to balance responsibilities for child protection with child health surveillance and, increasingly, community health (Lupton et al., 2001). Hanafin (1998), referring to Irish public health nurses, argues that if public health nurses themselves and other professionals are not clear about the limitations of the health visiting role, then a mismatch can occur between actual and perceived or anticipated roles, which can undermine rather than support child protection work.

Despite the acknowledgement of their role in identifying and assessing child neglect, Truman (2004), who is a health visitor, identifies the problems that health visitors are likely to encounter when identifying child neglect. These include:

- Lack of definitional agreement and operational consistency.
- Different perceptions of children's needs and thresholds of significant harm.
- Different professional perceptions of neglect.
- Cultural values and beliefs.
- Failure to recognise the signs of neglect because of a belief that neglect will not occur on their caseload.
- Believing possible signs of neglect are the result of childhood accidents.
- Focusing on current parenting behaviour and ignoring frequency, chronicity and severity.
- Lack of clarity regarding the significance of a range of factors that may contribute to neglect and possible variables to be targeted for interventions.
- Uncertainty about proving neglect legally.

Nadya (2002) identified further problems, amongst public health nurses in South Australia. They were more tolerant of emotional abuse and neglect than other forms of abuse. They also found difficulty in discerning the difference between wilful neglect and a failure on the part of carers to meet middle class expectations. As a result of this, they try to find ways of supporting carers to avoid the situation deteriorating and referring to child protection services. This support can take the form of 'monitoring' or 'keeping an eye on the family'.

Monitoring

Over half of the public health nurses, in the Health Board Study, favoured 'monitoring' situations of child neglect. However, whilst health visitors, or public health nurses, may decide to monitor the situation, they may be unclear as to what 'monitoring' means and indeed may be 'monitoring' inappropriately.

For example, Hanafin (1998) cites an Irish case where a child died from neglect despite the attempts of the public health nurse to refer the case to social workers and other medical personnel. The public health nurse was left visiting the family, offering advice that was ignored by the carers and unable to convince other professionals of the vulnerability of the children in the family. In this type of situation, the health visitor can be drawn into attempting to support families that require more specialist services such as social work. Health visitors can be left monitoring cases because of the need to ration the limited resources available in social work departments. The result is that cases that may previously have received social work services are no longer receiving them and practitioners, such as health visitors, are by default being drawn into the task of supporting families in place of social workers (Lupton et al., 2001).

Educational Professionals

Education professionals, whether school teachers or early years workers, spend more time in direct contact with children who may be suffering child neglect then any other group of professionals. Neglect may become evident in schools and early years services in a variety of ways (Briggs & Hawkins, 1998):

- The physical presentation of the child. Through poor hygiene, inappropriate clothing, etc.
- Poor nutrition. The child is always hungry and may present as fractious and tired.
- Lack of supervision This is likely to present in three different ways to education workers: 'children locked in, locked out or left to their own devices' (ibid, p. 62).
- Parenting issues. Educational staff are often the first to recognise changes in the carer's behaviour as a result of drug or alcohol misuse, mental health problems, etc.
- Negligence amongst affluent carers. Discussing child neglect with often articulate and confident carers can be challenging. In addition, this type of abuse is likely to occur in more affluent state schools and independent schools. These education professionals are often not as familiar with the signs and indicators of neglect as their colleagues who work with cases of neglect on a more regular basis.

Formal or Informal Actions

Despite their contact with children, teachers may judge it inappropriate to make a child protection referral because of unsuccessful previous attempts to refer cases. However, they are reluctant to do nothing (Baginsky, 2000). This was borne out in the Health Board Study. Preschool and education professionals were the least likely to refer immediately to social work services. As a preschool professional in the study stated:

> Referrals are made to to social workers as a last resortbecause oftne they do more damage.
>
> (Horwath & Saunders, 2004a, p. 69)

often

And a teacher commented:

> Only make referrals if there is a marked deterioration after the school has addressed the issues.
>
> (Horwath & Saunders, 2004a, p. 69)

The findings indicate that teachers and preschool workers prefer informal interventions over formal reporting. This is similar to findings from other studies (Abrahams et al, 1992; Tite, 1993). Building on the work of Pelcovitz (1980), Tite (1993) explores the reasons why this maybe the case. She notes that teachers appear to distinguish between the broad multi-faceted concept of maltreatment and narrower, reportable abuse. Child neglect is more likely to fall into the former category. Thus, unless the neglect is marked by a significant incident, that places it into the reportable and punishable category, it remains managed within the school.

However, Tite (ibid) found when teachers do consider that a case has entered the reportable category, and report child neglect, they are often criticised by social workers for making inappropriate referrals. What worries teachers and places the neglected child in the reportable category may be different to what worries social workers. This was evident in the Health Board Study. The consequence is that teachers become reluctant to report cases of neglect. When this occurs, teachers often find alternative ways of managing the case, either by referring to other agencies or managing the situation themselves.

Section 175 of the Education Act 2002 has placed education services' responsibilities for making child protection arrangements, in England, on a statutory footing. This means that schools, further education institutions and Local Education Authorities now have a duty to safeguard and promote the welfare of children in relation to all functions relating to the conduct of a school (Fiddy, 2002). This legal duty was introduced following the death of Lauren Wright who, while attending school, showed visible signs of neglect and physical abuse, which were not reported. Her mother – a playground assistant at the school – lied to teachers convincing them that the injuries and neglect were a result of clumsiness and poor health. One wonders to what extent the relationship between the mother and the staff influenced their judgement and whether statutory responsibilities would actually make a difference in such a situation.

Briggs and Hawkins (1998) recognise that in Australia despite mandatory reporting of child abuse a number of barriers exist that make teachers reluctant to report abuse and neglect. These include:

- Teachers' personal values and beliefs about the rights of parents and family privacy. These can influence views that parents have the right to treat children as they see fit.
- Beliefs about the role of the teacher as purely an educationalist with no responsibility for the wider welfare of the child.
- Distrust of child welfare services. This includes perceptions of the services ability to handle sensitive issues such as confidentiality.
- Previous negative experiences of involvement with child welfare services.
- Lack of training about neglect.
- Little confidence in one's ability to identify neglect and fear of making a mistake.
- Poor support from within the school.
- Concerns about relationships with carers particularly fear of repercussions from carers and the community.
- Stereotypical views of child neglect. For example, it only exists in poor, problem areas. This means that teachers in middle class schools do not recognise the need to even consider child neglect as a possibility within their classroom.

Baginsky (2000) identified further barriers that exist at an organisational level. She found that teachers', engagement in child protection work, is associated with the relationship between the school and social services. In addition, the priority given to this work by the school can either promote or inhibit engagement. Baginsky found child protection practice was positively influenced if the school and social services had a shared understanding as to what constitutes an appropriate referral.

The barriers to working with child neglect in a way that promotes better outcomes for children, are not just erected by teachers. Gilligan (1998) argues social workers do not always appreciate the central role that teachers have in children's lives, not only in terms of identifying possible maltreatment but in providing a positive school experience. These positive experiences can have a long-term effect on social as well as educational development and act as a potential preventative and protective source for children experiencing social adversity.

The Police (known as Garda Síochána in Ireland)

'The main roles of the police are to uphold the law, prevent crime and disorder and protect the citizen' (HM Government, 2006 p. 31 para 2.97). Hence, the role of the police in cases of child neglect is to both protect children from negligent carers and investigate possible criminal offences associated with neglecting a child. These roles are considered in further detail.

Safeguarding children is a fundamental part of all police officers' duties. It is not solely the role of Child Protection Unit (CPU) officers (these officers normally take primary responsibility for investigating child abuse cases). For example, uniformed officers, detectives and drugs squad officers may well meet neglected children when investigating crime. These officers should also be aware that certain criminal activities such as domestic violence, drug dealing and drug misuse could have a negative impact on children (the impact is described in detail in Chapters 2 and 4). In addition, police officers should be mindful that persons committing other criminal acts may have problems such as learning disabilities or mental health issues that affect the individual's ability to meet the needs of any children in their care.

The second duty of the police, in relation to child neglect, is to investigate cases of child neglect when they believe that a crime has been committed. The Children and Young Person Act 1933 c12 Cruelty to Persons under Sixteen Section 1 states:

> (1) If any person who has attained the age of sixteen years and has the custody, charge, or care of any child or young person under that age *wilfully* assaults, ill-treats, neglects, abandons, or exposes him, or causes or procures him to be assaulted, ill-treated, neglected, abandoned, or exposed, in a *manner likely to cause him unnecessary suffering or injury to health* (including injury to or loss of sight hearing, or limb, or organ of the body, and any mental derangement), that person shall be guilty of a misdemeanour, and shall be liable
>
> (*Note*: Author's italics)

Under s 1 para 2 of the Act neglect includes failure to provide adequate food, clothing, medical aid or lodging (sic) and exposing children under the age of twelve to risk of burning.

As can be seen from the italics, the crucial questions that need to be answered when the police are investigating cases of possible child neglect are, first, is the act of neglect wilful? Second, has it caused the child unnecessary suffering or injury? When considering whether the act was intentional or wilful the following questions should be asked:

- Did the carer mean to do this?
- What evidence is there that they knew this behaviour could cause harm?
- What warnings had the carers received and from whom about the possible outcome of their behaviour?

These kinds of questions can rarely be answered without consultation with other practitioners. Practitioners who have worked with the carers to develop their parenting skills, are likely to have evidence about the carers understanding of the developmental needs of the child and their ability and motivation to meet these needs. Thus, accurate recording by practitioners working with the carers can provide crucial evidence. However, the emphasis on 'wilful' means that the police are likely to view child neglect in a very different way to other professionals. As discussed in Chapter 1, increasingly the focus, when working with child neglect, is the impact on the child rather than the intentions of the carer. This means that the police and other professionals could be at cross-purposes when making joint inquires in cases of possible child neglect.

Practitioners are likely to feel on more familiar territory when considering whether the child has experienced unnecessary suffering or injury. The police need to determine whether the health and well-being of the child has been impaired, as a result of child neglect. The following evidence is likely to demonstrate this:

- Medical evidence of the impact of the neglect on the developmental needs of the child.
- Evidence of the living conditions. For example, video or photos of the home; state of hygiene in kitchen toilet and bathroom; loose wires; condition of food.
- Actual house contents. For example, the child's mattress, bedding, etc, may be physically removed to show in court.

The police will attempt to build up a case to demonstrate what life is like for a child living within this family environment. However, as with care proceedings, building up a case of child neglect can be difficult. It is much easier to proceed with criminal proceedings if there is detailed evidence of abuse through a specific incident, such as physical neglect or child sexual abuse. Indeed, evidence from a child witness regarding a specific incident is easier to obtain then attempts to gain evidence from a child that describes the way chronic wilful neglect has affected the child. With this in mind, it can be useful to gain information from a child about a day in their life (see Chapter 8 for more detail on obtaining this information).

Although police clearly have a duty to identify and refer cases of child neglect there are a number of reasons why police officers may fail to notice child neglect. First, as with teachers and other professionals, the police may hold particular views about the families they visit and the children in these families. For example, perceiving children as 'criminals in the making', or 'little thieves already'. As Stevenson (1998) notes, young people are often labelled as 'villains' without consideration of the lack of care and control these young people may be experiencing at home. Second, police officers are accustomed to visiting impoverished homes and may become desensitised to the possible indicators of neglect that exist in some of the homes, such as squalid conditions, lack of food and bedding. In addition, when a crime has been committed the police focus on arresting the possible perpetrator. In this situation, it is all too easy to marginalise or forget about the needs of the children present in the home. Finally, The Joint Chief Inspectors (2002) in their report *Safeguarding Children. A joint Chief Inspectors' Report on Arrangements to Safeguard Children,* found uniformed police officers were not receiving any basic child protection training. Without training police are unlikely to recognise the signs and indicators of neglect or understand their role in identifying child neglect.

Police officers, like other practitioners, are expected to inform social services if they have concerns that a child may be suffering from child abuse. Most police forces in England have notification forms that police officers complete when they believe a child is at risk of harm. These tend to be used routinely to inform social services of a child living in a home where the police were called out. For example, officers will complete the form following an incident concerning domestic violence or a drugs raid where children are present in the home. The routine completion of notification forms, by the police, means that social services can be overwhelmed by these notifications. The result is that social workers are frequently placed in a situation where they are unable to identify, from the number of forms and the way they are completed a specific cause for concern and may well take no further action.

maybe there is no cause in the referrals received- or +

Paediatricians

> To some extent children's outcomes when presenting to medical practitioners as a result of child abuse or neglect is no better than a lottery, dependent on which doctor they happen to see.   Hareingen et al., (1998, p. 159)

This description of practice in Queensland could as easily be a description of practice in the United Kingdom and Ireland. There are a number of reasons as to why this may be the case with regard to neglect (Johnson, 1993). The way + in which a case is presented influences the approach taken by the doctor. For example, Gelles (1982, cited in Shor, 1998) found that physicians took different approaches towards child neglect and malnutrition depending on whether the situation was presented to them as wilful neglect or due to parental ignorance. Whilst Shor (1998) found, when paediatricians were aware of the consequences of an act or rationalisation for the act, this influenced their perception of level of risk to the child. For example, a case of educational neglect was ranked at the highest level of risk when the consequences of the neglect for the child were described. However, when rationalization of the parent's act was included the case was ranked as less concerning. Third, paediatricians appear to operate a hierarchy of abuse. Shor found that educational neglect and psychological abuse were ranked lower by paediatricians than other forms of abuse, in terms of risk to the child. These forms of abuse were less likely to be reported to welfare agencies or the police. Shor also found that signs associated with physical abuse were ranked as more likely to lead to a suspicion of child maltreatment than signs associated with child neglect.

Similar barriers to those identified by the GPs in the Health Board Study affect paediatricians reporting of abuse (Socolar & Reives, 2002; Vulliamy & Sullivan, 2000). Lamb (2003, p. 1475) notes that cases of serious child abuse are only 'a fraction of the workload of a general paediatrician in the UK'. He believes not more than one case in 1000 is child maltreatment. However, he argues the work generated by the cases is disproportionately high and extremely stressful. Paediatricians also have concerns about the quality of child welfare services and lack of feedback from social workers and uncertainty as to whether referrals result in better outcomes for children. The paediatricians like their colleagues the GPs, are confused about confidentiality and information-sharing. In addition, they are anxious about the legal ramifications of engaging in child protection work (Lamb, 2003). A survey completed by the Royal College of Paediatrics and Child Health (2004) showed that complaints against paediatricians rose dramatically since 1995. Although only 3% of complaints were upheld, the Royal College concluded in the survey report, that complaints against those engaged in child protection work may act as a deterrent to involvement.

Pre-Referral Assessment

Although, as described above, there can be a reluctance amongst professionals to refer possible cases of child neglect to social work services, this does not mean that nothing is done to identify and meet the needs of the child. Whilst community care professionals and the Garda Síochána (police), were most likely to refer to social workers, without completing detailed pre-referral assessments, others, such as education professionals and public health nurses, made detailed pre-referral assessments before making a decision to refer a case to the social work teams or other professionals. The reason for this difference could be that working directly with children is not the core business of professionals, who work primarily with adults, and they do not consider themselves to be in a position to make a detailed pre-referral assessment. However, the introduction of a Common Assessment Framework (CAF) (Department for Education and Skills, 2005) could have a significant impact on this practice. The CAF is designed to be used by any practitioner, irrespective of discipline, at the first sign of concerns about emerging vulnerability of a child. It is to be the main method for establishing whether, and to whom, a referral should be made. CAF, which at the time of writing is still being introduced in England, begins an identification and assessment process of vulnerable children which continues with the *Framework for the Assessment of Children in Need and their Families* commonly known as the 'Assessment Framework' (Department of Health et al., 2000). Together they provide a conceptual framework for identifying vulnerable children and children considered to be in need under s17 of the Children Act 1989.

Despite the lack of a common assessment framework, professionals in the Health Board Study use a variety of assessment tools as part of the pre-referral assessment process such as direct observation and taking a family history. For example:

> I would look at the history of the family and see whether they are dysfunctional, with a history of alcohol or drug abuse, poor parenting skills, eg. diet, interaction with child. I would look at the history of the other children and whether they had been in care or any history of physical abuse. (Public health nurse)
>
> (Horwath & Saunders 2004a, p. 68)

are all these factors associated with poverty?

> We use staff observations and records when identifying. (Pre-schools worker)
>
> (Horwath & Saunders 2004a, p. 68)

As part of this assessment, professionals spend time gathering information about the child and family both intra and inter-agency. In addition, discussions in teams and with managers were identified by the majority of professionals, who attended the focus groups, as an essential part of the process of identifying child neglect. For example, a head teacher said:

> We try and create a culture of care within the school, so that we all can identify neglect and that collective wisdom will prevail.

Referring Child Neglect to Social Work Services: Barriers and Dilemmas

Buckley (2005, p. 113) argues, in cases of child neglect, social workers have 'no monopoly on expertise'. However, there are some situations when professionals should refer directly to social work teams irrespective of the services the family have or have not received from other agencies. These are situations where there are indicators that the child may be, or is, at risk of suffering significant harm. Findings from the Health Board Study and the child deaths associated with neglect described in Chapter 9, indicate that referrals in these situations do not always occur.

A number of subjective factors would seem to influence the decision of professionals to report cases of child neglect to social work teams in these cases.

These include:

- Perceptions of social work services.
- Personal fears.
- Knowledge of the community.
- The battle of thresholds.

(Horwath, 2006)

Each of these are discussed in detail.

From the Outside Looking In: Perceptions of Social Work Services

Although some professionals, in the Health Board Study, described positive experiences when reporting potential cases of child neglect to the social work teams, the majority of the case finders in the study described negative experiences of referring cases to social work teams. This description from a hospital professional summarises the feelings:

> Frustration, non-supportive, anger, lack of communication, not enough liaison, anxious, slow, poor follow-up.   (Horwath & Saunders, 2004a, p. 70)

Respondents indicated that they did not believe the social work teams took their concerns seriously or met the needs of families. This resulted in one of two responses: either referrals were made out of a sense of obligation, with no real conviction that they would result in better outcomes for children and families. In other words the professionals were 'covering their own backs' in case the child suffered significant harm; or alternatively, professionals were reluctant to refer, attempting to work with the child and family outside the formal child protection system and in these situations they only referred to social services as a last resort measure.

Referring professionals, in the Health Board Study, were also asked how many child neglect referrals they had made to social workers in the past 12 months: 52% (n = 204) had not made a referral in the last year and a further 18% had referred only one case of child neglect. This raises questions about the evidence-base used by the majority of respondents when answering the questions regarding social work practice in cases of child neglect. It may well be that their opinions are based on impressions or the experiences of colleagues not their own experience. If this is the case, hearsay, myth and organisational folklore, rather than actual experience, is influencing the way in which these professionals approach social work services. Alternatively, the professionals may have experience of making other types of referrals and are anticipating responses to concerns about child neglect on the basis of those experiences.

The professionals in the study identified four issues related to the current operation of social work services that acted as inhibitors to referral (Horwath, 2006).

Lack of Communication and Feedback

Limited communication and feedback from social workers following a referral was evident in the case audit and identified as a barrier to referral by professionals. These findings are commensurate with the findings of Ferguson and O'Reilly (2001) who studied the processing of child protection cases in the Mid Western Health Board area. If professionals, who remain in contact with the child and family, do not receive feedback on a referral they are left in a vacuum not knowing what is happening to the child and what if anything they should say to the child and family. Which, as Cleaver et al., (2004) found left professionals feeling ineffectual and powerless.

Lack of Continuity of Staff

Respondents in the focus groups described the importance of established relationships with social workers. They emphasised the value of picking up the telephone to talk over concerns with a worker they knew or indeed popping into the office for a discussion about situations that were worrying them. High staff turnover was seen as a real issue that prevented this occurring. As a GP put it:

> I need to put a face to a name and strike up better liaison so there is room for informal discussion and to instil more confidence.
>
> (Horwath & Saunders, 2004a, p. 71)

and a Garda said:

> High turnover of staff is a major problem in continuity of contact and communication – never know who to speak with. (Public health nurse)
>
> (Howard & Saunders, 2004a, p. 7)

The importance of ongoing multi-disciplinary relationships in order to build up trust and an understanding of different roles and responsibilities is well documented in the literature (see for example Calder & Horwath, 1999). Not only were professionals concerned about the impact of a high turnover of staff on their working relationships with social workers, they also felt this affected social workers ability to build up relationships with families and the outcomes for children. Their concerns are justified as the devastating consequences of high staff turnover for children and families is well documented in reports into child deaths (Cm (5730), 2003; Reder et al., 1993; Sinclair & Bullock, 2002).

The professionals were also concerned that skilled, experienced staff are leaving social work teams, resulting in cases remaining unallocated or complex cases being allocated to inexperienced staff. The result is that workers are managing cases without the appropriate level of knowledge and skills. The possible consequences of this situation are highlighted in the Victoria Climbié case. The social worker who worked with Victoria in the months leading up to her death, was recently qualified and had gained little experience of undertaking child protection inquires or working with a child in hospital, experience crucial to the appropriate assessment of Victoria's needs (Cm (5730), 2003).

Lack of Clarity Regarding Social Work Processes

Most professionals in the study, understood the referral process to social work services. However, professionals in the focus groups were confused as to their ability to have 'informal discussions' with social workers prior to making a formal inquiry. At least 16 professionals described how they had believed they were holding informal discussions with social workers, which were responded to as formal referrals by the social workers. This is an issue for professionals who may wish to seek advice and guidance from social workers regarding their concerns, without making an actual referral. A solution would be for professionals to describe the situation, without giving the actual name of the child, until it is clear a referral is appropriate, as outlined in the *What to Do If You are Worried a Child is Being Abused* Guidance (Department for Education and Skills et al., 2003). ✓

There was a sense amongst study respondents, that once professionals have made a referral to social workers it goes into a 'black hole' and they were unclear what followed. Some professionals were not even sure who took their referral. Experience indicated that in some cases it was a receptionist, in others a trained duty worker. When they knew it was a social worker they were still unsure about the level of qualification or experience of the worker. This can influence professionals' willingness to refer cases. For example, (Burton, 1996) found GPs were reluctant to refer cases to social services if they did not have confidence in the expertise of the person receiving the referral.

Lack of Access to Social Workers

Only 29% (n = 115) of respondents stated that they never had a problem contacting social workers. Professionals described the frustration of leaving telephone messages for social workers who failed to respond. Findings from the study indicated that professionals who are in physical contact with social workers because they work in the same building were more likely to make a referral or seek informal advice from social workers than those who needed to telephone or write. However, some referring professionals recognised close proximity brought its own issues as informal discussion can result in important information not being recorded and assumptions being made about who will do what as a result of the informal discussion.

Lack of direct access creates a number of problems. First, the invisibility of social workers reduces professionals' ability to build effective working relationships with them. Second, informal discussion about cases, between professionals, can often clarify thinking about the needs of the child. If social workers are not readily accessible these discussions will not take place, which may result in an inappropriate response to identifying and meeting the needs of the child (Burton, 1996; Lagerberg, 2001).

Personal Barriers to Referral

There are a number of personal factors which appear to influence practitioners decisions as to whether to refer possible cases of child neglect.

Fear of Violence

Professionals in this study demonstrated that the impact of potential aggression from parents affects their attitude towards referring possible cases of child neglect. For example, members of all the focus groups expressed anxiety about their own personal safety, when reporting concerns about child neglect. These fears centred on verbal and physical aggression and threats to workers and their families from the referred families. Indeed, several professionals in the focus groups, described situations where they had been verbally intimidated and physically attacked by carers because they had made a referral to the social work teams. Fear of aggression was identified by the case finders as negatively influencing decisions to report neglect (23% n = 90). Stanley and Goddard (2002) note that managers often minimise the impact of violence on the assessment process. They argue that workers who are fearful of actual or perceived threats may act as if they are helpless, or may engage in defensive practice and reality distortion, commenting that 'these behaviours may shield the worker against high levels of stress, but the cost may be borne by the child, whose safety may not be accurately evaluated' (ibid, p. 127).

Knowledge of the Community

Professionals who work closely with small communities indicated that reporting cases of child neglect was an issue as they feared members of the community would not trust them if they knew that they reported concerns to social work services. Those who ran private businesses such as nurseries had other concerns. For example:

> We also have to consider that our business could be affected and we could lose our livelihood if a referral is made and there are negative repercussions (owner of a private nursery).
> (Horwath & Saunders, 2004a, p. 70)

The respondents were also asked whether personal knowledge and associations with children and families in the community, influenced their decision to refer. Almost 25% of respondents felt that it did with five out of the six drug outreach workers stating that it influenced their decision not to refer. These responses raise questions about the dilemmas encountered by professionals, who either work in small, rural communities or are employed in community-based jobs. Other professionals considered the stigmatising effect of referral on families once the community know that social work services are involved with the family. If professionals decisions to refer are influenced by their position in the community, or that of the family, they are likely to delay or fail to report concerns about child neglect, which can place the child in a vulnerable situation.

Personal Feelings

As described above, fear of violence can influence the responses of practitioners to child neglect. Other feelings have also been found been found to influence practice. For example, Pollak and Levy (1989) argue that feelings of fear, guilt, shame, anger and sympathy will influence decisions to refer. Feelings of helplessness can be added to this list. If this is the case, these feelings need to be recognised and their impact on referral practice explored. Building on their work Box 6.1 outlines types of referral practice and the possible underlying concerns, fears and anxieties that inform this practice.

Pollak and Levy (1989) make three suggestions that could assist practitioners manage their underlying fears and anxieties:

1   Training that takes into account the emotive nature of child protection work and its impact on workers.
2   Consultation with others to share both personal and professional concerns and gain support.
3   Guidance regarding roles and responsibilities in terms of reporting child maltreatment should not merely focus on task but recognise the impact of referral on professionals. Why ?

The Battle of Thresholds

Findings from the Health Board Study indicate, a social worker's concerns about child neglect may be different from that of another professional. For example, differences in terms of concerns regarding the home environment were noted. All the professionals were asked questions relating to how they would define an 'unacceptable home environment' for a three-year-old child. The most concerning factor for 84.1% (n = 328) of respondents, who refer to social work services, were health and safety risks in the home. However, only

15% (n = 6) social workers were concerned about environments which posed health and safety risks. For example, loose electrical wires were considered a significant hazard by 75% (n = 293) of referring professionals, whereas only 10% (n = 4) of social work professionals were concerned about loose electrical wires. The findings indicate that whilst professionals recognise similar general

Table 6.1 Underlying Concerns and the Possible Impact on Referral Practice

Referral Practice	Underlying Concern
Fear Avoid making referral because of actual or perceived threats from family and/or community	*Underlying cause: lack of relevant training* Fear of lack of competence to manage the family situation Fear of one's own anger about the situation and own response to abuse Fear of reprisal and judgement if the report is unsubstantiated
Guilt and shame Do not refer as a betrayal of family's trust Avoid referring family as the family are poor, needy and disempowered Decide to contain concerns and manage the case	Unable to compromise on professional principles regarding confidentiality Want to be seen as caring, supportive and non-intrusive Lack of confidence in role; feel should be managing the situation
Anger and control Referral to social work is an intrusion and challenges professional autonomy Do not want to refer as no feedback from social workers Delay reporting in the hope that situation can be contained	Anger at not being able to manage the situation Feeling of being out of control Reporting itself is perceived by referrer as an aggressive or invasive act
Sympathy Make excuses for the family to avoid making a referral	Over-identify with the family Guilt that worker is in a better position than family members
Helplessness Overwhelmed and refer all cases irrespective of nature Underwhelmed make very few referrals	Sense of despair at the size of the problem Feelings of hopelessness that little, if anything can be done to improve the situation

factors as indicators of child neglect the *emphasis* placed on the specifics varies. This indicates that the case finders and gatekeepers hold different views on what constitutes 'a critical level of jeopardy' (Wattenberg & Boisen, no date p. 8). The case audit showed that when professionals made a referral they describe the situation, leaving social workers to make the classification as to whether the case is one of child neglect. This means that social workers decide whether a case reaches the threshold for further assessment by the social work team (Buckley, 2003). Based on the findings of the Health Board Study, whilst a common assessment framework for referrals may standardise the information that is gathered and introduce a common language for describing the needs of children, the information gathered will still be open to interpretation.

If professionals have differing opinions about what is concerning in cases of child neglect, it is likely to have one of three consequences. First, acts of omission that could potentially have a serious impact on the child may be ignored or minimised if they are not considered significant by the referrer. Second, if referrers do not consider their concerns are being taken seriously they may exaggerate or up the anti (Scott, 1997). Finally, social workers may dismiss the concerns of certain professionals believing that they are over-reacting to situations. The danger, when professionals hold differing opinions, is that the social worker may ignore behaviour that can potentially have a negative effect on the well-being of the child.

Differences, with regard to thresholds for concern, are also influenced by limited resources, staffing shortages and the shear demand for services. This can result in child welfare agencies operating thresholds that seem to be forever moving upwards (Little, 1995). The issue for professionals, and indeed families wishing to access services, is that the criteria are not always specific and may vary depending on team and individual workers interpretation of need. The *Framework for the Assessment of Children in Need and their Families* (Department of Health et al., 2000), used in England and Wales, is designed to provide professionals with a common language and a shared understanding of the factors that should be taken into consideration when referring possible cases of maltreatment. Professionals have found that the Assessment Framework has provided a structured way to record information and created a greater willingness to share information. However, other issues have hampered collaborative work such as lack of agreement over definitions, including the criteria for defining a child in need (Cleaver et al., 2004). At the time of writing Ireland does not have a national assessment framework and disagreement over thresholds is common (Buckley, 2003; Buckley, Skehill, & O'Sullivan, 1997; Ferguson & O'Reilly, 2001).

Disagreement over thresholds may be reduced if practitioners recognise that effective communication about children's needs 'involves the transfer of information *and* the attribution of meaning' (Reder & Duncan, 2004, p. 108). Reder and Duncan believe this can be achieved by:

- Making information readily accessible.
- Presenting it in a form that is clear and avoids misinterpretation.
- Indicating the meaning the referrer has ascribed to the information albeit tentatively.
- Using an evidence-base and distinguishing observations from inferences.
- Recording unambiguously, allowing others to draw their own inferences or revisit and alter own view in light of subsequent information.

Summary

All professionals who come into contact with children and their families have, as a minimum, a responsibility to identify and refer to appropriate agencies concerns about child neglect. Members of primary health care teams, education professionals and the police are particularly well placed to identify possible neglect. However, the very nature of child neglect means that professionals may disagree amongst themselves as to the specific concerns about a child that warrant a referral. In addition, a number of subjective factors influence their responses to child neglect. These include personal values and beliefs, understanding of role, personal anxieties about working with child neglect, fear of the impact on the family of referral to statutory agencies and disillusionment with the child protection system. Professionals also have some very specific concerns about making referrals to social work services. These include negative perceptions of social work often associated with poor communication, lack of

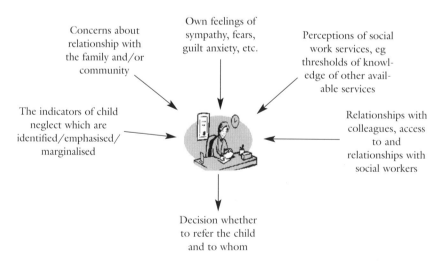

Figure 6.1   **Factors Influencing Decisions to Refer Possible Cases of Child Neglect to Social Work Services**

staff continuity, lack of clarity regarding social work processes and lack of access to social workers.

The subjective factors that can influence referral practice are summarised in Figure 6.1.

What appears to happen, to the neglected child and their family, is that they inadvertently enter a lottery. The child and family's 'win' – a referral to the appropriate agency – will be determined by where they 'buy' a lottery ticket – that is the agency and particular professional who becomes aware of concerns and the 'pick and mix' of numbers selected by the professional on their behalf. The pick and mix being the variables identified in Figure 6.1.

Note

1 The local specialist professional with responsibility for advising colleagues on child protection matters.

7

The Assessment Task and Process: Factors that Promote and Inhibit a Child Focus

Introduction

When I first read the report into the death of Paul who died because of neglect, I was astonished to find that practitioners had not completed a full or systematic assessment in all the 13 years that child welfare agencies had been involved with Paul's family (The Bridge Care Consultancy Service, 1995). It is all too easy to believe that this would not happen now-a-days as so much emphasis is placed on multi-disciplinary assessment. Yet, I believe it is still possible for practitioners to complete superficial rather than thorough assessments in cases of child neglect For example, assessment of child neglect may not be seen as an urgent priority if professionals are 'under-whelmed' by the situation (Graham, 1998). This can occur, for example, when neglect is equated with poverty and the impact on the child is minimalised. Alternatively, professionals may be 'over-whelmed' by child neglect. In this situation, identifying and indeed addressing, the multi-dimensional problems associated with child neglect, is considered an impossible task, so practitioners complete a superficial assessment or take no further action. Whatever the reason for failing to complete a systematic assessment the outcome is the same: the needs of the child are marginalised. Hence, in this chapter we consider the factors that promote and inhibit effective assessment practice following referrals about possible child neglect. The chapter begins by considering the evidence-base that informs assessment practice, in terms of both the assessment task and process. Having identified good practice when assessing neglect, we consider how individuals do not fit neatly into boxes. In exactly the same way as personal and professional values, perception of role and the working context influence practitioners' referral practice, as discussed in Chapter 6, these factors influence the way in which practitioners' complete assessments following referral. In other words, assessments of child neglect are a combination of 'head' or technical-rational activity and 'heart' practice-moral activity. i e a lottery

Assessing Child Neglect: Frameworks and Tools

Although this may appear obvious it is worth stating that the aim, when assessing cases of child neglect, is to identify the needs of the child and their family and to establish ways in which these needs can be met. There are a number of different frameworks and tools, which have been developed at national and state level to assist practitioners complete this task. The advantages and disadvantages of these assessment aids are considered below.

Assessment Frameworks

Assessment frameworks consist of a series of guiding principles and prompts designed to promote effective assessments by sharpening thinking about factors that should inform the assessment of a child in need. For example, in 2000 the English Government introduced the *Framework for the Assessment of Children in Need and their Families* (Department of Health et al., 2000). The Assessment Framework, as it is known has three 'domains': the developmental needs of children; parenting capacity and family and environmental factors. Each domain is divided into 'dimensions', which describe the key areas that should be assessed under each domain. The Assessment Framework and the accompanying Guidance (Department of Health, 2000), are designed to assist professionals in the task of understanding what is happening to a neglected child in order to inform judgements and make decisions to safeguard the child and promote their welfare.

While assessment frameworks offer guidance as to the areas that should be considered when assessing a vulnerable child, the quality of the assessment, depends on the way in which the framework is used by practitioners. For example, I worked with Area Child Protection Committees[1] (now known as Local Safeguarding Children Boards) and social service departments in England to assist in the implementation of the Assessment Framework. This work highlighted some of the problems encountered by practitioners when using the Framework to assess cases of child neglect (for a fuller discussion see Horwath, 2002). The problems identified include:

1   *Practitioners failing to pay equal attention to all three domains of the Framework.* The result of this failure is that the assessment becomes distorted with one aspect of the child's world dominating the assessment.

For example, in cases of child neglect, professionals may become preoccupied with the parenting issues and opportunities described in Chapter 3 and 4 and consequently minimise the needs of the child.

2   *Professionals ignoring the specific needs of members of minority groups.* As described in Chapter 5 practitioners often struggle with assessing the needs of children from minority groups. Government has produced guidance to accompany the Assessment Framework designed to assist practitioners assess the needs of children with disabilities and complex health needs and children from ethnic minority groups (Department of Health, 2000). However, this Guidance is not always readily available or professionals do not regard it as an essential tool when assessing children. In addition, the Guidance is limited and does not, for example, consider assessment of children from different religious groups.

3   *Failing to recognise the multi-disciplinary nature of assessment.* Local Authority child care social work staff have a lead responsibility for implementing the Assessment Framework (Department of Health et al., 2000). Whilst social workers may understand their role, other professionals, who have a less prominent role and have not received training, are often confused about their responsibilities. In addition, systems may not be in place within many organisations to enable staff to contribute to the assessments in a meaningful way.

Organisations that have developed joint initiatives such as inter-agency referral forms, are more likely to engage professionals from different disciplines (Cleaver & Walker, 2004). Hence the introduction of the multidisciplinary Common Assessment Framework (described in Chapter 6) should assist in engaging practitioners in the assessment process.

4   *Inappropriate use of recording forms.* The recording forms, used to accompany the Framework, have in some organisations become *the* Framework. That is, practitioners focus on form-filling and see the Framework as yet another procedure to be followed. In these cases, practitioners allow form filling and recording to dominate practice (Cleaver et al., 2004).

5   *Constraining timescales.* In England, timescales have been introduced for assessment completion. Social workers have seven working days to complete an Initial Assessment (a brief assessment of each child referred to social services with a request to provide services for the child and family) and 35 days to complete a Core Assessment (a detailed assessment of a child with complex needs or a child who is suffering or likely to suffer significant harm). The experiences within the social services departments, referred to above, indicate that some assessments are shaped by the timescales rather than the needs of the child.

6   *Completing assessments in over-burdened organisations.* All social service departments are currently under-staffed and are frequently dependent on

inexperienced workers or recently arrived staff from overseas to deliver front-line services. Many of these workers do not have the knowledge and skills to complete the complex assessments required in cases of child neglect in England. In addition, the overwhelming demands for services means that the focus of the work becomes the 'hard visible end of child protection – crisis-driven and incident-led' (Horwath, 2002, p. 206), with cases of child neglect going to the bottom of the pile.

Assessment Tools

In the USA, rather than using holistic assessment frameworks, the emphasis is on developing risk assessment tools, which are designed to improve the quality and consistency of decision-making. Over 40 states have adopted a risk assessment tool (English, 1999). Tools are developed in one of two ways. 'Actuarial tools' are based on established empirical relationships between predictable variables and outcomes – that is they use actuarial methods and statistical formulae for working out the degree of risk. Other tools are based on a review of the literature or variables agreed by experts as indicating risk and are called 'consensus tools' (English, 1999; Gambrill & Shlonsky, 2000; Munro, 2000).

In England, the Department of Health have developed, alongside the Assessment Framework, assessment tools, questionnaires and scales based largely on consensual models. These are designed to assist professionals assess the needs of the child and their family. Some of the tools are particularly relevant for assessing child neglect. These include:

Tools Designed to Increase Professionals' Understanding of the Home Environment

The HOME (Home Observation for Measurement of the Environment) Inventory. This is a set of tools for assessing a child's home environment. It comprises groups of scales for different age ranges that are scored as present or absent. Scoring is completed using a mixture of observation of the home and carer–child interaction as well as parental report. This tool covers aspects of parenting required to meet the developmental needs of the child and is useful in drawing the professional's attention to the neglected areas. For example, the Early Childhood HOME Record Form includes 55 'items' covering various learning materials, language stimulation, physical environment, responsivity, academic stimulation, modelling, variety and acceptance (Cox & Walker, 2002).

The Family Assessment. This comprises a range of methods and instruments designed to aid the assessment of family competence, strengths and difficulties. The Family Assessment comprises a model of family functioning, family competence, strengths and difficulties scales and recording forms. In addition, the tools include interview schedules designed to explore family organisation, character and history and a range of family tasks to assist families to talk or do things together. The tools should assist in the assessment of child neglect by identifying 'the nature and degree of any difficulties in family functioning and relationships which may be contributing to possible harm. It can also help to identify strengths in the family upon which it may be possible to build a planned intervention' (Bentovim & Miller, 2001, p. 6).

Home Conditions Scale. This lends itself to assessing potential cases of child neglect as the focus is on the physical home environment.

The Family Activity Scale. This is designed to explore with carers the environment they provide for their children. This gives practitioners some insight into the daily life of a child in this family. It is particularly useful in cases of child neglect, when professionals are attempting to identify the way in which the ongoing experiences of the child in the home are affecting their well-being.

Assessing Parenting Capacity and Parenting Issues

There are also some specific tools designed to assist practitioners in assessing the impact of aspects of parenting capacity and parenting issues on the parents' ability to meet the needs of the child (Department of Health, 2000):

The Parental Daily Hassles Scale assesses the frequency and intensity of 20 potential daily 'hassles' carers experience when caring for children. This questionnaire is useful in identifying with neglectful carers some of the daily child-rearing tasks that they find difficult to manage.

The Recent Life Events Questionnaire designed to assist the compilation of a social history. This assists in assessing the impact of past events in carers' lives on current parenting.

The Adult Well-being Scale explores the feelings of the carer in terms of depression, anxiety and irritability, which can be useful, bearing in mind, as described in Chapter 4, the impact that depression can have on a carer's ability and motivation to meet the needs of their child.

The Alcohol Scale seeks to establish how alcohol consumption impacts on the individual and to identify those with hazardous drinking habits. As outlined in Chapter 4, the number of referrals regarding child neglect that are associated with alcohol consumption is significant and the Alcohol Scale tool is useful in establishing the carer's drinking pattern and the possible impact that this can have on ability and motivation to meet the needs of the child.

Assessing the Impact of Neglect on Children

Finally, tools exist designed to explore the impact of maltreatment on children:

> *The Strengths and Difficulties Questionnaire* focuses on the child's emotional and behavioural strengths as well as their difficulties.
>
> *The Adolescent Well-being Scale* is designed to gain some understanding as to how an adolescent feels about their life.
>
> (Cox & Bentovim, 2000)

The Graded Care Profile

A tool that is specifically designed for assessing cases of child neglect is the *Graded Care Profile (GCP) Scale* (Srivastava et al., 2005; Srivastava et al, 2003).

> *The GCP* is designed to assist professionals assess different aspects or 'areas' of care – physical care, safety, love and esteem against predetermined criteria. These areas are broken down into 'sub-areas' and specific 'items'. For example, under 'love' a sub-area is the carer's approach, which is broken further into different components or 'items'. One of these is the 'sensitivity' of the carer to the child. To complete the assessment the practitioner grades each item on a five-point scale. For example 'sensitivity' is graded from 'anticipates or picks up very subtle signals of verbal or non-verbal expression or mood' through to 'insensitive to even sustained intense signals' (ibid, p. 244). Each point on the scale has such a description enabling the practitioner to rate what they have observed. The scores are then recorded for all the items and areas of strength and weakness identified. The GCP has been piloted in two local authorities in England. Professionals found that it promotes working in partnership with families; is user-friendly; results in less subjective assessments than 'free-form approaches' (ibid, p. 231); focuses on strengths as well as deficits and can be used with the Assessment Framework. What is particularly valuable about this tool is that professionals in a variety of settings can use the GCP to identify their cumulative concerns about a neglected child to support a referral to social services or elsewhere. *but . . . p 136–137*

The Limitations of Tools and Frameworks

Scales and tools can be useful in assessing cases of child neglect as they provide specific indicators for measuring the different aspects and severity of neglect and in addition, they also assist in highlighting areas for observation (Stevenson, 1998). However, these tools are not the Holy Grail; they will not automatically provide practitioners with the right answers. Many of the questions, linked to the tools, are dependent on making a judgement regarding acceptable standards of care, and family strengths and deficits. Yet, our knowledge of child-rearing is not sufficiently accurate to reliably predict the positive or negative behaviours that relate to specific outcomes for children and more research is required to adequately describe the correlates of child neglect (Connell-Carrick, 2003; Gershater-Molko et al., 2003; Murphy-Berman, 1994). *So, you do not know what you are looking for.*

In the absence of clear criteria for measuring child neglect, individual professionals are left to establish their own standards (Gershater-Molko et al., 2003) and, as indicated in Chapter 6, as professionals hold different views with regard to 'good enough' parenting these standards will vary. For example, 'acceptance' of a child is described in the HOME Inventory Guidance as 'parental acceptance of less than optimal behaviour from the child and the avoidance of undue restriction and punishment' (ibid, p. 10). What one professional may consider acceptable punishment may be different to another professional, depending on the individual's values and beliefs. Professionals may also hold different views as to the weight they should give to the scores for each section of the assessment tool and whether some negative scores are more concerning than others (English, 1999).

Practitioners also need to balance what they observe with what the family tell them. There is a danger that carers and children may be over-optimistic in their responses when answering questions from professionals as they have a vested interest in creating particular impressions of the situation (Gershater-Molko et al., 2003; Murphy-Berman, 1994; Stone, 2003). Thus, it is important to bear in mind what is said by whom and for what possible purpose. Practitioners are more likely to gain an accurate view of the situation if they use a range of methods to gather information (Murphy-Berman, 1994). *So your approach is gather all sorts of information in case you need it...*

Another issue, regarding the use of tools and frameworks, concerns cultural sensitivity. Practitioners should ensure that the tools that are used are relevant for all cultural groups. This means checking out with the family that the questions being asked are meaningful to the family, rather than presuming relevance. Moreover, as discussed in Chapter 5, it is important to recognise that culture and religion may influence perception of possible risk factors and indeed what constitutes child neglect (Munro, 2000; Murphy-Berman, 1994). Professionals also need to be aware that their own cultural values and worldview may influence the way they interpret and grade the information received.

If tools are to be used effectively when assessing child neglect, then practitioners need to have the relevant training to use the tools confidently and appreciate their value (Cleaver et al., 2004). In addition, they should be aware that the tools are not a quick and easy way of making an assessment: they are time consuming. Moreover, their effectiveness in assessing child neglect depends on using the information gained, from the selected tools, in the context of information gained from other sources. Finally, it is important to remember that tools are designed to support the professional in their task. Hence, assessment tools can only assist in informing judgements and decisions about the child and family. With this in mind, the following may be useful prompts for practitioners using assessment tools to assess child neglect:

- Think about the purpose of the assessment and choose the assessment measures that best evaluate the specific family situation.
- Focus on the knowledge, skills and abilities of the carers to meet the needs of the child.
- Consider the impact of the neglectful behaviours on the child.
- Use a range of different methods such as observation of child-carer inter-action, parent-specific measures.
- Be familiar with and comfortable using the assessment tool and be aware of its limitations.
- Be cautious interpreting the findings and consider the results in the context of information gathered from other sources.

(Gershater-Molko et al., 2003, p. 581)

The Assessment Process

Frameworks and tools are designed to assist professionals gather and make sense of information in order to gain insight into the nature of the family situation and the life of the child. If professionals are going to maximise the use of tools when assessing child neglect, they need to pay attention not only to the assessment task but also the assessment process and the judgements that need to be made at each stage of the process. The process is summarised in Figure 7.1 as are the types of judgement made at different stages of the process as identified by Hollows (2003).

Each stage of the process and the type of judgement that needs to be made is described in detail below.

Identifying Purpose and Gathering Information

The first stage of any assessment is to gain a common understanding with the family and other professionals, as to why an assessment is being completed and the questions that need to be answered. Once this is clarified, then everyone can be clear about the type of information that needs to be gathered. The

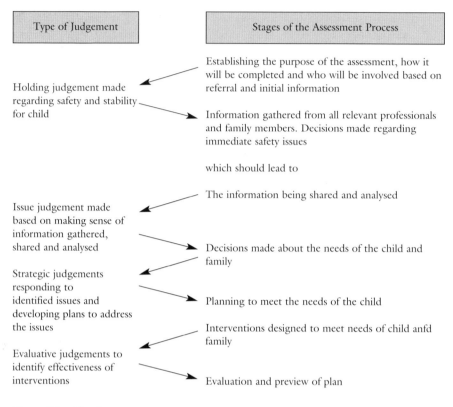

Figure 7.1   The Assessment Process

framework in Box 7.1 is designed to assist professionals in identifying the type of information that should be gathered in cases of child neglect. It draws on the work of the social workers who participated in the Health Board Study as well as practice developments and research into child neglect assessments (Horwath & Bishop, 2001, Horwath, 2005a).

Making Sense of the Information

A crucial part of the assessment is to make sense of the information gathered, in order to make decisions about the child and their situation. This should inform planning and service delivery. Making sense of information, in cases of child neglect, is a difficult task. Indeed Cleaver and Walker (2004) found that practitioners were anxious about their ability to analyse information gathered using the *Framework for the Assessment of Children in Need and their Families*. As neglect is multi-faceted, professionals can be overwhelmed by both the amount of information obtained and also the significance of the information. This creates three problems. First, information gathered may not always be used to inform decision-making (Cleaver & Walker, 2004). We tend to focus on the vivid detail that makes the case different (Munro, 2000). Second, professionals may find it difficult knowing when sufficient information has been gathered to make an informed assessment of the needs of the child (Macdonald, 2001). Finally, making sense of the information requires a strong theoretical and research based approach. However, for hard pressed practitioners it is difficult keeping up to date with research. Yet without it, 'information gathered about a case hangs loose and directionless' (Howe et al., 2000, p. 154).

Making Judgements and Decisions

Once professionals have made sense of the information, then they need to make judgements about the nature of the information and its implication for the health and well-being of the child and family (see Figure 7.1). However, it is naïve to think that judgements are only made at a discreet point of the assessment process. Professionals make different types of judgements at different points of the process (Hollows, 2003). The first type of judgement is what Hollows (ibid, p. 68) refers to as a '*holding*' judgement. These should be speedy judgements, often made at the point of referral. These judgements are designed to ensure safety and stability for the child without reducing other options in terms of more long-term judgements. However, in busy social work departments cases of neglect may never get beyond a holding judgement. The response to neglect can be to offer a 'quick fix' without considering the underlying problems. The family is literally put on hold until an incident occurs that is considered to be sufficiently significant to warrant more detailed work.

The second type of judgement is the '*issues*' judgement. These are judgements based on a thorough analysis of the information gathered, using a framework such as the *Framework for the Assessment of Children in Need and their Families*. The following questions are designed to assist professionals with issue judgements in cases of child neglect:

- What are the pre-existing and current factors that indicate the child is being neglected?
- What type of neglectful behaviour on the part of the carer/s is of concern?
- Are these behaviours impacting on the health and well-being of the child? If so how?
- What evidence is there to support these judgements?
- What are the pre-existing and current strengths that protect the child from neglect and promote their welfare?

Box 7.1 Framework

Assessment Focus	Child's Needs: Consider	Parents' Ability and Motivation: Consider	Relationship With The Outside World: Consider
Basic Care	Appearance and quality of clothing, seasonal, fit and level of cleanliness and repair Physical presentation including level of cleanliness, condition of hair, body odour, skin infections, regular dental and optical care Medical care and attention commensurate with needs of child Child immunised as appropriate Receiving necessary medical checks Child's physical development using centile charts Child's attitude towards food Whether child feels warm/cool as appropriate	Provision of clean, fitting clothes appropriate for weather conditions Ability to recognise when the child needs help with basic care Prompt response to child's needs, for example, nappy changes, treating infections Commitment to routinised care such as bathing, mealtimes Modelling of good practice in terms of own basic care by carers Meeting medical care requirements such as attendance at clinics, appointments, etc Provision of regular and nutritious meals Ensuring food available Ability to recognise and respond when child is hungry or satiated Approach to feeding. For example, encouragement to eat; force feeding; child left to own devices Awareness of and ability to respond to child's physical state, for example illness, Financial ability of carers to improve home conditions	Response of significant people in child's world such as teachers, peers to their appearance The condition of the home for example, human/animal excrement; soiled bathroom and toilet; old, decaying food in kitchen, evidence of infestation; damp; sources of heating; broken windows and doors; bedding Sleeping arrangements adequate enabling the child to receive sufficient sleep for example, cot, pram or bed available and clean State of housing in contrast to other homes in neighbourhood Adults available to meet the basic care needs of the child or support carers in meeting these needs

Ensuring Safety	Child feels and is safe and secure within the home The child is protected from abuse Child protected from inappropriate behaviours such as domestic violence	Management of money and budgeting to meet needs of child Priority of spending Ensuring child protected from hazards in the home such as open fires and heaters; alcohol; drugs, etc. Ability to recognise potential unsafe adults and children, including siblings and protect child from them Teaches child life skills to keep the child safe	Home environment is safe. Hazards for child in street and neighbourhood such as syringes, broken glass etc Support for child outside home in situations of domestic violence, etc.
Stimulation	Level of school/preschool attendance Freedom to play with toys Time given for play Interaction between the child and appropriate adults Variety of activities to stimulate curiosity and exploratory behaviour Particular educational needs of the child Child needs opportunities to explore and find out about the world around them	Importance attached to educational activities by carer Encourage regular schooling and support attendance Social opportunities provided for interaction Ability and commitment to interact with child through play etc Engaging child in verbal communication Ability and commitment to listen to and communicate with the child Encourage intellectual development Provision of toys, books and opportunities to use them Recognise and respond to the special needs of the child Hold appropriate expectations of the child	Engagement in learning at school/pre school. To include attendance, behaviour in class, ability, concentration, responses to adults Access to activities outside the home Relationships with peers Opportunities for extra curricular school and social activities Provision of services to meet special needs

Box 7.1   Framework (continued)

Assessment Focus	Child's Needs: Consider	Parents' Ability and Motivation: Consider	Relationship With The Outside World: Consider
		Readiness to answer child's questions and provide them with new learning experiences	
Emotional Warmth	Child has secure attachment with strong feeling of self-confidence and self-worth	Forms secure attachment	Positive relationships outside the home
	Having a sense of being valued, self-esteem	Ability and commitment to show child consistent love and acceptance and to respond to their emotional needs	Attitude of teachers and significant others to the child
	Able to have fun	Encourage a sense of identity	Relationship with significant others
	Respond appropriately in different emotional contexts	Provide appropriate physical contact	Identity in out of home settings
	Positive sense of identity, including race, gender, disability, culture and sexuality	Demonstrate love for the child	Activities that increase child's sense of self-worth
	Secure, stable and affectionate relationships with significant others	Able to say positive things about the child	
	Appropriate physical contact	Show consistency, reliability, dependability	
	Sense of belonging to a family and other relevant groups	Realistic expectations of the child in line with emotional maturity	
	Child senses emotional mutuality between self and carer	Demonstrate a sense of belonging and togetherness	

Guidance and Boundaries	Able to regulate own emotions and behaviours Develop values, a conscience and appropriate social behaviours Grow into an autonomous adult Explore and learn Manage anger	Provides supervision and guidance balancing being lax with being over-protective Realistic expectations of the child in terms of age and ability Provides consistent, clear and fair guidance and rules Appropriate methods of discipline used and followed through Ensures guidance is consistent and indicates clear boundaries Offers appropriate models to child	Community norms provide acceptable boundaries, for example, leaving children alone Groups and members of the community engaged with young people to provide guidance and supervision School recognises and is able to meet the needs of the child in terms of levels of supervision and guidance Good contacts with neighbours Community activities are seen as safe (crime/drug safety) Community is perceived to be safe (roads, buildings)
Stability	Able to trust others Sense of stability about family in contact with family members Maintains a secure attachment with carer Child feels secure and able to express herself	Provides a stable home environment Provides a secure relationship with the child Maintain relationships with significant others in the child's life Recognise and respond to the changing needs of the child Create a stable home environment with harmonious family relationships	Stable neighbourhood with effective established community groups designed to meet the needs of the child and carer Established and supportive social networks Children feel valued and parents supported

Sources: Horwath, 2005; Iwaniec, 1995; Iwaniec & McSherry, 2002; Rosenberg & Cantwell, 1993; Stone, 2003, Jack & Gill, 2003

- What is there about the current situation that increases or decreases the likelihood that the health and development of the child will be affected through neglect?
- How does the current situation fit with past patterns of carer/s neglectful behaviour?
- What are the child's views on their situation? What do they want to change?
- What insight does the carer/s have in relation to the impact of their behaviour on the child?
- What would need to change if the carer/s were to meet the needs of the child?
- What are the indicators that carer/s have the ability and motivation to make the changes required to promote the welfare of the child?

(Adapted from Buckley et al., 2006).

Based on the answers to the above, practitioners should make decisions that take into account which of the child's needs are being met, those that are not and the impact on the child of failing to meet these needs. Howe et al., (2000, p. 154) emphasise that decision-making should be based on an understanding of the 'mechanisms that drive children along particular developmental pathways'. In cases of child neglect an attachment perspective as outlined in Chapter 2 can ensure that the outcome of an assessment is more than a concern for the physical care of the child.

Having reached a decision about the health and well-being of the child, professionals are required to make further judgements called '*strategic*' judgements (Hollows, 2003). These involve professionals deciding how to respond to the identified needs of the child and family and developing plans that safeguard and promote the well-being of the child.

Needless to say, judgement making does not stop here. Professionals should continue to make '*evaluative*' judgements regarding the effectiveness of interventions for the child and family. The questions that should be asked are:

- In what way are the services provided meeting the identified needs of the child and the family?
- What evidence do we have to support this?
- Are the interventions addressing our original and any emerging concerns?
- Is progress being made at a pace that will safeguard and promote the well-being of the child in both the short- and longer-term?

One of the biggest challenges, encountered by professionals working with child neglect, is to systematically evaluate the progress being made by the child and family. It is all too easy to slip into routinised visiting or monitoring that has no

Why would you visit if there is no reason to?

clear aims and objectives against which to evaluate effectiveness. This is discussed further later in this chapter.

In this first part of this chapter we have explored assessment as a technical-rational or 'head' activity. In the second part we consider the way in which the 'heart' can influence practice.

Factors that Distort Assessments in Cases of Child Neglect

Although the assessment process, described above, appears logical, assessment of child neglect is open to a range of influences that can distort the assessment and affect the outcomes for children and families. The most common factors identified from the Health Board Study are discussed below (for further discussion see Horwath, 2005 and Horwath, 2005a).

Inter-Professional Practice

As identified above, an effective assessment of child neglect requires successful collaborative working between professionals. However, as we know, this is more easily said than done. There are a number of barriers which can affect multi-disciplinary practice. The findings from the Heath Board Study indicated that the following factors influence working together in cases of child neglect.

The Assessment Role of Professionals

Evidence from the Health Board case audit indicated that multi-disciplinary work was limited when social workers initiated assessments of neglect, with only a minority of professionals being involved in decision-making and planning. These findings are commensurate with those of Holland (2004) who completed a study of assessment practice in Wales. One explanation for this could be that 67% of non-social work professionals in the Health Board Study did not consider it was their role to assess cases of child neglect. The breakdown of professionals perception of role is shown in Box 7.2.

What is concerning about these findings, is the number of professionals who are in daily contact with children who did not consider they had a role in assessing child neglect. One of the reasons for this could be the lack of training available to professionals, regarding their child protection role. For example, Baginsky (2000) notes child protection training is minimal on teacher training programmes, leading to a poor understanding of role. It is perhaps more understandable, although not acceptable, that professionals working in adult services and the police did not consider they had an assessment role. The lack of understanding amongst adult service professionals, about their child protection role, has been well documented. Once again lack of training, as well as

---

Box 7.2   The Breakdown by Professional Groups of the 67% of Professionals (n = 261) Who Said It Was Not Their Role to Assess Neglect

- n = 48   (96%)   Garda Síochána
- n = 40   (71%)   primary schools
- n = 39   (68%)   GP's
- n = 30   (71%)   preschools
- n = 25   (66%)   post primary
- n = 17   (71%)   speech and language therapists
- n = 16   (29%)   public health nurses
- n = 15 (100%)   mental health
- n = 7   (64%)   child psychiatry
- n = 6   (100%)   drugs outreach workers
- n = 5   (50%)   accident & emergency nurses
- n = 5   (45%)   clinical psychologists
- n = 4   (80%)   disability
- n = 3   (75%)   area medical officers
- n = 1   (12%)   paediatrics

---

anxiety about working with child protection concerns and a sense of not being equipped to assess children in need, are all reasons given for not engaging in assessments (see for example, Falkov, 1996; Forrester, 2000; Hester et al., 1999). When professionals from adult services do contribute to an assessment Budd et al., (2001) found lack of understanding about the assessment task can lead to the assessments being completed in a single session. They also found these professionals rarely visited the home and used few sources of information, other than information from the parents. They found reports lacked context and often disregarded the impact of the carer's behaviour on the child's relationship with the carer. ⇨ paperwork exercise

There are two developments in England which are designed to improve multi-disciplinary working. First, all staff in contact with children and families will be expected to receive training focusing on a common core of skills, knowledge and competence (HM Government, 2006). Eventually this will be extended to underpin all qualifications for working with children and families.

The aim is through training, to introduce a common language amongst practitioners and begin to break down some of the cultural and practice barriers existing between different professionals working with children. The core competences include multi-disciplinary working. Unfortunately, this training does not extend to staff working in adult services. In addition, the split between statutory adult and children's social care services is likely to lead to further confusion about role. However, the second development makes clear that all staff have to recognise they have a responsibility to safeguard children. Under s11 of the Children Act 2004 all agencies have a duty to 'ensure that their functions are discharged with regard to the need to safeguard and promote the welfare of children' (HM Government, 2006 p. 10, para 2.4). Although this development is designed to engage staff in multi-disciplinary working, agencies could potentially still argue that participating in assessments is not a key role and responsibility.

Communication between Professionals

Professionals' lack of understanding about their assessment role, in relation to assessing cases of child neglect, may also be due to the mixed messages given to them by social workers about roles. For example, although in 39 of the 57 cases included in the case audit, social workers in response to referrals of child neglect did contact professionals who knew the child and family in question, in 14 cases, not all relevant professionals were contacted. In these cases there was no indication on the file as to why certain professionals were selected for contact and others ignored. If social workers do not routinely and systematically approach practitioners and engage them in the assessment process, they may well be confused about social workers' expectations. This can lead to a passive response: practitioners only contributing to the assessment if invited to do so by social workers (Calder & Horwath, 1999).

When social workers in the study did contact professionals the methods used for contact varied and had an impact on the quality of the information obtained. For example, detailed information was obtained when social workers had face-to-face contact, or telephone discussions, with professionals. However, social workers often communicated by letter. These letters rarely elicited information that could assist the assessment. The letters did not give details of the case, rather professionals were asked to inform social workers of any 'concerns' they had about a family or child. This placed the onus on professionals to interpret what social workers mean by 'concerns' and to respond accordingly. What?!

It was not clear, from the audit, why some professionals were contacted by telephone and others by letter. When questioned about this in the focus groups, social workers highlighted the problems of attempting to contact busy professionals. Professionals who could be contacted easily, by direct communication or telephone were contacted in those ways, whereas those that were not usually available tended to be contacted by letter. Social workers explained that they did not want to waste valuable time attempting to contact these professionals by telephone. Needless to say, few professionals responded to the letters, meaning that significant information may have been excluded from the assessment. Cleaver and Walker (2004), evaluating the implementation of the Assessment Framework in England, also found that poor social work practice, particularly failure to communicate with other professionals, hampered collaborative assessments.

Child Protection Conferences

The recognised multi-disciplinary arenas for sharing information and making decisions about child neglect in England and Ireland are the case planning meeting and child protection conference. The focus in the Health Board Study was on the conference. However, similar issues are likely to arise in case planning meetings.

Both social workers and other professionals in the Health Board Study considered that these conferences were both important and useful. However, the professionals themselves identified a number of issues related to conference attendance. First, they were often unclear as to both the criteria used for inviting professionals to the conference and how information regarding conference decisions was disseminated. This confusion is likely to add to misunderstanding about role in relation to assessing child neglect. For example, conference attendees who do not receive minutes of the meeting may believe they are not expected to contribute further to ongoing assessments and interventions. Second, the respondents also identified practical problems, such as limited warning of conferences and conflicting workload pressures, making it difficult to prioritise taking time away from the workplace to attend the conferences. The fact that conference venues were often a distance from professionals' workplace exacerbated the situation. In addition, working in partnership with families was a barrier as some respondents had experienced verbal and physical aggression from parents at conferences and others were concerned that parents would use verbal and physical aggression against them if they said negative things about the family at conferences. Others, particularly the police, found it difficult sharing information with parents present.

Contact with the Child and Family

Sharing information with the family, both within the conference setting but also in response to a referral, was an issue. In most cases the initial contact with the family took place after professionals had been contacted. It is worth noting that in only five cases was there evidence on the files that family members had been asked if they agreed to professionals being contacted for information, despite the fact that this study took place at the time of the implementation of Freedom of Information legislation and the Board had local guidance indicating that good practice was to consult with children and families before contacting other professionals. Once professionals did make contact with families the way in which they worked with members of the family as part of the assessment process varied, as described below.

Communicating with Children

The nature of the contact between the workers and the child varied, from case to case. Guidance issued by the Board (North Eastern Health Board, 1994), like the Assessment Framework (Department of Health et al., 2000), recognises that children have a right to be heard and should be consulted and involved in all matters and decisions about their lives. Of the social workers, 80% that responded to the questionnaire believed that decisions, in cases of child neglect, should be based on what the child wants (provided they have the ability to understand and make informed choices). However, other professionals were not so sure, with only 28% agreeing with this statement. These findings would indicate a difference of opinion between social workers and other professionals as to the attention that should be given to the child's wishes and feelings.

Although social workers stated in the questionnaires and focus groups that it was important to make decisions, based on the views of the young person, the review of case material showed a lack of meaningful communication with children about their lives. First, children were physically seen on only 21 of the 48 home visits made by social workers following referral. In only 15 cases where children were not seen was a reason given: such as the child was asleep or at school. Even when the child was seen it appears that it was more by accident than design. The workers did not include details that indicated that they had made any meaningful observation of the child, such as comments on weight, appearance demeanour, etc. In fact very few case files held any descriptions that gave the reader a clear picture of the child. Rather, as Holland (2004, p. 73) found in her study, the child assessments were two-dimensional 'which made them [children] objects of the assessment rather than subjects'. The records indicate that the social workers rarely spoke to the children to ascertain their views and feelings. Thus workers gained little insight into the child's experience of family life. In three cases, children make explicit comments about their experiences. The comments were recorded, but there was no evidence on the files that the views were taken into account when assessing the children's needs.

As neglect centres on the interaction between the child and their carer (Dubowitz, 1999b; Iwaniec, 1995), it is difficult to see how workers can assess neglect without at the very least seeing the child. The practitioners themselves felt they were poorly equipped with the skills to communicate competently with children regarding such a complex area as child neglect. In addition, they believed workload pressures often prevented them from spending time with children. As one of them put it:

[handwritten: What do you mean workload pressures? This is your job.]

> No communication may be better than getting the child all worked up and not having the time to see things through.   (personal communication)

However, it is not only practical problems that prevent communication, practitioners' personal feelings can also impact on direct work with children and act as a barrier to communication. As the same practitioner put it:

> I really can't cope with asking a child to tell me about their miserable lives when I know there is little, if anything, I can do that will improve things.
> (personal communication)

Practitioners need to find ways of communicating with children: the aim being, as Lord Laming (Cm (5730), 2003) made clear in his report into the death of Victoria Climbié, to establish what a day in the life of the child is really like. Box 7.3 lists questions indicating the type of detailed information that professionals require in order to understand what life is really like for the child. This information may be obtained through a range of methods, which should be selected based on both the age and ability of the child and also what appeals to the child. For example, discussion, using toys or through getting the child to draw a strip cartoon of a day in their life. Alternatively, the practitioner could use a clock and ask the child what happens at particular times of the day and night (Samra-Tibbetts & Raynes, 1999).

Cleaver and Walker (2004) who interviewed children, who had been involved in assessments using the Assessment Framework in England, found that children felt excluded from the assessment and planning process. These children wanted professionals to:

- Take time to explain to them what is happening and why.
- Listen and respect their views and experiences.
- Believe what is said.
- Talk to the people they think are important.
- Provide them with something to remind them of what was decided.

(Ibid, p. 248)

Observing carer–child Interaction

The case recordings, from the Health Board Study, highlight that some workers are able to describe, in vivid detail, what they observe when they have contact with family members, whilst others struggle to portray a picture of the family situation and family interactions. Yet it is important. As described in Chapters 1 and 2, neglect is an omission on the part of the parent to meet the needs of a child; therefore it is necessary to understand the relationship between the carer and child in order to identify strengths and weaknesses. One of the most effective ways of achieving this is through observing the carer and child together. If workers do not observe and make sense of this interaction then they may not understand the difficulties the carer has in offering reliable and adequate care.

Effective observation should be based on three key principles: context, purpose and consent (Holland, 2004). Holland expands on this, stating that the observer should consider how their role and the context in which the observation is taking place, may influence the family interactions. Particular attention should be paid to the impact of ethnicity and gender on the worker/family dynamics. Second, practitioners need to be honest with the family as to what they intend to observe, why and how this will be done. And finally, they should also be clear about what will be recorded and the opportunities available to the family to comment on the recording. It is also important to obtain the family's consent to the observation. Professionals may routinely do this if they decide to observe a particular situation, such as a mealtime. However it is all too easy to fail to inform the family of the ongoing observations that practitioners continually make and may record whilst visiting the family.

Contact with Carers

Of social work respondents to the questionnaire, 85% (n = 30) believed decisions about neglect should be based on workers and families exploring possible issues and outcomes, together. And 72% believed that decisions should be made according to information obtained from families. Despite these beliefs the *nature* of contact and engagement with carers varied from case to case. In the case audit there were nine cases where there was no evidence on the file of any contact with the carers. In two cases the family had moved and despite worrying referrals about the needs of the children, there was no attempt to track the families down. This could leave children in vulnerable positions as families may use 'flight' as a way of avoiding contact with professionals (Reder et al., 1993). Five cases were closed as professionals, who when contacted by social workers did not express concerns in response to the referral and, in a final two cases, no reasons were given for case closure.

In a further seven cases the follow up to a case was by letter inviting the carer into the office to discuss the 'issues'. There were no clear criteria operating across the Board indicating which cases should be managed by sending a letter to the family or arranging a visit. Indeed in some cases sending a letter was thoughtless. For example, a letter was sent to a mother with a learning disabil-

Box 7.3 Establishing a Day in the Life of a School-Age Child

Question	Factors to Consider
Do you get yourself up in the morning?	Is the child expected to get themselves up? Is there a regular routine or does it depend on the motivation of the carer? Does the child have to take responsibility for carers and/or siblings in the morning? Is an alarm clock/mobile phone used to make sure child is up in time for school/play school etc?
Do you have anything to eat?	Is there usually food in the house? What is available to the child? Does an adult/sibling or child themselves take responsibility for preparing breakfast? Is child given money to buy something on way to school? If so what do they tend to buy?
What happens about getting dressed?	Are clothes readily available, clean and in a good state of repair? Does the child have to find their own clothes? Do they have their own clothing? What happens about washing, etc? Does the child wash and brush their teeth in the morning? Is this appropriately supervised? Are there facilities available, eg tooth brush?
What happens if you are going to school?	How does the child get to school? Who is responsible for getting the child to school? Is the child responsible for other children?
What happens at school?	What is the nature of the child's relationships with their peers, teachers and support staff? What do they enjoy at school? What do they find difficult? What makes them happy and sad at school? Do they have friends? Are they bullied? What do they do at playtime?
What happens if it's the weekend or school holidays?	Is the child expected to look after other children and or the carer? Are they expected to do errands, etc, for the carer? How do they spend their time?

Do they have any friends?

Are they left unsupervised or allowed to undertake inappropriate activities?

What happens about food? (consider areas below)

What happens after school?	Are they collected from school and if so on time?
	Do they stay for after-school activities?
	Are they responsible for other children?
	Do they have friends that they see?
	What is the journey home from school like? (consider opportunities for bullying, etc)
	Is there anyone at home when they arrive back?
	What happens when they get home?
	Do they have any caring responsibilities?
	Is food available when the child gets home from school?
What happens in the evening?	Is there food available?
	What kind of food does the child eat in the evening?
	What does the child enjoy eating best? How often do they have this?
	Does anyone prepare an evening meal? If so does the family eat together?
	If not does the child get their own food and/or get food for others?
	When does the child usually have their last meal/snack?
	What happens if the child says they are hungry?
	Does the child spend their time watching TV? Do they go out where and with whom?
	Does the child enjoy games and toys which ones? Do they have toys?
	What do the carers do in the evening? What does the child think about their activities?
	Does anyone talk to the child or give them any attention?
	Is the child left alone or expected to supervise other children in the evenings?
What happens at bedtime?	Does the child have a bedtime?
	Who decides when the child goes to bed?
	Where does the child sleep?
	Do they change their clothes before bed?
	Do they have a wash and brush their teeth?
	Does the child get disturbed? Eg carers making a noise, child sleeping on settee
	Is the child left alone at night and/or expected to look after other children?

ity when it was not known if she could read, or if she could read, whether she would be able to comprehend the contents of letter. These findings are commensurate with those of Thoburn et al., (2000) who found that 37% of cases in their similar sample were closed with no face-to-face contact with social workers, the contact being confined to a letter or telephone call. These researchers note that parents receiving letters were likely to be deterred from asking for help and contacting social workers even if the offer was made in the letters. Why?

Avoiding Meaningful Contact

Other cases were filtered out of the system, when the carers appeared to avoid meaningful contact with the social workers. Whilst being reluctant to categorise these cases the different ways in which they avoided meaningful contact appear to reflect the different characteristics of the neglectful family types described in Chapter 3. For example, carers cancelled or failed to attend office visits or were not in when workers had arranged planned home visits. Carers also managed to avoid assessments by keeping workers on the doorstep or not engaging with the worker when they did visit. This would fit with the behaviours of the emotionally neglectful families. Other carers would be physically available but would have friends present or keep the TV on, which would fit with the disorganised neglectful carers. This group may also be superficial compliant, when responding to requests from a social worker. In five cases superficial compliance resulted in case closure without an initial or in-depth assessment. For example, records on one child's file indicated a long history of non-school attendance. The case was closed after the social worker recorded the mother and daughter '*assured us that Jade would go to school in the morning*'. There was no follow up to see if attendance had been resumed and sustained. Depressed neglectful carers are likely to be the ones that practitioners can physically access but they may fail to engage in any meaningful dialogue because everything washes over them. Workers in a minority of cases did not identify a pattern of superficial contact, which was evident from reading the case files. In these situations, failing to identify lack of engagement as an issue means concerns about the child or children in the family are never addressed.

Selection of Family Members Contacted

A further variable centred on *which* family members were contacted by the social worker. For example, in 11 cases in the case audit, there were concerns about the neglecting behaviour of both carers however, only the mother or the father was seen by social workers. In some cases (n = 5), men who were described as '*aggressive and intimidating*' came to the office to see the social worker and consequently kept the professionals away from the home so that the mothers and indeed the children, were never seen. However, in other cases (n

= 6) the social worker only saw the mother even though the concerns centred on the behaviour of the father. When workers fear aggression and intimidation from the male partner it is all too easy to focus on the mother (O'Hagan & Dillenburger, 1995; Stanley & Goddard, 2002). In all cases where there were two carers and only the mother was involved in the assessment, workers did not record why the father was not seen. What is concerning, in these cases, is that the child and their situation is forgotten. If practitioners are frightened and intimidated by the carer what must it be like for the child? Finally, the lack of engagement with fathers can result in stereotyping the role of fathers so that men in the household are seen either as marginal to caring for children or dangerous to children as discussed in Chapter 3.

Lack of Co-Operation

The case records from the Health Board Study, gave some indication as to why carers were unco-operative. Some had already had children removed, others were frightened that removal was a possible outcome of the current assessment. However, practitioners may interpret the lack of co-operation by families, at the start of the assessment process, as a sign that the carers will not engage with professionals. Social workers may make judgements about carers' commitment, based on their presentation. For example, carers who are co-operative, motivated and articulate are seen as easy to work with. However, those who are inarticulate, unmotivated and unco-operative, are often seen in a negative light (Holland, 2000). Bearing in mind what is known about carers in chronic neglectful families, they are most likely to present in a negative light. What is concerning is that Munro (2000) found first impressions stay in the minds of professionals. Therefore, the label of lacking motivation is likely to remain with certain families; not only in the mind of the worker but, as was demonstrated in the case audit, in the case notes and case summaries. This creates an impression amongst new workers taking on a case of carers being unco-operative before the workers have even met the family.

Use of Information

Making Use of Material in Case Files

The child neglect families are the ones that are likely to have a lengthy history of involvement with social workers and other professionals (Stone, 1998). Indeed, in the Irish study, 60% of the families had had previous involvement with the Board. These files hold a wealth of information about the children and their carers. However, most of the case records were hand written and difficult to read. The workers occasionally referred in the records, to other practitioners by their first names, so it was not evident which profession they represented. In addition, dates of events and ages of family members were recorded inconsistently in the family files.

Workers in the study also relied heavily for background information on past summaries prepared for case closure or transfer. In addition they used typed reports from case conferences or specialist assessments prepared by other professionals. This in itself appears to be innocuous, however the information recorded in these summaries and reports, was often inaccurate and in some cases, unsubstantiated opinion became fact. For example, a public health nurse stated at a case conference held five years previously, '*this is a chaotic, dysfunctional family*'. No evidence was given to support this statement. However, subsequent records continually referred to this family in these terms – the family had become labelled. There is another problem about workers becoming over-dependent on summaries from reports or case transfers. That is, inevitably, certain information may not have appeared relevant at the time. If workers do not read case records this information, which may be relevant in the context of current concerns or recurring patterns of behaviour, is lost. For example, in one case included in the audit, a mother with two young children had had intermittent contact with workers over a period of five years. Referrals and assessments had focused on emotional and physical neglect of the children and on occasion, resulted in short-term service provision on other occasions, no further action. However, the workers failed to identify a pattern of neglect associated with binge drinking. As the mother did not present as having an ongoing drink problem her drinking habits were not referred to in case summaries. It was only by reading the case records that the pattern became apparent.

Failure to read case records in detail can also mean that professionals are unaware of factors which should influence the way in which they engage with families. For example, it was evident from records in one case, that the children in the family were intimidated and frightened of their father. One child had actually mentioned this to a previous social worker. This information was not used by the social worker responding to the most recent referral. She asked the children if everything was fine in front of the father and accepted their positive reply. This led to case closure.

Focus on Current Incidents

Despite the wealth of information on the files, the focus for assessment and intervention, in ten cases in the Health Board Study, appeared to be the carer's current behaviour, rather than the ongoing nature of the issues. This resulted in short-term interventions or case closure. Cleaver and Walker (2004) also found that a concerning minority of multi-problem families (very likely to include families suffering chronic neglect) received no services as a result of an Initial Assessment. This approach reflects what has been observed in both England and Western Australia. Families are drawn into the child protection system as a response to a specific incident. Limited, if any work, is done with the family and the case is closed, only to be reopened in response to a further specific incident of abuse (Department of Health, 1995). Thoburn et al., (2000) refer to the families treated in this way as the 'revolving door' cases. They note that the families have long-term problems and either keep on trying to access services or act in ways that continue to raise concerns for professionals resulting in further referrals. The families in the Health Board Study tended to fall into the second category.

Summary

In order to effectively assess cases of child neglect practitioners should have a clear understanding of the assessment task and process. Assessment guidance emphasises an evidence-based approach towards assessment, indicating that assessment is a 'head' or technical-rational activity. There are a wide range of frameworks and tools available to practitioners to assist them in gathering information about a child and their family and making sense of this information. However, tools and frameworks can do no more than act as a series of prompts and practitioners are still required to make professional judgements in light of the information obtained about the family. When assessing child neglect practitioners are required to make a range of judgements at different stages of the assessment process.

What is evident from practice, is that assessment in cases of child neglect is influenced by a number of factors over and above research and guidance, such as organisational context, management expectations and the approach of individual workers, which can be described as 'heart' or practice-moral activity. These factors influence the assessment and can lead to a loss of focus on the child. For example, effective assessment of child neglect requires a multi-disciplinary approach. However, professionals may be reluctant to engage in the assessment process through lack of understanding of their role, inadequate training or fear of child protection work. Lack of engagement in the assessment can result in crucial information being lost. The type of contact workers have with a child and family will also influence the type of information obtained and the sense made of that information. For example, if practitioners do not have a meaningful communication with the child in the family how can they establish what life is like for that child? Information can also be obtained from files. However, these are often lengthy and practitioners may not have the time to read them in detail. This means information about past patterns of behaviour and family strengths is lost.

Note

1 At the time of the work the ACPC was responsible under *Working Together to Safeguard Children* (Department of Health, et al., 1999) for co-ordinating local agencies work in relation to protecting children from harm.

Part IV

Moving Practice Forward

In the first half of this book we considered the complex task facing practitioners when identifying and assessing the needs of the neglected child and their family. We then proceeded in Part III, to explore the ways in which practitioners manage this complexity, paying particular attention to professional roles and responsibilities and the personal, professional and organisational factors that influence practice. This final section of the book is designed to build on the previous sections. The aim is to identify best practice and to consider ways in which practitioners can develop their own practice in cases of child neglect. We also consider how managers, at all levels in organisations, have a responsibility to create an environment which promotes best practice.

In Chapter 8 we consider aspects of neglect which practitioners find particularly difficult to assess. Drawing on the literature, we consider 'what works' and the ways in which practitioners and managers can use this information to develop their own knowledge and skills when working with possible cases of child neglect.

The final chapter of the book moves away from individual cases to consider the context in which practitioners operate. The focus here is on the ways in which the working context influences practitioners' capacity to identify and assess neglect. In this chapter, consideration is given to recent reports and serious case reviews into death and serious injury from neglect and the lessons that can be learnt. The role of supervision and training are explored as well as the changing context in which children's services are being delivered.

8

The Assessment Challenges and Best Practice

Introduction

Assessing child neglect is rather like looking at the stars. If one just uses the naked eye some stars are obvious while others are invisible. When one takes a pair of binoculars and focuses on the same part of the sky, one sees a great many more stars. However, if one exchanges the binoculars for a powerful telescope, even more stars are visible. The same is true of child neglect. A superficial engagement with the child, family and other professionals alerts practitioners to some of the consequences of neglect for the particular child. Using assessment frameworks and tools, as outlined in Chapter 7, assists practitioners to gain more detail of the problems. However, in certain circumstances it is necessary to explore the finer detail; to look closely at specific issues and their consequences. It is frequently the assessment of the finer detail in complex situations that poses the greatest challenge to practitioners. Moreover, it is this crucial detail, which really tells us what life is like for a child, day in day out. This is all too easily overlooked when practitioners are expected to complete assessments to short, unrealistic timescales.

In this chapter we consider the finer detail in relation to specific aspects of assessment task and process. In terms of task this includes assessing chronic neglect, failure to thrive and lack of supervision. It also includes groups of children who are particularly vulnerable to neglect if the context is not supportive and designed to meet their specific needs: for instance refugee children and children in asylum-seeking families as well as disabled children and children with complex health needs. We consider ways in which their needs should be considered. In relation to process we explore two particularly challenging requirements: assessing motivation and potential for change and planning interventions.

Types of Neglect: Assessment and Best Practice

In this section, we draw on the research and literature in the field to identify best practice.

Assessing Chronic Neglect

Macdonald states (2001, p. 52), 'assessment should be an organised, purposeful activity which comprises a discrete phase of work, as near to the point of referral as possible, and revised as and when appropriate'. The problem for practitioners working with chronic neglect, is determining when assessments should be revised. Evidence from the case records, in the Health Board Study (for detail see introduction to Part III), indicate that re-assessments of chronic neglect tend to take place when the family are experiencing a crisis, which results in a new referral. And, when this occurs, the assessment tends to focus on the current incident. Yet, it is not the isolated incident, but the extent and continuity of the maltreatment that is most likely to have a detrimental effect on the child (English et al., 2005).

The problem, when working with chronic neglectful families, particularly the disorganised or depressed neglectful families, as described in Chapter 3, is that professionals can begin to become desensitised to the issues: the visits become routinised and lose a focus. These are the very cases where heart can rule over head as discussed in Chapter 7. Practitioners may have built-up relationships with the carers and find certain aspects of their behaviour endearing (this is particularly likely to occur with disorganised neglectful carers who, at times, can treat professionals as important members of the family). Alternatively, practitioners may believe perseverance will bring about change, without any tangible, consistent evidence to support this belief. Under these circumstances, as recorded on the case files in the Health Board Study, professionals 'monitor' the situation or follow up routine visits with a brief case recording 'all well', 'things as normal'. However, ongoing re-assessment in these kinds of cases, using a framework such as the one included in Chapter 7, often shows that actually all is not well.

If this type of situation is to be avoided, then professionals should have clear strategies for not only assessing the needs of the children regularly, but also finding ways of responding to those identified needs. There are a number of ways in which this can be achieved. For example, professionals in England are expected to keep chronologies as part of the Department of Health's *Integrated Children's System* (2002). However, whilst these forms are useful in providing an overview of the progress of each child in the family they do not lend themselves to capturing the chaotic lifestyles associated with chronic neglect. Moreover, they do not, by themselves, provide a vehicle for assessing the impact of events on the health and well-being of the children. To achieve this, a chronology of relevant events, combined with an assessment of the needs of the child and the carers' response to these needs, could assist practitioners in identifying the changing need of the child and their family in cases of chronic neglect. Box 8.1 provides such a format. Each professional can complete the form and share their ongoing assessment at a planning meeting. Alternatively, the form can be used as a vehicle to complete an ongoing multi-disciplinary assessment.

The questions included in Box 8.1, are designed to encourage professionals to remain child focused, both in terms of the ongoing assessment of the child's developmental needs and also by reflecting on the services provided to assist the family meet the needs of the particular child. Using the framework, professionals can make judgements about the current family situation and decide whether previous decisions about interventions remain appropriate. As we noted in Chapter 7, Hollows (2003, p. 70) refers to this type of judgement-making as 'evaluative' (see Chapter 7 for more discussion). Important areas to consider, when making these evaluative judgements, include establishing the carers' engagement with the changes required of them in order to meet the needs of their children and recognising the ways in which practitioners own attitudes towards the particular case are influencing the judgement (Horwath, 2005).

Assessing Failure to Thrive

Professionals in the Health Board Study (described in the introduction to Part III), were asked in the focus groups what they would do if they had concerns about:

> a family known to social workers, with a history of neglect and children in care, who had a three month old baby who is failing to thrive and there is no organic cause.
> (Horwath & Saunders, p. 74)

While all the hospital based professionals and many of the Garda Síochána (police), would refer the case to social workers, four of the five groups of teachers would refer elsewhere, normally to the public health nurse (health visitor). The public health nurses, themselves, were divided as to what they would do with the case. The majority of this group saying they would refer to social services whilst, a minority would refer to doctors or monitor the situation themselves. This finding highlights the confusion that exists about failure to thrive (FTT) and child maltreatment. If professionals do not believe that FTT is anything other than a medical condition then it is not surprising that assessment and intervention remain within the medical arena. However, as described

What is failure to thrive and do you deal with it?

Box 8.1   Ongoing Assessment of Child Neglect

Name of child:

Period covered by assessment:

Indicate contacts with carers (identify nature of involvement of each carer):

Indicate contact with child (specify when child seen, form of communication and under what circumstances):

What significant events have occurred during the period?
(Consider: family achievements as well as concerns; missed contacts with professionals; professionals meetings; attendance at school and health appointments; specific incidents identified by professionals as significant; incidents identified by family as significant)

Date	Event	Consequences for Child

Bearing in mind the ongoing developmental needs of the child and the impact of the significant events, what are the current concerns about the health and well-being of the child?

What indicators are there that the carers have worked towards meeting the needs of the child over the identified period?

Are there indicators that the carers *have not* worked towards addressing the concerns identified above over the period?

Have parenting issues and socio-economic factors influenced the carer/s ability and or motivation to meet the needs of the child over the identified period?

Bearing in mind the responses to the above questions:
- How does the current situation fit with past patterns of behaviour?
- What are the implications of the information gained over this period for the child?
- What is the likely outcome for the child given the current circumstances if the involvement of professionals remains as it is?
- Is it necessary to consider changing the services provided to the family?
- If so, what services are required, with what purpose and to achieve what outcomes?

Date for next ongoing assessment:

of my comment

P189

in Chapter 2, some forms of FTT are associated with child neglect and in these cases, can have a devastating effect on the child.

Taylor and Daniel (1999) found professionals are confused as to cause and effect in cases of FTT. However, a distinction can be made between under-nutrition, which may be the result of illness or feeding difficulties, and under-nutrition, which is linked to a range of psycho-social factors. It is these cases that may be associated with child neglect. For example, as described in Chapter 4, mental health problems and drug and alcohol misuse may result in the carer being emotionally unavailable to the child, forgetting to feed or being erratic in their response to the hungry baby. In order to establish any association between FTT and psycho-social factors, Williams (1994) suggests that an initial assessment of FTT should provide an understanding of feeding behaviours, interactions between carer and child, the temperament of the child, dietary history and growth as well as a social background.

Iwaniec (2003) believes that the *Framework for the Assessment of Children in Need and their Families* (Department of Health et al., 2000) lends itself to assessing FTT. However, she draws attention to particular areas that should be considered as part of this assessment, notably establishing the child's height, weight, head circumference and feeding behaviour. She also emphasises the importance of assessing the interaction between the parent and the child. This involves recognising that the mothers themselves may have experienced childhood abuse, which in turn influences their interactions with the child (Iwaniec & Sneddon, 2002).

Hobbs and Wynne (2002, p. 148) offer some useful tools for assessing feeding behaviours and the interaction between the child and carer. These include:

- *Three day diaries.* These could include the time, food amount, method of feeding, time taken and mother's feelings (Iwaniec, 2003).
- *Dietary recall.* Asking the carer to describe the food provided to a child on a recent day. This provides some insight into the attention the carer gives to feeding.
- *Mealtime observation.* This involves observing the interaction between the child and the carer focusing on the carer's feeding style, the behaviour of the carer and the reaction of the child (Iwaniec, ibid).

FTT children require regular monitoring of their growth and development. Professionals will be required to make ongoing evaluative judgements, based on these findings. It is also important that practitioners recognise that FTT, when associated with child neglect, is an area where over-optimism in the face of clear evidence that the child is not gaining weight, can be literally fatal.

and here

is

the

answer for p 189

In Chapter 1, we considered not only FTT but also nutritional neglect. Practitioners should be aware of the impact of FTT and nutritional neglect on children's eating behaviours, when planning appropriate family interventions. For example, a family support worker, in the North East Health Board, described working with a neglectful family where there had been concerns about malnutrition. The parents were taught to cook a basic meal and with great pride placed it before their children. The children, who were not used to eating anything other than snacks throughout the day, were unable to eat the meal. They were over-whelmed by the quantity of food. The parents were upset and ready to give up, concluding that the children did not like the food and would only eat what they were used to – junk food. The family support worker had to adapt the plan encouraging the parents to offer small portions of simple foods, such as sandwiches, egg on toast. They gradually built up to providing proper meals, which the children eventually ate with relish.

Assessing Lack of Supervision

Lack of supervision, arguably engenders more debate amongst practitioners in terms of what is acceptable than most other forms of neglect. Some practitioners and members of the public perceive lack of supervision purely in terms of the age of the child, believing there should be national guidance regarding the age at which children should be allowed at home alone and for how long. Others, consider the problem to be far more complex and believe that focusing on age alone does not take account of the other variables that could impact on safeguarding the welfare of the child.

Coohey (2003, p. 822) concludes that professionals are confused about supervisory neglect 'because of the amorphous nature of supervision problems'. She compared cases where children were registered for supervisory neglect with those that were not. She found that the cases that were most likely to be registered involved a child being harmed, the mother (the carers were predominantly mothers) failing to take responsibility for the problem, no extenuating circumstances existing and the family having had prior involvement with the child protection services. Based on her findings, Coohey offers a three dimensional conceptual model for assessing supervisory neglect. The model has been adapted and a forth dimension – the child's perspective added (see Figure 8.1).   Fourth?

One of the areas that practitioners find most challenging when assessing supervisory neglect, is the supervision of the teenager. This is usually thought about in terms of the young person being left in charge of younger siblings or left to cook a meal. However, supervisory neglect as described in Chapter 1 goes far beyond this and includes adolescents being left to their own devices and/or the carers being unaware of their whereabouts. Practitioners should take this into account when exploring the young person's exposure to, or engagement in, anti-social or criminal activity. In addition, consideration

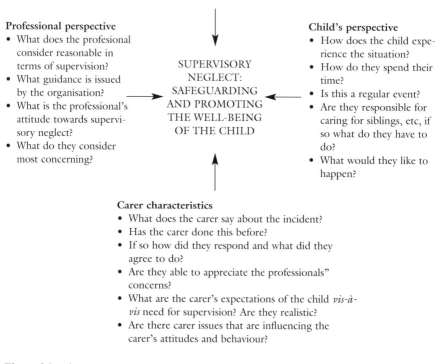

Severity of the incident
- Has the child suffered actual harm?
- What is the likelihood that the child could have suffered harm?
- Does the lack of supevision occur frequently?
- Is the child near dangerous objects?
- How long is the child left alone?
- Are other people around?
- Are they able to meet the needs of the child?

Professional perspective
- What does the profesional consider reasonable in terms of supervision?
- What guidance is issued by the organisation?
- What is the professional's attitude towards supervisory neglect?
- What do they consider most concerning?

SUPERVISORY NEGLECT: SAFEGUARDING AND PROMOTING THE WELL-BEING OF THE CHILD

Child's perspective
- How does the child experience the situation?
- How do they spend their time?
- Is this a regular event?
- Are they responsible for caring for siblings, etc, if so what do they have to do?
- What would they like to happen?

Carer characteristics
- What does the carer say about the incident?
- Has the carer done this before?
- If so how did they respond and what did they agree to do?
- Are they able to appreciate the professionals" concerns?
- What are the carer's expectations of the child *vis-à-vis* need for supervision? Are they realistic?
- Are there carer issues that are influencing the carer's attitudes and behaviour?

Figure 8.1   Assessment Framework for Assessing Supervisory Neglect

should be given to ways in which lack of supervision can expose the young person to possible abuse through prostitution and illegal sexual activities as well as drug and alcohol misuse.

Knutson et al., (2005) found an association between supervisory neglect, care neglect (poor hygiene and inadequate clothing) and harsh discipline on the part of carers and aggression amongst children. They also found that social disadvantage exacerbated the situation. It is not a surprising finding but one that is worth bearing in mind when assessing supervisory neglect, particularly amongst school age and adolescent children. Carers whose parenting is borderline and are already coping with social disadvantage, plus the stresses of parent-

bear in mind how?

ing, may well find it difficult not only meeting the physical needs of the child but also providing guidance and boundaries for children. Under these circumstances it is all too easy to see how carers resort to harsh discipline in an attempt to control their children. Children provided with this kind of role model may well exhibit aggressive behaviours in their own relationships with family and peers.

Asylum-Seeking and Refugee Families and Neglect

Arguably, one of the most taxing situations in which to assess child neglect, is amongst asylum-seeking and refugee families. These families are likely to have experienced forms of loss, trauma and change that are unimaginable to most of us. The children and their families, at the very least, will have been 'stripped of their anchors' (Rutter, 2001, p. 124). Rutter goes on to describe the refugee experiences which are likely to result in children suffering long-term psychological stress. These include inconsistent child-care; economic insecurity and poor housing; isolation; low self-esteem and being unable to talk about the trauma. These are all features which can result in carers neglecting their children because of their own past experiences and current situation. Soetendorp (2005 p1-3), describing his experiences as a child of Holocaust survivors, vividly illustrates the detrimental affects of his parents situation on his health and well-being. He says:

> I cried my first cry into the silence and grieving all around my family ... There was no room for me in this extremely pre-occupied household. The only comfort I found in those early years was in the care of helpers and in food: these were the only things that gave me the feeling that I existed at all.

If children come to the attention of professionals because of their parents' distressing experiences of torture and loss, these practitioners may be reluctant to identify child neglect: over-identifying with the parents and their distress. This can leave children, who have specific needs, in a vulnerable position. As is evident from Soetendorp's account, the experiences produced a very confused and unhappy child. albeit a very articulate one.

Melzak (2005) considers the impact of exile from a child rather than a parent's perspective. She summarises the four different types of difficulties a child may have that can affect their health and development, when making the transition from country of origin to country of exile. These include, past experiences in the country of origin, such as violence, scape-goating, persecution, witnessing atrocities and separation. Second, on their journey into exile, the young people have had to deal with separation from their community and possibly their carer, possible further abuse and exploitation and uncertainty. from whom?

Third, in the country of exile itself difficulties are likely to include being treated as an asylum seeker rather than as a young person or child with needs. Finally, these young people may have difficulty with their ongoing imaginary or real relationship with their country of origin and their home. This can include feelings of shame, grief, moral and ethical conflicts. It is also worth bearing in mind that parents too will have had difficulties making the transition into exile. Put the two together and the experiences can result in needy families: parents preoccupied with their own situation, coming to terms with loss and the practicalities of building a new home and children who are likely to have very specific needs. It is not surprising that these specific needs may be ignored or minimised because it is too difficult and painful for the carer to begin to address them. or they may be acknowledged and met

Assessing Possible Neglect Amongst Asylum-Seeking and Refugee Families

Torode et al. (2001) describe the barriers that are likely to affect the assessment process with refugee families. These include language barriers and the difficulty of accessing accurate current and background information (Torode et al., 2001). The families themselves may recognise they have problems but might be reluctant to ask for help out of fear that contact with 'official' agencies could lead to deportation or imprisonment.

Lack of understanding of asylum seeking families' situations was apparent in the study of child neglect I completed in the Republic of Ireland (for further detail of the study see the introduction to Part III). A child neglect referral was received, by the child care team, about a lone parent refugee who was allegedly struggling to meet the needs of her children. Letters were sent to the mother on official notepaper, inviting her to come to the social work office to discuss the situation. She failed to respond and the case was closed with no further action. No consideration was given to the possibility that she may not have been able to read English, may have been frightened by the formal letter or may have been afraid to come to the offices of an official department. We can only begin to guess at the additional stress and anxiety placed on this mother by a letter from an agency that was, ironically, attempting to offer help and support.

The following should be considered when assessing neglect amongst asylum-seeking and refugee families. These are based on the work of Torode et al. (2001):

- Be honest about the concerns and offer an explanation as to why agencies are concerned.
- Listen to the family's explanation and understanding of the issues.
- Seek appropriate cultural advice and support.
- Recognise that there will be gaps in knowledge about the family history.
- Attempt to minimise language and communication barriers.

- Appreciate that the child and family may find it difficult talking about past experiences, conflict and abuse.
- Recognise past and current stresses.
- Families need a clear understanding of the roles and functions of the welfare agencies involved.
- Carers need information enabling them to distinguish this assessment process from any asylum procedures.
- Make time for families to contribute to the assessment and identify their own possible solutions.

Child Neglect and the Disabled Child or Child with Complex Health Needs

'A disabled child is not simply a "child" but a child which has the additional issues of impairment and disabling barriers' (Kennedy & Wonnacott, 2003, p. 189). It is this combination that makes disabled children and children with complex health needs more vulnerable to neglect than their non-disabled peers. Sullivan and Knutson (2000) found in a study of 40,211 school aged children in the USA, disabled children were 3.76 times more likely to be neglected than their peers. They also found that when they broke down the risk of neglect into different types of disability that children with behaviour disorders were 6.7 more likely to be neglected than non-disabled children, those with a speech and language disability 4.7 times as likely and those defined as 'mentally retarded' (sic) 3.7 times. They also found that some disabilities such as communication and 'health and orthopedic' (ibid, p. 1270) seemed to place children at increased risk of maltreatment in early years while other disabilities such as behaviour disorders appeared to be both a risk factor and possible consequence of maltreatment in later years.

Kennedy and Wonnacott (2003; 2005) argue that practitioners need to be aware of the way in which 'disabling barriers' (2005, p. 230) affect perceptions of disability and distort assessments of child neglect. Disabling barriers include discrimination and prejudice, lack of service provision, pity for carers who are managing the 'burden' of a disabled child and a perception that disabled children are worth less than other children. These barriers are likely to influence parenting opportunities. Moreover, they can act as blocks to high quality assessments of the needs of the child. Kennedy and Wonnacott (2005) believe practitioners can address these barriers by asking themselves the following questions:

- What is there about the child's environment that makes them vulnerable to neglect?
- How is service provision or lack of it contributing to neglect?

- Are there factors in the family circumstances such as poverty that are contributing to neglect?
- What is it about society's perception of disabled children that contributes to the neglect?

Although assessment frameworks, such as the *Framework for the Assessment of Children in Need and their Families* (Department of Health et al., 2000) is designed for use with all children, practitioners should be particularly aware of the additional needs of a child resulting from their impairment. For example, specific feeding needs such as gastrostomy feeding, medication and treatment requirements and special educational needs. It is also important to consider ways in which, not only the family but also the extended family and community, are able to meet these needs. For example parenting opportunity to meet the needs of the child may be affected if resources, such as computer-aided systems or other technological communication systems, are not available. H ow ?

Assessments, involving disabled children, pose specific challenges. It can be difficult differentiating cause and effect in terms of neglect and the disabled child. It may well be that the child is developmentally delayed as a result of their disability, neglect or a combination of both. For example, it can be very difficult ascertaining to what extent the impact of neglectful behaviours, such as poor feeding regimes, has further exacerbated a delay due to a disability. Moreover, challenging behaviours in disabled school children can be a result of the disability, the neglect or a combination of the two (Sullivan & Knutson, 2000). In this context, the impact of neglect on the child can become minimised, by professionals, and neglectful behaviours allowed to continue, because the disability masks the neglect. To prevent this occurring, practitioners should try and gain a sense of what a day in the life of the child is like and use this as a basis for identifying neglectful behaviours on the part of carers (Box 7.4 in Chapter 7 can be adapted for this purpose).

A further challenge centres on recognising that a significant number of professionals can be involved in the assessment. These practitioners may view the disabled child in very different ways, depending for example, on whether they take a social or medical model of disability. Moreover, the practitioners engaged in the assessment are likely to have differing professional status and power. This can lead to some practitioners deferring judgement to those who are perceived to have most control over the process (Kennedy & Wonnacott, 2003).

In addition, disabled children are likely to have experienced both a significant number and also a diverse range of assessments including medical assessments, assessments for special education, assessments for financial and other resources. This assessment history will affect both the child and parents' attitude and understanding of the assessment task.

Finally, it is all too easy to empathise and over-identify with the carer to the extent that we accept parents doing their best rather than being good enough (Horwath, 2002). Therefore a key question that practitioners should be constantly asking of themselves, when completing the assessment, is whether they would accept this level of parenting for a non-disabled child.

Kennedy and Wonnacott (2005) offer some useful guidance for practitioners working with disabled children and neglect. Based on this guidance, practitioners should ask themselves the following questions:

- What is our attitude to disability? How can we ensure a positive attitude towards disabled children, their lives and achievements as part of this assessment?
- What is the relationship between the child, their peers, family and significant others?
- How can we ensure that we recognise the emotional and psychological needs of the child as well as their physical development and carer? *care ?*
- What is the child's view of their experience? How do they describe a day in their life?
- The carer may love the child but what evidence do we have that they are competent carers for this specific child?
- What impact is the parenting context having on parenting capacity? For example, parenting issues, the accommodation, finances etc.
- What messages is this child receiving about being valued and wanted?
- Are we making decisions about interventions based on resources available or the needs of the child? *I would say resources based on p176*
- Would we accept this situation for a non-disabled child?

Assessment Process: Challenges and Best Practice

In this section we consider two aspects of the assessment process which are particularly complex and can be challenging for practitioners. Traditionally, practitioners have allowed some carers, who neglect their children, numerous opportunities to improve their parenting capacity to little avail. This can leave children in vulnerable situations (see for example The Bridge Child Care Consultancy Service, 1995). As described in the introduction to Part III of this book, parenting capacity is dependent on opportunity, ability and motivation. If the needs of the child are not being met it is obvious that practitioners should consider all three aspects of parenting capacity when undertaking an assessment. The aspect that can be particularly difficult to assess is motivation and the potential for change. It is for this reason that this is considered below.

what are the three aspects of parenting capacity?

answer p209

If change is to be successful, practitioners should determine, during the assessment process, the services which are most appropriate in terms of meeting the needs of the child. As neglect takes so many forms, individualised approaches will be required that address the specific issues associated with each family (Macdonald, 2001; Stevenson, 1998; Wekerle & Wolfe, 1993). This means that it can be a complex process for practitioners to reach agreement on plans of intervention designed to meet the identified needs of the child and their family. With this in mind, we consider 'what works' when intervening to meet the needs of the neglected child and their family.

Assessing Motivation to Change: What is 'Good Enough'?

Effective change does not occur instantly, rather it is a process consisting of a number of stages (Horwath & Morrison, 2001; Protchaska & diClementi, 1982), which are described below using an example from a case of child neglect:

> *Pre-contemplation.* At this stage the carer is either unaware of or has a vague notion that all is not well. When an incident occurs, or concerns about their parenting are brought to their attention, carers do not necessarily recognise that their behaviour needs to change. At this stage carers tend to respond to professional concerns in a variety of ways: denying the problem, being angry towards professionals or being passive and helpless in their interactions.
>
>> I don't know why everyone is getting so worked up. Amy is six years old. She is quite capable of getting herself up and off to school in the morning. It's not my fault I don't have the energy to sort her out in the morning.
>
> *Contemplation.* At this stage the carer begins to recognise that there is a problem and that change may be necessary. At this point they weigh up the pros and cons of making changes.
>
>> I never thought about it before but the teacher is right. I do treat Amy like an adult rather than a child. Perhaps I shouldn't ask so much of her.
>
> *Determination.* Once a carer decides to change their behaviour they then begin to think of ways of doing this.
>
>> I'll try and be more organised. I'll start getting up in the morning and getting her some breakfast. I'll also make sure I do the washing so that she has clean clothes.

Action. This describes the process of attempting to put the changes into practice.

> I can do it. I've sorted out a routine and it works. Amy is so much happier now I'm paying her some attention.

Maintenance, Lapse and Relapse. New behaviours need to consolidate so they become routinised. This is difficult to achieve and it is normal for people to lapse into old ways of behaving if faced with a crisis or a situation that is new and unexpected. Sometimes the new behaviours are so difficult to sustain that the carer relapses permanently to their old behaviours. This is most likely to occur if they do not have the support and encouragement to maintain the changes.

> I was able to look after Amy but I've had a bad time and I'm getting depressed again. It's all so much effort I'm sure it can't really be doing Amy any harm leaving her to get herself sorted for school.

At any stage the person engaged in the change process may exit and revert back to the old behaviours.

Carers may use a variety of defence mechanisms to avoid contemplating meaningful change. For example, blaming others for the situation, justifying their behaviour or denying there is a problem. In addition, carers may demonstrate different levels of commitment and engage in activities designed to bring about change in different ways as shown in Figure 8.2.

As can be seen from Figure 8.2, meaningful, long-term changes are only likely to occur if the carer can 'walk the walk and talk the talk'. However, as Corden and Somerton (2004) point out some carers begin by 'walking the walk' for example, by attending parenting classes. They then find that they actually do learn from this and consequently change their behaviours towards their children. Hence, on occasion, initial tokenistic engagement in the change process can positively affect commitment to change. However, it is all too easy for practitioners to live in hope believing there is some indication of change when in fact the carer does not actively engage in the process, because they are for example, just 'talking the talk'.

It is important to bear in mind, when using this model of change that it has not been subject to longitudinal research in the area of child welfare. Rather, it is offered as a tool to assist practitioners in making sense of the change process and some of the factors that they should take into account when assessing the parent's capacity for change. It should be used cautiously, bearing in mind that assessing motivation and ability to change with neglect-

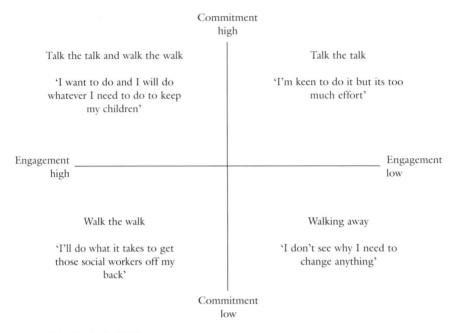

Figure 8.2   Walk the Walk

ful carers can be difficult for a number of reasons. First, people do not neces-sarily make an orderly progression through the change stages and changes in behaviour may occur at different rates (Corden & Somerton, 2004). For example, a carer may find it relatively easy to make some changes towards their child-rearing practices whilst others may be much harder to make. Second, the types of behaviours and attitudes that need to change are likely to be deeply embedded meaning that change will be a very slow process. This is a real dilemma for practitioners who need to assess whether sufficient change is likely to occur at a pace that will meet the needs of the children in the family. *Their~~but~~ all the child welfare system needs revising to accommodate slow change* In addition, the opportunities for change, through the input of services within the current child welfare system, are not geared up for slow change. Organisational performance indicators tend to be designed for quick through-put and immediate results: not for providing services to support carers through a lengthy change process. Finally, and perhaps the biggest challenge for practitioners, is being realistic about the type of change that can be achieved with chronic neglectful families. Patterns of chronic neglect can be so embedded within the family's style of functioning – carers having ~~learning~~ *learnt* these behaviours from their own parents – that practitioners expectations of what can change and at what pace are often unrealistic.

'What Works' in Meeting the Needs of Neglected Children: Implications for Assessment

As neglect is multi-faceted, cases of neglect usually require multi-faceted interventions. These interventions should be designed to 'increase the ability of families to successfully nurture their children by enabling families to use resources and opportunities in the community that will alleviate stress, overcome knowledge and skills deficits, and build and maintain care-giving competences' (DePanfilis, 1999, p. 220)

DePanfilis (1999) identifies five different types of intervention for neglecting families which are described below. However as the focus of this book is on identifying and assessing child neglect what is provided are just briefly summaries of the different types of intervention.

Concrete Resources

As described in Chapter 5, many neglecting families are living in situations that provide them with little opportunity to meet the needs of their children through poverty, poor housing and harassment. These families need basic resources such as housing assistance, clothing and household goods, transportation, child-care and financial support to enable them to meet the needs of the child.

Social Support

As already discussed in Chapter 5 support is a blanket term that describes a range of different forms of support. Neglecting families need formal and informal support networks that reduce isolation and increase both parenting ability and motivation However, in Chapter 5 we noted the limited informal support networks available to most neglecting families are often perceived as dissatisfying by carers, offering little emotional support. If support interventions are to be effective it is important to identify the type of social support that is missing for the carers, such as emotional support, and respond accordingly. Ghate and Hazel (2002), in their study of parenting in poor environments, found that parents wanted support services that were well-organised and professionally run but treated the users as equals. Families also wanted services that are accessible and responsive to their needs and available in times of crisis. Gaudin (1993) found the following interventions are effective when attempting to enhance the networks of neglectful families:

- Direct interventions by professionals to improve the family support network, such as facilitating communication between family members.
- Use of volunteers and parent aides to raise awareness of what is available and to support families in accessing resources.

- Social skills training to improve carers ability to maintain relationships.
- Parent support groups to develop social skills and social networks.
- Linking families with existing community resources.

Social support through home visiting programmes, such as those provided by health visitors, may influence factors that lead to neglect such as poor attachments, social isolation and poverty (Macdonald, 2005). However, the importance of ongoing involvement and engagement with vulnerable families appears to be crucial in terms of the effectiveness of home visiting. For example, Olds et al., (1999; 1998), who completed a longitudinal study of home visiting programmes in the USA, found participation in the programmes had a positive effect on referral rates for child neglect and maltreatment. However, this effect reduced over time when the support was removed.

Cognitive-Behavioural Interventions

These are programmes designed to teach parents skills using behavioural approaches. There are a number of effective parenting programmes for neglectful carers:

The Triple P Parenting Programme This programme originated in Australia and its success has been supported by clinical trials (Sanders, 1999). The programme seeks to help parents with such issues as building relationships with their children, teaching children new skills and the effective use of discipline.

The programme has five levels of intervention:

Level 1: Information provision.
Levels 2 and 3: Brief consultations for parents and children regarding common behavioural problems.
Level 4 and 5: Ten or more structured sessions to address severe behavioural problems.

In addition, there is an enhanced programme providing intense services for families who have maltreated their children or are at risk of doing so.

Project 12-Ways and Project SafeCare These programmes are American in origin and are designed to ameliorate the social and ecological factors that appear to contribute to child neglect. Project 12-Ways offers 12 different services including parent training, money management, home safety training, parent–child training and behaviour management, Project SafeCare uses a one-to-one teaching format to focus on parent–child interaction, home safety and child health care (National Center for Injury Prevention and Control, 2004). As part of the programme staff use quizzes, role-play scenarios, checklists to guide parent behaviour in particular situations and record charts. They also provide parents with manuals and supplies necessary to complete the task. For example, a basic medical kit. Bigelow and Lutzker (2000) found, in a small scale study of methods used to improve parents child health care skills, the provision of the written materials alone did not improve parents' performance. Rather, the use of these materials with opportunities to test out through role plays, appeared to make a difference. That is, neglectful carers benefited from opportunities to consolidate their learning.

Interventions Focused on the Individual

Interventions for carers should address the specific parenting issues that impact on parenting capacity. In addition, neglected children require services in their own right such as play therapy, additional education support, speech and language therapy to help them manage the consequences of neglect on their health and development as described in Chapter 2. Daro (1988), in a review of 19 projects providing services to abused and neglect children, found providing direct services to the children improved functioning for over 70% of the children.

Family-Focused Home Based Interventions

These interventions should focus on all family members. They can be targeted at improving home and child management through the intervention of family support workers. Alternatively, they may be targeted at improving emotional functioning through family therapy.

Factors to Consider when Planning Community-Based Interventions

If interventions are to provide families with appropriate opportunities to make changes to their attitudes and behaviours towards child-rearing, three key points should be taken into account when planning interventions (Macdonald, 2005). First, interventions need to be multi-faceted. For example, Wattenberg and Boisen (no date) believe as part of multi-faceted packages professionals should consider in-home services, supportive professional relationships, parent groups for socialisation, parent training and services designed to address any specific issues such as housing, mental health concerns, etc. Second, consideration should be given to the length of time required for successful interventions to have an effect – there are no quick fix solutions – successful interventions often require long-term input (Browne & Lynch, 1998). However, DePanfilis and Dubowitz (2005), in a study of a multi-faceted, community-based programme, designed to prevent neglect amongst vulnerable families, noted positive changes amongst those that attended a three month programme and those that attended for nine months. Although the families had similar problems they found no additional advantages of a nine month intervention, for improving parenting capacity, over the three month programme. They noted families tended to disengage after six months, and at the end of the nine months these carers were less satisfied with services than the families that terminated after three months. This would seem to indicate that intensive, community-based, holistic, short-term interventions may contribute to improving parenting functioning. Finally, there will always be cases where these community-based interventions, whether short- or longer-term, fail to meet the needs of the child. In these cases, practitioners and their managers need to grasp the nettle and make decisions about the effectiveness of the interventions rather than let cases drift.

Gaudin (1993) offers some general guidance for practitioners planning interventions for neglected children and their families. This includes recognising the uniqueness of each family and devising interventions that are culturally sensitive. Neglectful carers are often immature and needy, as discussed in Chapter 3, and may therefore need to be parented. If this is the case then it is important to avoid fostering dysfunctional dependence. Neglectful families often lack structure and benefit from the setting of clear, limited, achievable goals. As part of this process, the responsibilities of both professionals and family should be clearly outlined as should legislative mandates and their enforcement. Finally, neglectful carers are no different from any of us in as much as we all flourish when provided with positive feedback and reinforcement of achievements.

Out-of-Home Placement

One of the biggest challenges, encountered by practitioners when working with carers who neglect their children, is making the decision that despite efforts to work with the family, the parenting is not good enough to meet the needs of the child. The change required to meet the needs of the child has not, or is unlikely to take place, and out-of-home placements are necessary. This decision is never easy to make. Nevertheless, if the carer has been provided with all the appropriate services, within the context of supportive relationships with professionals, and has still failed to make significant changes in terms of effectively meeting the needs of the child, then the choices available are limited. The decision to remove the child from the family home is even harder to make if the carers have been expected to work with an ever changing group of professionals and the resources have not been available, or only available on a short-term basis. In this situation a focus on the child and their needs is crucial. If this is lost, practitioners can continue working with the situation, excusing or rationalising the carer's behaviour.

Removing children does not necessarily have to be permanent. Out-of-home-placements can be short-term. The Children Act 1989 encourages the use of respite care to safeguard and promote the welfare of children and support families under stress. Aldgate et al. (1996) stress that this experience can be valuable but the social worker has a crucial role in assisting parents and children make sense of and learn from the respite care experience. This in turn can lead to change. In a study of respite care, they found benefits for both child and carer. For example, increasing parents' self-esteem, reducing their social isolation and teaching them new skills. The benefits for children in terms of promoting their health and well-being can be considerable as well as giving them respite from their home situation.

However, in cases where carers do not make sufficient changes at a pace that ensures the needs of the child are met, children will require more permanent placement with extended family or friends, foster care, adoption or placement in group care.

When out-of-home placement is being considered, Thoburn (2002) suggests that practitioners consider the following:

- The type and length of placement most likely to meet the needs of the child.
- The appropriate legal status that is required to safeguard and promote the well-being of the child.
- The type of contact the child should maintain with the family.
- The services required by the child, family and carers and the financial help and practical support needed to maintain the placement.

Summary

Effective assessment of child neglect is both demanding and time consuming. There are however aspects of the process of assessing neglect which are particularly complex. Assessing the way in which the carers are able to change their attitudes and behaviours in order to meet the needs of the child is a particular challenge. Models of change can provide practitioners with a useful tool to assist them in identifying the carer's motivation to change. However, these models have limitations in as much as people do not necessarily make an orderly progression through the various stages of the process. They may be able to change certain aspects of their behaviours, whilst other behaviours remain entrenched and resistant to change. The task for the practitioner is to ascertain whether sufficient change has occurred to ensure the ever-changing needs of the child will be met.

If assessments are to be completed effectively, practitioners should have some understanding of 'what works' in cases of child neglect. Armed with this information, practitioners can ensure that as part of the assessment interventions are planned to meet identified needs. As neglect is multi-faceted a range of interventions should be considered by practitioners. These include concrete resources, social support, cognitive-behavioural interventions, one-to-one and family-focused interventions. The assessment task does not end when services are provided, rather the focus shifts from identifying need to assessing ways in which the services meet these needs. In some cases community-based services will not meet the needs of the child and family and practitioners should consider out-of-home placements.

There are some neglectful situations that practitioners find particularly difficult to assess; chronic neglect; failure to thrive, supervisory neglect and neglect of disabled children, and refugee and asylum-seeking children and families. Whilst each of these situations requires professionals to consider very specific aspects of neglect what is crucial, in each of these situations, as in any case of neglect, is to keep a focus on the child. It is only by trying to understand the particular circumstances of the child, the causes of the neglectful behaviours and the impact on the child that one can begin to make sense of the way in which the particular behaviours of the carer are affecting the child.

9

Working with Child Neglect: Developing Practitioner and Organisational Capacity

Introduction

Throughout this book I have emphasised the responsibility of practitioners to safeguard and promote the welfare of children. Indeed, safeguarding is now a statutory duty for all practitioners in contact with children and families in England under the Children Act 2004. This duty not only means identifying and referring concerns about a child but providing information on a child or family and where appropriate, offering a service (Department of Health et al., 2003). Some practitioners have additional roles that are more specific, such as assessing and planning to meet the needs of the child (Department of Health et al., 2003, p. 5 para 10). If practitioners do not carry out these roles and responsibilities appropriately, then at the very least the child may be deprived of opportunities to achieve their maximum potential but at the very worst, the child may die. In these situations it is not just the carers but the professionals who are acting neglectfully. Professional neglect can be defined as a failure on the part of a professional to satisfactorily safeguard and promote the welfare of children, in line with their professional role and responsibilities.

However, it is not always fair to blame the practitioner when cases go wrong. In exactly the same way as neglect by carers may be a combination of failure by carers to meet the needs of the child plus lack of resources, the practitioner's capacity to carry out their duties in relation to child neglect, or indeed other forms of maltreatment, is dependent on the same three inter-connected components as parenting capacity which we discussed in the introduction to Part III: that is ability, motivation and opportunity. In exactly the same way as parents are unlikely to promote the welfare of their child if the three components are not in place, the same is true of practitioners. Yet, a worker's capacity to meet the needs of children is often forgotten about until a case goes badly wrong and a child dies or is seriously injured. Arguably, practitioner capacity to promote and safeguard the well-being of the child is the forgotten domain of the *Framework for the Assessment of Children in Need and their Families* (Department of Health et al, 2000) and other assessment frameworks and tools (Horwath, 2006).

The first half of this chapter explores the motivation and ability of practitioners to safeguard and promote the welfare of the neglected child. This is discussed by drawing on findings from recent English reports and reviews into child deaths, where neglect was the primary cause, or a contributing feature, of the child's death. These findings include published reports following the deaths of Paul (The Bridge Child Care Consultancy Service, 1995) and Victoria Climbié (Lord Laming, 2003) with reference to the findings of serious case reviews (Chapter Eight Reviews)[1] following the deaths of Rikki Neave, Lauren Wright, Ainlee Labonte and Toni-Ann Byfield and serious harm to the 'W' children. Whilst recognising that these children's deaths were associated with both physical abuse and neglect, the focus in this chapter is on system and professional failure to identify and work with child neglect.

In the second part of the chapter we consider the opportunities available to practitioners to meet the needs of neglected children. That is, the organisational context in which practitioners operate and the systems required to promote effective practice.

We begin this discussion by considering practitioner ability to identify and assess the needs of neglected children.

Practitioner Ability

'Ability' in this context, describes the knowledge and skills that practitioners require and possess, which enables them to safeguard and promote the welfare of the child. If professionals are to safeguard children who are suffering from child neglect, they need to be able to both identify possible indicators of neglect and be able to respond to any identified concerns in line with their role. However, Lord Laming, in his report following the death of Victoria Climbié[2] (Lord Laming, 2003, p. 40, para 4.12), found 'gaps in the competence of staff'. While Reder and Duncan (2004, p. 109), analysing Laming's findings, believe staff demonstrated 'a lack of clarity of thinking'. Unfortunately, the lack of clarity of thinking applied to very basic tasks which lead Lord Laming to conclude that practitioners failed to do the simple things well. Reder and Duncan (2004, p. 100) argue that obvious tasks were not completed in the Victoria Climbié case because the practitioners did not think about their significance. They include social workers not appreciating the value of reading files and assessment interviews being set up by inappropriately qualified staff. In addition, they identified confusion about task in relation to multi-disciplinary practice including membership of strategy meetings[3] not specifying who should do what and when; workers failing to ensure all information was available to inform decision-making and hospital staff making inaccurate assumptions about social services role. Many of these issues were discussed in Chapters 6 and 7 in relation to the findings from the Health Board Study.

A number of these tasks could be completed effectively if practitioners are aware of and follow the local child protection guidance and procedures issued by Local Safeguarding Children Boards (previously Area Child Protection Committees). However, practitioners are often unaware of this guidance (Commission for Social Care Inspection, 2005; Joint Chief Inspectors, 2002; Lord Laming, 2003; Sinclair & Bullock, 2002). This can lead, not only to a failure to complete basic tasks, but also misinterpretation of role (the guidance usually outlines the different roles and responsibilities of various professionals). For example, Lord Laming (Cm (5730), 2003) criticised both police officers and hospital social workers, amongst others, for failing to act to protect Victoria because they had misinterpreted their roles and responsibilities.

The findings, from the reports, indicated that practitioners had some specific knowledge gaps in relation to child neglect. These included a lack of awareness of indicators of neglect; lack of understanding about different forms of neglect and working with neglected children. These are discussed in detail below.

A Lack of Awareness of Indicators of Neglect

In the case of Victoria Climbié, a number of professionals, from a range of agencies, saw her on numerous occasions. The professionals noted Victoria's shabby appearance, contrasting this with that of her aunt, who was well dressed. However, they did not recognise or respond, to possible indicators of neglect, despite the fact that one worker described Victoria as looking as if she was an advertisement for a third world charity (Cm (5730), 2003). Six-year-old Lauren Wright[4] weighed just over two stone in the weeks before she died and her hair was falling out through malnutrition. She was also covered in bruises. Yet, members of staff at Lauren's school did not recognise and respond to obvious indicators of neglect and physical abuse (Bowcott, 2002). In the case of the 'W' children, on the day the children were removed from the home, ambulance and police services described the home conditions as 'appallingly dirty and their living and sleeping environment totally inadequate. Two of the children ... were found in a poor physical condition, seriously malnourished and under-weight' (Sheffield Area Child Protection Committee, 2005, p. 8, para 4.10). Yet, the day before police had visited the home and taken no action.

Lack of Understanding about Different Forms of Neglect

As was noted in Chapter 6, practitioners often concentrate on identifying physical and supervisory aspects of neglect. Practitioners, according to findings from the reports, also tended to focus on physical neglect, thus concentrating on poverty and the child's physical needs and practical interventions to meet these needs. For example, the report following the death of Toni-Ann Byfield[5] notes that 'the primary focus of professional work was on the assessment of Mr Byfield's parental capacity and the practicalities of the arrangements for him to undertake the parental role and that inadequate attention was paid to the full and necessary assessment of Toni-Ann's needs' (Birmingham Area Child Protection Committee, 2004, p. 5, para 1.3). In the case of Paul[6] (The Bridge Child Care Consultancy Service, 1995), the emphasis was on assessing and meeting the practical needs of the family, such as providing funding for bedding, furniture and food. This may have assisted the parents to meet the children's physical needs but little was done to establish whether the parents were meeting the other developmental needs of the children. As described in Chapter 6 and 7, some carers, who neglect their children, can be verbally and physically aggressive, as was evident in the cases of Ainlee Labonte and Lauren Wright. Yet, practitioners in the Labonte case lacked a conceptual understanding of work with dangerous families (Kenwood, 2002).

Practitioners working with the 'W' children also failed to distinguish between the effects of poverty and deprivation and neglect. For example, the school had sufficient evidence to ascertain that the 'W' children were vulnerable. However, the school in a poor deprived part of the city had a number of pupils who also appeared to be in this vulnerable situation because of the level of care they were receiving. For example the 'W' children and other children attended school wearing no underwear. This appeared to desensitise staff to the needs of all these children and they failed to recognise that these standards of care were not acceptable for any child (Sheffield Area Child Protection Committee, 2005).

Working with Neglected Children

Turning to work with neglected children themselves, the reports highlighted a number of important gaps in knowledge and skills. First, as was noted in the Health Board Study discussed in Chapter 6, a number of practitioners did not recognise the importance of detailed observation of children and did little more than record that they 'saw' the children (Kenwood, 2002; Lord Laming, 2003; The Bridge Child Care Consultancy Service, 1995). Second, when practitioners did record their observations of children in more detail they failed to integrate theory with observation. For example, numerous professionals saw

Victoria Climbié shabbily and inappropriately dressed and observed the 'master-servant' relationship between the child and her aunt. However, they did no more than record the observations without thinking through what the information meant in terms of the needs of the child. Third, and perhaps most concerning, was the misinterpretation of observations. For example, one of the most striking findings from the reports is that so many of the children were described in case files as happy because they were smiling (Cm (5730), 2003; Kenwood, 2002; Lord Laming, 2003; The Bridge Child Care Consultancy Service, 1995). Professionals equated smiling children with happy children. However, as described in Chapter 3, children with insecure attachments may handle their interactions with others through 'smiling' and superficial engagement, as a strategy for managing an uncertain world. Neglected children smiling and appearing to engage with the practitioner does not necessarily mean contentment, rather it can indicate attachment problems as considered in Chapter 2.

Knowledge and Child Neglect: The Challenges

As discussed in previous chapters, one of the problems of identifying, assessing and intervening in cases of child neglect is that different practitioners hold different opinions as to what neglect is and the ways in which concerns about neglect should be addressed. The knowledge used to make assessments is dependent on the particular professional training and perspective of the individual (Upton, 1999). For example, Shor (1998) found that doctors, because of their medical training, focus on physical symptomatology. However, this can be to the exclusion of other significant factors such as psychological and social difficulties. This means that practitioners apply limited professional knowledge to cases of child neglect and consequently may discount indicators that do not fit with the particular professional perspective. This focus on physical symptomatology, resulting in a failure to identify possible indicators of child neglect, is well illustrated in the case of Victoria Climbié (Cm (5730), 2003). In June 1999, Victoria was registered with a GP. She attended for a new patient check, which was completed by the practice nurse. The check covered various aspects of medical care such as general health and past medical history. Victoria was also weighed and her height was measured. The check did not incorporate questions related to her social circumstances, such as whether she attended school. The result was that information that could have indicated possible child neglect was never obtained by the nurse. This focus on physical symptomatology, was also evident in the case of the 'W' family. The hospitals that provided the mother with care during her pregnancies and for the post-natal care of the children, focused on physical care and there was little evidence that the emotional, psychological and social needs of the mother and her family were

[handwritten margin notes: It should not be Assessment tools should be standardised]

considered. Even though as discussed in Chapter 3 a number of antecedents linked to neglect were apparent, such as the mother being 16 when she had the first child and having five children by the time she and her partner were 24-years-old (Sheffield Area Child Protection Committee, 2005).

We should also be aware that a narrow focus on a particular type of knowledge can result in neglect being erroneously identified. For example, D'Cruz (2004) describes a case of child neglect in Australia where the focus on the physical body of the child and perceived physical abnormalities identified by doctors labelled the case as child neglect. Once the diagnosis was made it became fixed in the minds of workers. This limited meaningful dialogue between professionals with regard to the psychosocial factors that could have contributed to the child's poor condition.

It is not only health professionals who take a narrow focus. A social services spokesman, commenting on the serious case review into the scalding of a two-year-old who pulled a kettle of boiling water over himself, found that a range of professionals did not think outside their narrow professional remits. These professionals came from disciplines in both adult services and children's services (Valios, 2004b). This was also evident in the 'W' case (Sheffield Area Child Protection Committee, 2005). 'DA', the carer involved with the 'W' children, had a social worker in his own right. This worker was aware of 'DA's' poor attachment with his own birth mother and a series of experiences of separation from and loss of family members. These experiences, as described in Chapter 2, were likely to have an impact on his ability to become a good parent. However, social workers did not anticipate that this was likely to affect his ability to parent. Moreover, although the social worker was aware of early indications that 'DA' and his partner were struggling to cope with managing the home and care of the children, other than a request to the health visitor to monitor the situation, no referral was made for ongoing support services. Cantrill, who prepared the serious case review, concludes that it was likely that 'DA', rather than the children, was viewed as the client by these workers. This narrow focus, on the adult, was also evident in the police response to a domestic violence incident involving the 'W' family. The police officers, who visited the home following the complaint of domestic violence, did not talk to or check the children. This occurred even though the officers had information indicating that the eight-year-old may have witnessed the alleged incident, and as described in Chapter 4 this can have a devastating effect on children.

Ability is not only about professionals having the right knowledge and skills to work with child neglect, it is also about being able to apply the knowledge and skills appropriately. Many front-line staff are newly qualified. They may have acquired the theoretical knowledge necessary to work with child neglect on their qualifying training, however, they lack the experience and confidence to manage complex assessments of child neglect. For example, Lisa

Arthurworrey, the social worker working with Victoria Climbié at the time of her death, had only 19 months' experience. Yet, she was expected to complete a Section 47 inquiry into possible significant harm, with the police on Victoria, whilst the child was in hospital. She had little support and no experience of completing such an assessment.

The current staff shortages, in many agencies, can result in practitioners being expected to possess knowledge and skills that go beyond their particular role. For example, Kenwood (2002), in her report, following the death of Ainlee Labonte, found deficits in the professional knowledge of family support workers. This was most evident with regard to both their understanding of families that abuse and also their ability to integrate knowledge with observations. This begs questions about the knowledge these unqualified workers should be expected to possess.

The practitioners involved in the Health Board Study (described in detail in the introduction to Part III), were asked to list the knowledge and skills that they considered were necessary to work effectively in cases of child neglect. These have been developed, in light of the findings from the case reviews, and are listed in Box 9.1. What is interesting, about this list, is that it includes not only specific knowledge about neglect but basic skills required to work with families: something that on occasion, as highlighted in the reports, is forgotten. Both practitioners and managers can use this list, which is by no means exhaustive, to begin to audit practitioners' knowledge and skills and to identify areas for future staff development and training.

Practitioner Motivation

Motivation, in this context, describes the factors that induce a professional to act in a certain way. These are likely to be influenced by the powerful feelings engendered by child protection work and the stressful nature of the job (Morrison, 1990, 2001; Munro, 2000; Reder & Duncan, 1999; Reder et al., 1993). The coping strategies that professionals adopt to manage both their feelings and also the stress of the job, will influence the way in which they work with cases of child neglect. 'The more effective strategies combine a sense of optimism with a realistic level of pessimism' (Morrison, 2001, p. 237), or, as Lord Laming puts it, 'respectful uncertainty' (Cm (5730), 2003, p. 205) and 'healthy scepticism' about a case (ibid, p. 322). The less effective coping strategies do not achieve this balance and distort the way the worker perceives the case. This means that healthy scepticism can become over-optimism and collusion and respectful uncertainty gives way to a fixed idea or avoidance. These responses are considered in detail below.

Box 9.1   Knowledge and Skills Required of Practitioners when Working with Child Neglect

Knowledge

Understanding the indicators of neglect in terms of acts of omission by carer and their impact on the child

Awareness of the long-term nature of child neglect and the implications for assessment and intervention

Recognition of professional role when identifying, assessing and working with cases of child neglect

Appreciation of the different types of evidence that can be used when assessing child neglect. For example, observation, self-report, practice experience and research

Understanding the defence mechanisms used by children and families to distance professionals

Awareness of what works in cases of child neglect

Knowing when to consult with colleagues and manager

Awareness of the personal, professional and organisational factors that can distort identification, assessments, planning and interventions in cases of child neglect

Skills

Problem-solving skills

Skills enabling the practitioner to communicate and engage with the child and family in a meaningful way

Ability to develop relationships with, while able to challenge both colleagues and the family

Ability to assess and make an appropriate response when a carer is verbally or physically aggressive

Ability to apply evidence obtained about a child and family to inform referral, assessment and plans for the child as per professional role

Ability to name and work with the defence mechanisms used by families to distance professionals

Ability to encourage and motivate while being realistic about the carer's ability to change

Ability to focus on one issue at a time thus enabling the carer to make sense of chaos

Ability to make a case to secure resources that reflect the needs of the child and family

Ability to negotiate with colleagues to acquire appropriate resources

Ability to relate observations to an understanding of possible indicators of child neglect

Ability to work collaboratively with colleagues, the child and family

Ability to recognise when identification, assessment and planning in cases of child neglect may become distorted because of personal, professional and organisational factors

Ability to seek appropriate consultation and advice

Over-optimism

Over-optimism occurs when the practitioners working with child neglect have a misguided positive belief in the carers' ability to meet the needs of their children. In the case of Paul, a 'fixed perception' dominated for eleven years. The professionals accepted at face value the information received from the family that they could care for their children, whilst the actual evidence indicated that this was clearly not the case (The Bridge Child Care Consultancy Service, 1995, p. 154, para 100).

Collusion

Workers can also collude with carers, choosing to believe what they had to say, despite evidence to the contrary. For example, Ainlee Labonte's mother convinced practitioners to remove the name of her son from the Child Protection Register. She persuaded professionals that she would keep appointments and seek health care despite evidence on case files that indicated that she had a history of failing to do so (Kenwood, 2002). Moreover, there was little evidence to indicate that her present attitudes and behaviours were different to previous ones. The professionals working with Lauren Wright accepted her mother's explanations that Lauren was a sick, clumsy child who was continually hurt in domestic accidents or bullied at school. However, there was clear evidence of failure to thrive and injuries that indicated this was more than a sick, clumsy child (Bowcott, 2002). In neither of these cases did workers question the basis for being optimistic about the carers' capacity to meet the needs of the child, nor look for evidence to support these views. Reading the files to identify the carers' past patterns of behaviours may have introduced a more realistic sense of pessimism.

Fixed Idea

Workers can take a distorted approach to child neglect when they hold a specific idea about a case that does not change despite evidence to the contrary. For example, in Victoria Climbié's case, social workers pre-judged the situation from the very first contact with Victoria. They focused on the presenting problem of homelessness and consequently labelled Victoria as a child in need. This framed all subsequent responses to Victoria. This meant that child protection issues were ignored and the focus remained on finding the family suitable accommodation (Cm (5730), 2003; Lord Laming, 2003; Reder & Duncan, 2004). In the case of the 'W' children, the focus at the school became the poor attendance of one of the children. This resulted in a failure to recognise indicators of concern about other aspects of the children's lives (Sheffield Area Child Protection Committee, 2005).

Overriding Beliefs

Overriding beliefs can remain in professionals' minds despite evidence of accumulating risk to the child. The Bridge Child Care Consultancy Service (1995, p. 151, para 81) note that professionals working with Paul's family held an overriding belief that with material support the family could manage. The consequence was that they failed to identify recurring patterns that 'again and again provide[d] indicators of the neglect that the children were suffering'. Worryingly, Sinclair and Bullock (2002) found in eight of the 40 Serious Case Reviews, they examined, that practice short-comings resulted from a limited or dominant perspective on the part of professionals.

Avoidance

Avoidance, on the part of practitioners, can result in decisions being made about a child without all the evidence being available. This was evident in a variety of ways in the case reports. First, professionals avoided challenging the opinions of professionals perceived to have more knowledge and status than themselves. For example, although the GP and social workers suspected that Lauren Wright may be suffering abuse, and she was showing signs of neglect, such as being underweight, they accepted the opinion of the consultant paediatrician that he thought it was plausible that her injuries were accidental (Bowcott, 2002). In the case of Victoria Climbié, there were frequent disputes and disagreement about her medical symptoms and their cause. Social workers, police officers and medical personnel were criticised for accepting uncritically the medical diagnosis (Parton, 2004).

Professionals also avoided meaningful contact with carers where the carers had a history of aggression and violence, as was the case with the carers of Rikki Neave[7], Lauren Wright and Ainlee Labonte. When this occurs, as is discussed in more detail in Chapter 6 and 7, practitioners are unable to establish the developmental needs of the child and consequently can do little to realistically safeguard and promote the well-being of the child. In Ainlee's case Kenwood (2002, p. 18) comments that the 'fear with which the family are regarded leads to almost paralysis in terms of action'. The professionals can walk away, but the children cannot.

Avoidance can also result in selective information being gathered and included in assessments and progress reports (Munro, 2000). Workers may gather information they feel comfortable obtaining and avoid asking questions about subjects that cause them discomfort. Alternatively, they may avoid asking relevant questions which may lead to a violent response from the carer. For example, in Ainlee's case, workers focused on assessing the health care needs of the children but did not explore or consider the impact of the carers' violence on the children (Kenwood, 2002).

If workers do as above they should consider another vocation

Ignoring Difference

Social workers in the Health Board Study did not routinely record the ethnicity or religion of children referred for possible neglect. Sinclair and Bullock (2002) found this lack of recording was also evident in cases subject to serious case reviews. Failure to record and acknowledge different religious and cultural beliefs raises a number of issues. First, practitioners may ignore the impact of culture and religion on child-rearing, which as discussed in Chapter 5, can influence attitudes and behaviours towards child neglect. Second, supervisors may not be aware of the particular family's needs and consequently fail to challenge practice, which does not take particular needs into account. Finally, disregard of ethnicity and religion, means that issues such as racism and harassment may be ignored by professionals working with the family. We also need to be aware that the alternative may happen, as occurred in the case of Victoria Climbié. In this case, the carers and child were black and the professionals working with the child and family were also black. It was presumed, that the issues of ethnicity were being addressed (Cm (5730), 2003). This is a naïve approach and ignores differences between cultures and indeed in individual interpretations of the same culture or religious persuasion.

Practitioner Opportunity: The Organisational Context

It has long been recognised that the nature of the working environment contributes to the way in which professionals practice (Dale et al., 1989; Reder & Duncan, 1999; Reder et al., 1993). Glisson and Hemmelgarten (1998) go further and state that the capacity of members of an organisation to work collaboratively with members from another organisation is determined by the resources, stability and management of their own organisation. They compared 12 child welfare social work services in the USA, which were given additional resources for collaborative endeavours, with 12 that had not received additional resources. They measured the outcomes for children who received these services. Glissen and Hemmelgarten found that the strongest association with better outcomes for children was the internal culture of the organisation. It was only in those organisations that had a positive culture that collaborative practice promoted better outcomes for children. This is particularly relevant in cases of child neglect as multi-disciplinary practice, as described in Chapter 6 and 7, is crucial if the needs of a neglected child are to be identified and met. Thus, the third component influencing professionals' capacity to work effectively in cases of child neglect is 'opportunity'. This refers to the organisational context in which professionals are operating and the way in which this environment facilitates or prevents effective practice. The organisational context affects child neglect practice in three different ways.

Resources

Members, attending the seminar on service provision and delivery, held by Lord Laming as part of his inquiry into the death of Victoria Climbié, painted a grim picture of the current working context. They described under-resourced organisations with high vacancy rates, inadequate information technology and administrative systems and inadequate training. Working in an under-resourced organisation will influence both practitioner ability and motivation to work effectively in cases of child neglect. For example, lack of information technology and effective administration systems meant that in Victoria's case, information was not immediately accessible, files were lost and faxes not processed (Cm (5730), 2003). Hence, professionals were making decisions about cases without all the necessary current information at hand and without access to information about the past history.

In many organisations lack of resources, in terms of staffing, means that agencies are dependent on the employment of agency staff. Many agency and temporary staff have recently arrived from aboard and therefore are likely to have little understanding of local and national policies and procedures and the cultural context. In this context, taking on a complex case of child neglect can be daunting. Staff within many teams also carry high caseloads. The result is that workers are overwhelmed by the conflicting demands of the cases and work long hours to keep up to date (Cm (5730), 2003). In this situation, workers may well know what they should be doing, but are unable to do the job properly because of the conflicting demands made on their time. In addition, working long hours is stressful and can lead to burn out. Burn out leads to practitioners using coping mechanisms that distort perceptions of neglectful families and result in a loss of focus on the child (Morrison, 2001).

Limited resources means that inevitably demand for services outweighs supply. In this context, as described in Chapter 6, cases of possible maltreatment that have immediately observable indicators of harm, such as occurs with physical abuse and sexual abuse, are likely to be given priority over neglect (Iwaniec & McSherry, 2002; Minty & Pattinson, 1994; Stone, 1998). Cleaver and Walker (2004) found lack of resources can also influence an assessment, with practitioners shaping the outcome in recognition of the lack of resources available, or the eligibility criteria required to access certain resources. They found that a small number of multi-problem families did not progress beyond an initial assessment, of the needs of the child, for this reason. As Iwaniec and McSherry (2002, p. 43) put it 'these children are simply patched up and left without appropriate assessment and long-term action'.

Thoburn et al. (2000) conclude, from their study of family support services in cases of emotional maltreatment and neglect, that if the maximum benefit is to be obtained from available resources, then the role of multi-agency planning groups in identifying local need and co-ordinating responses to meet those needs is crucial. This should be more easily achieved than in the past in England through the introduction of a new organisational requirement. Local authorities are now responsible for producing a single, strategic, over-arching Children and Young People's Plan, which seeks to ensure services are effective and targeted at promoting the health and well-being of children (Cm (5860), 2003). In addition, as part of the planning process senior managers should gather information about the types of families needing services and the actual services required. Service providers are therefore in a position to recognise the need for longer-term services as well as shorter-term intervention, and advice services. However, managers and practitioners will require guidelines for prioritising the more expensive intense and/or longer-term services. To be effective the guidelines should be based on need, rather than reason for referral or the request for a service.

Commitment of Senior Management

Lord Laming, in the Victoria Climbié Report (Cm (5730) 2003), found an absence of direction, effective procedures and efficient management at a senior level. Managers can be distant from front-line practice and fail to appreciate the nature of the work and its impact on staff. In addition, the performance indicators and targets that are used to measure the success of the organisation shape the managers' perceptions of a successful organisation. The social work practitioners in the study completed by Jones (2001, p. 552) described being concerned that 'budget management and control had become the key concern of the agency, stripping out its welfare ideals in the process'. These controls, together with performance indicators, are often quantitative short-term measures that do not readily lend themselves to meeting the long-term needs of neglected children. Indeed the focus throughout the organisation can become completing the required forms and paperwork to demonstrate quantifiable targets are being met with little attention being paid to targets that qualitatively demonstrate improvements to the life of children.

Demoralised Staff

Finally, staff themselves find the demands of their caseloads overwhelming and are demoralised by working in under-funded and under-staffed organisations (Reder & Duncan, 2004). Jones (2001) describes the impact that this can have on front-line social workers (the description applies equally to practitioners in other disciplines). He found colleagues in tears; practitioners going sick on a regular basis as a stress survival strategy and recurring and serious health problems amongst front-line staff. These responses contribute to a viscous cycle: staff off sick increases the burden on those remaining, adding to their stress and increasing staff sickness rates.

It is against this backcloth that the ability and motivation of front-line staff to identify and meet the needs of neglected children has to be considered. As Reder and Duncan (2004) note, inadequate resources and a pressurised working environment have a negative effect on professionals' ability to think. Add to this, lack of support in managing the stressful and emotional nature of the work and the capacity to think is reduced even further.

Having considered the factors that influence practitioners' capacity to work effectively in cases of child neglect, we conclude by exploring the opportunities available to practitioners and managers working in hard-pressed organisations to improve practice.

Promoting Effective Practice in Cases of Child Neglect through Organisational Development

There are changes currently taking place within child welfare organisations in England that should assist practitioners to work more effectively in cases of child neglect. These include a move towards integrated service provision. In addition, organisations already have systems in place that used effectively can improve practice. This includes supervision, consultation with colleagues and training.

Service Integration

As noted earlier in this chapter, the ability of practitioners to work together in cases of child neglect will be influenced by the organisations in which they operate. To date, attempts to bring agencies together to promote multi-disciplinary practice have included informal arrangements through to formal partnerships supported by joint funding arrangements. More recently, integrated local services have become the desired model for encouraging multi-disciplinary practice. For example, in the USA formal collaborations, often mandated, have influenced the development of child welfare programmes at regional and community levels for the past ten years (Hogan & Murphy, 2002). In England, the Green Paper *Every Child Matters* (Cm (5860), 2003, p. 60, para 4.24), called for the integration of services 'around the needs of children rather than providers'. This lead to the Children Act 2004, which provided the legislation for integrated services centring around Children's Trusts. These Children's

Trusts bring together all services for children and young people in an area to focus on improving outcomes for all children and young people. As discussed in Chapter 7 and 8, both assessment and interventions in cases of neglect should be multi-faceted. Thus systems that promote multi-disciplinary working should enhance practice in these cases.

Every Child Matters (Cm (5860), 2003) also emphasises the importance of establishing integrated systems for information-sharing and the Children Act 2004 has legislated for this development. As described above, one of the challenges encountered by practitioners is knowing when and how to share information without the child or carers' consent. At the time of writing, the Government in England is introducing an information-sharing index holding core data on every child in England. A parctitioner with a concern about a child would be able to check this index and find out who is involved with the child, access contact details and make connections. The system should also hold information regarding the 'lead professional' who should act as a single point of contact for a child and family to ensure an integrated response when a range of services are required. Whilst this system should ensure that significant information is shared amongst practitioners, what is clear when assessing child neglect is that snippets or pieces of information in isolation about a child may appear insignificant, but placed together with other information they can become very significant. It is questionable whether the introduction of the information-sharing index will address this issue, bearing in mind the detailed and systematic piecing together of information required in cases of child neglect (Stevenson, 2005). It should as there is a lead professional to integrate the

However, whilst national policy may aspire towards integration, the working context within each agency may militate against it. For example, concentration on agency core tasks, performance targets and corporate goals challenges the service shared, collaborative approach of partnerships (Barton, 2002). In addition, multi-disciplinary working has been dogged in the past by communication problems; poor understanding of roles and responsibilities and mistrust amongst professionals (Calder & Horwath, 1999; Department of Health, 1995; Hallett, 1995; Hallett & Birchall, 1992; Murphy, 1995). These will not go away merely be placing practitioners together in the same worksite or setting up integrated systems. Whilst system change should support multi-disciplinary practice, front-line practitioners from different disciplines and professional backgrounds will still need to find effective ways of working together. This will only occur if senior managers create a climate where practitioners from different disciplines are given a clear message that working together and engaging in dialogue with practitioners from other agencies is crucial if we are to meet the needs of neglected children. Moreover, they need to recognise this is not an overnight development; rather it takes time to build up trust between members of different professionals, learn about and understand the different roles and

professions?

responsibilities of various professionals and their different professional perspectives and world-views.

Supervision

Supervision and professional consultation are crucial in both providing front-line staff with a sense of direction and enabling practitioners to think about and reflect on their practice. Supervision should identify gaps in knowledge and skills and ensure that factors influencing motivation do not result in actions that have a negative impact on the health and well-being of children. A lack of regular, high quality consultation and supervision was evident in a number of the reviews following child deaths from neglect. This meant that 'no one was standing outside of their day-to-day work and reflecting upon what was happening in terms of the events that were unfolding' (The Bridge Child Care Consultancy Service, 1995, p. 182, para 286). Lisa Arthurworrey, the social worker allocated to Victoria Climbié's at the time of her death, did not receive regular supervision. She should have received supervision every two to three weeks. In reality, she received it once every seven weeks. This gave her no opportunity to reflect on cases on a regular basis.

The Climbié report and the case review following the death of Toni-Ann Byfield (Birmingham Area Child Protection Committee, 2004), both indicate that the quality of supervision is as important if not more so than the quantity of supervision. For example, with regard to Toni-Ann, the supervisor did not detect that the Core Assessment undertaken on Toni-Ann was incomplete and a supervisor never challenged the quality of the work of the professionals concerned (Birmingham Area Child Protection Committee, 2004).

In only 13 out of the 57 files in the Health Board Study, were there comments on the social work file relating to supervisory advice regarding case management. In four cases the advice was general '*check on progress*'. In only six cases was comprehensive advice provided giving the social worker specific directions as to how to progress the assessment. Responses in the study by social work respondents to questions about the impact of the supervisor on assessment raise some interesting points. A slightly higher proportion of practitioners (76%) than managers, (66%) who responded to the questionnaire, believed that decisions in cases of child neglect *should* be made taking account of the views of the supervisor. When asked whether the views of the supervisors *actually* influenced decisions, both managers and practitioners gave responses that indicated that in practice they had less influence than they should have. This was explored in detail in the focus groups. The participants noted that supervisors, like themselves, are over-worked and under pressure, supervision is constantly cancelled or interrupted and when it does take place the focus is on cases in crisis.

> ### Box 9.2 An Example of Supervision 'On the Hoof'
>
> In a 46 minute period a supervisor discussed 16 cases and made 14 discernible decisions. These included:
>
> - Advice re continuing role in a neglect case
> - Checking compliance with internal audit
> - Two decisions to proceed with an assessment
> - Decision re urgency of a another assessment
> - Decision to reallocate case because of sickness
> - Advice to clerk re format of report
> - Decision to write case review personally because of worker's inexperience
> - Decision to cancel case review because worker sick
> - Request for finance under s17
> - Negotiate with worker to stand in for another at a case meeting
> - Advice to unqualified worker regarding possible child abuse referral
> - Advice to worker on letter to court
> - Consultation with worker regarding investigative interview exploring disclosure of CSA
> - Advice to worker regarding allegation of strangle marks on child
> - Advice regarding proceeding with possible concerns of child neglect

Supervision 'On the Hoof'

When regular supervision is difficult to access practitioners are reduced to making decisions without consultation. Alternatively, they obtain advice from supervisors as and when the supervisor is available. That is, supervision becomes informal, reactive, ad hoc and provided 'on the hoof'. In a study, I recently completed on the role of the front-line manager in social work access teams in England, I found that significant discussion of cases occurred 'on the hoof'. Typically, the supervisor would pass by the practitioner who would stop her 'just to check something out'. Box 9.2 summarises a typical 46 minute 'on the hoof' interaction between a supervisor and her team.

During the 46 minutes referred to in Box 9.2, the supervisor discussed 16 cases: an average of one to three minutes was spent on each case. In that time, she made 14 discernable decisions. These included such decisions as providing advice to a worker regarding allegations of strangle marks on a child and agreeing to reallocate a case because of worker sickness. Amongst those decisions, one related to a case of child neglect. The worker wanted to check out her continuing role in the case. This type of consultation raises questions as to how much information can be shared in a meaningful way in such a limited time. It is impossible for staff to make meaningful case decisions in this context and timeframe. Cases of child neglect usually require consideration of a complex

I wonder would that be the case if social services had to care for wealthy / influential families?

family history and both practitioners and supervisors need time to contextualise and make sense of what may appear to be a minor incident. When consultation is given 'on the hoof', practitioners are likely to select the information that they consider most significant. Munro (2000) found that this is likely to be the vivid detail rather than the mundane; concrete information; emotionally laden detail and the most recent information. Indeed, the practitioner may only share information that is likely to lead to the case decision that they consider most desirable. This can lead to distorted decision-making. For example, if as described above, a practitioner is over-optimistic about a case, or holds a fixed idea, they are likely to select the information that supports their view.

Meaningful Supervision

Box 9.3 developed with supervisors, is designed to provide a list of prompts that supervisors can use when discussing a case of child neglect with a worker 'on the hoof' and in regular supervision. The prompts take into account not only the specifics of a case but also the role of the worker and the factors that can prevent a 'healthy scepticism' about a situation.

Not only do practitioners need opportunities to explore the details of a neglect case, they also need to be able to explore the emotional difficulties that accompany work on neglectful cases (Stone, 1998; Horwath, 2006). To this end, questions regarding worker capacity are included in the list of prompts. As described above, the emotional challenge of the work together with the stress and burn out associated with current child welfare practice can lead to distorted decisions, which in turn affect the worker's ability to safeguard children. Smith et al. (2004) explore these emotional difficulties in terms of worker fear, stating that a number of fears influence the way in which social workers practice. Again, this would apply to other professionals. The fears include fear of being over-worked; fear of getting it wrong; fears about working with abusive and aggressive service users and fears of being publicly attacked by the media. The workers in their study identified the type of supervision that they considered helpful in this context. It included the supervisor being available, listening and not criticising. The practitioners wanted a supervisor to recognise the worker's position and provide an opportunity to discuss the position without being judgemental. Finally, they valued being supported and having their position validated.

Team Consultation

Not all practitioners who work with child neglect are in settings where they are offered the type of supervision that is traditional in social work. Many professionals make decisions about child neglect through discussion with colleagues and members of their team. Different teams will perceive child neglect in different ways. For example, The Health Board Study case audit showed that workers from one team made rigorous assessments of child neglect that focused on incidents and immediate safety issues. Another team, which was the most pressurised in terms of workload, completed more varied assessments. And members of the third team, which had most resources, undertook more comprehensive assessments. The initial perceptions of neglect, taken by the team, set the standards for thresholds, content and process of case assessment and interventions for the child and family. Based on the findings of the Health Board Study, insufficient data have been obtained to establish the extent to which it is the team manager, team members, resources, workloads or a combination of all of these that influences the team approach towards working with cases of child neglect.

Irrespective of what factors influence the team approach, there are lessons that can be learnt by drawing on theory related to group process. Brown (1996) analysed the social influences that operate within groups. He found individuals tend to conform to the attitudes and behaviours of the majority. This can result in individuals denying the evidence of their own senses to conform to the group perspective. The need for approval, arising out of not wishing to seem different, places pressure on members of a team, encouraging them to conform to the group perspective. Alternatively, members may perceive the team perspective to be the only and right perspective. This has particular consequences for newly qualified workers who are particularly vulnerable to adjusting to team standards. For example, Daley (1999) in a study of decision-making amongst newly qualified nurses found a reluctance to learn from experience. Rather, the nurses tended to focus on using memory, accumulating information and waiting for others to tell them what to learn. Hence, newly qualified workers are likely to be guided by the standards set by the more experienced team members. In addition, members of a team will be influenced by the need to achieve the group goals. These may be explicit in line with performance targets such as completing assessments in the specified time. Then again, the goals may be implicit. For example, the team may be overburdened and the implicit goal becomes managing cases in such a way as to avoid adding to the workload. The focus on these types of team goal can distort perceptions of child neglect, with practitioners adjusting their own standards to meet those of the team.

The teams that are most vulnerable to 'groupthink' (Janis, 1972) are those, which are very cohesive; are insulated from information outside the group; rarely search systematically through alternative options; are often under stress and are dominated by a directive group leader. If teams are to avoid losing the focus on the child in cases of child neglect then it is important to ensure that consultation takes place with others outside the team. In addition, managers should be mindful of the thresholds operating within the team. It is important that the managers have opportunities to compare and contrast their thresholds with those with similar teams to ensure standardisation.

The following tasks are designed to assist teams of social work professionals, team managers and practitioners explore these issues.

Box 9.3   Prompts for Supervisors Supervising Cases Of Child Neglect

Supervision on the hoof
- Do I have sufficient information to make an informed decision on the hoof?
    Consider: past history of the case; information about current situation; professionals consulted; knowledge of the worker.
- Based on the information I have received, is it in the best interests of the child to make a decision now?
    Consider: the immediate safety of the child; the nature of the decision; the likely impact of making or not making a decision on the child; the factors that may be influencing you such as workload pressures.
- Are there alternative ways of reaching a decision about this situation that are likely to lead to better outcomes for the child?
- How am I going to ensure accurate recording of this process and the decisions made?

Formal supervision
Supervision of cases of child neglect should include discussion on the following areas:

The developmental needs of the child
- What are the concerns about this child?
- How are they believed to be affecting the health and well-being of the child?
- Are there immediate safeguarding issues?
- Does the child have any additional needs?
    Consider: the impact of religion, ethnicity and disability.
- What assessments and plans are in place?
- How will these ensure that the developmental needs of the child are assessed and/or met?
- How will the practitioner measure the outcomes for the child?

Parenting capacity
- What do we know about the carer/s ability to meet the needs of the child?
- What do we know about the carer/s motivation to meet the needs of the child?
- Have assessments/plans demonstrated an ability to change?
- What are the blocks and barriers that are preventing the carer/s meeting the needs of the child?
- How can these be addressed?

Family and environmental factors
- What role do family, community and other practitioners have in supporting this child?
- To what extent are they able to provide sufficient support to address the concerns about child neglect?
- What support are the carer/s receiving from family, community and other practitioners?
- Is this support sufficient to enable them to meet the needs of the child?

These discussions should keep in mind the chronic nature of child neglect. Hence discussions should include:

- Reflection on ways current carer behaviours are repeat patterns of past behaviours.
- Setting current concerns in a broader context of ongoing and past concerns.
- The pace of any change and whether it is occurring at a speed that ensures the needs of the child will be met.
- Services provided in the past and lessons learnt regarding effective service provision.

Practitioner capacity
- Does the worker have the knowledge and skills to work effectively with this case?
- If not what can be done to either support the worker or ensure the case is managed by an appropriately skilled worker?
- What factors appear to be influencing the worker that may result in the focus on the child being lost?
     Consider: the coping mechanisms used by workers when under stress such as over-optimism and the fixed idea.
- What are the organisational constraints that are likely to influence the way in which practitioners can work with this family?
- How will this influence the services offered to the child and family?

Consideration should also be given to ways in which the discussion of the case and the decisions reached are recorded on the case file.

The Professional Team

As a team, select a number of cases of child neglect and audit the cases with the following questions in mind. Alternatively, devise a number of case scenarios, which team members consider individually in terms of ways they would assess and intervene in each case:

- Do we as a team tend to focus on the incident of neglect, safety issues or the developmental needs of the child?
- Do we always make a point of engaging both children and all key carers in the assessment process?
- How do we make judgements in this team? For example, team discussion with colleagues; discussion with manager 'on the hoof'; through regular case supervision?
- What organisational pressures influence our approach towards our work? How do they influence our work?
- How can we address issues of groupthink?

Team Manager

As a group of managers, audit a number of cases of child neglect from each team. Alternatively, devise case scenarios, which team managers initially consider individually in terms of ways their teams would assess and intervene in each case then share their findings by considering the following:

- What are the differences between the teams?
- What accounts for these differences? Consider organisational; professional and personal factors.
- How can we develop a standardised approach towards child neglect?
- How can we obtain professional support to encourage an objective approach towards assessment and intervention in cases of child neglect?

(Horwath, 2005, p. 95)

Training

Child protection training is often a low priority within organisations. For example, the school that Lauren Wright attended did not have a teacher trained in child protection and health professionals were criticised in the case review for their lack of training (Bowcott, 2002). Lord Laming (2003) found that both the GP and the school nurse involved in the initial patient registration of Victoria Climbié were both very experienced practitioners. However, they had never received child protection training. Without training on child maltreatment, and more specifically child neglect, practitioners will not be able to identify neglect let alone understand their duties in terms of reporting neglect and working with other professionals.

A recent development, designed to promote more effective and integrated service provison is the introduction of a common core of skills, knowledge and competence for all those working with children and families. The purpose of this 'common core' is to introduce training to agreed competences amongst practitioners working with children. It is envisaged that this will begin to break-down some of the cultural and practice barriers within the children's workforce (Cm (5860), 2003).

Multidisciplinary Training

A key theme throughout this book has been that effective practice in cases of child neglect is dependent on effective multi-disciplinary practice. One of the most successful ways of promoting this practice is through multi-disciplinary training (Charles & Hendry, 2000; Hallett, 1995; Horwath & Morrison, 1999). Multi-disciplinary training can be particularly beneficial in addressing some of the key issues associated with poor practice in cases of child neglect. For example, one of the issues, referred to in this book, is the lack of consensus amongst practitioners on various aspects of child neglect. Multi-disciplinary training can be an effective method for working towards a common consensus (Stevenson, 1998). In addition, earlier in this chapter, reference was made to the narrow professional perspectives taken by professionals in cases of child neglect. Opportunities to discuss case studies, in a multi-disciplinary arena, can assist in broadening practitioners' perceptions. Finally, both a lack of trust amongst practitioners and preconceived ideas as to how different professionals will respond to cases of child neglect, have been explored in Chapters 6 and 7. Locality based training that brings together groups of practitioners from a range of disciplines, who work together can begin to break down these preconceptions and begin to establish trust between these practitioners (Glennie & Norman, 2000).

The advantages of multi-disciplinary training for those working to safeguard children are well recognised (Department of Health et al., 1998). However, the logistics of ensuring that those who need training on child neglect receive that training is another matter. In addition, training is only going to be effective if those who have received the training have opportunities to both consolidate their learning in practice and to keep abreast of current developments through ongoing training (Horwath & Morrison, 1999). As our knowledge of the factors influencing carers' ability to meet the needs of children has increased, so has the need for training in specific areas such as the impact of drug misuse on parenting capacity. Most professionals, who encounter children and families, receive minimum training if they receive training at all. This training in line with *Working Together to Safeguard Children* (HM Government, 2006) should focus on signs and indicators of maltreatment and the role of the practitioner. However, the training generally covers all areas of possible maltreatment and in this context it is difficult to prepare practitioners for the unspecific ways in which neglect may present itself and the impact of parenting issues on ability to meet the needs of the child.

Summary

As outlined in the Introduction to this book, I set out to write a book on the identification and assessment of child neglect that not only drew on research and developmental theories related to neglect, but also recognised that practitioners and their managers are individuals with thoughts and feelings which will influence their practice. That is that effective practice, as described in detail in Chapters 6 and 7, is dependent on a successful interplay between technical-rational activity and practice-moral activity (head and heart). In this final chapter by exploring the factors that are believed to have contributed to the deaths and serious injuries of children from neglect we have considered what happens when practitioners fail to get the right balance and things go horribly wrong.

I have concluded that effective practice, which happens when practitioners effectively balance heart and head activities, is likely to occur when professionals have the 'practitioner capacity' to meet the needs of children and their families. This capacity – just like parenting capacity- is dependent on ability, motivation and opportunity. The ability to identify and assess child neglect is dependent on knowledge, skills and experience. Motivation will be influenced by personal, professional and organisational fears and anxieties, whilst opportunity is dependent on the culture of the organisation, workload, the approach of the team and supervisor. It is crucial that all three components are in place. Without them we are in a situation where too many workers will be able to identify with this comment from a participant at a seminar held to discuss the findings from the Health Board Study:

> As a worker I know what I should do, but there is so much that gets in the way of doing my best that the poor child gets forgotten and I leave work feeling demoralised and ineffective.

Notes

1 A review, completed by the local Area Child Protection Committee/Local Safeguarding Children Board, following the death or serious injury to a child where abuse or neglect is suspected. The purpose of the review is to establish the lessons to be learnt from the case about the way in which professionals and agencies work together to safeguard children.
2 An eight-year-old who died from hypothermia, she has also suffered from malnourishment, restricted movement and 128 separate injuries.
3 A multi-disciplinary planning meeting to identify how to undertake s47 inquires. This take place when there are concerns that a child is suffering or likely to suffer from significant harm.
4 A six-year-old, who died from physical abuse and at the time of her death she weighed just over two stone.
5 A seven-year-old shot while in the care of her father
6 A child who died at fifteen months suffering from burns through urine staining, septicemia and severe pneumonia.
7 A six-year-old boy who died from cruelty and neglect.

Bibliography

Abrahams, N., Casey, K., & Daro, D. (1992). Teachers' Knowledge, Attitudes and Beliefs about Child Abuse and Its Prevention. *Child Abuse and Neglect, 16*, 229–238.

Adcock, M. (2001). The Core Assessment – How to Synthesis Information and Make Judgements. In J. Horwath (Ed.), *The Child's World Assessing Children in Need*. London: Jessica Kingsley.

Adcock, M., & White, R. (1985). *Good-enough Parenting*. London: British Association for Adoption and Fostering.

Advisory Council on the Misuse of Drugs. (2003). *Hidden Harm – Responding to the Needs of Children of Problem Drug Users*. London: Home Office.

Ainsworth, M. D. S., Blehar, M., Walters, E., & Wallis, S. (1978). *Patterns of Attachment*. Hillsdale New Jersey: Erlbaum.

Aldgate, J., Bradley, M., & Hawley, D. (1996). Respite Accommodation: A Case Study of Partnership under the Children Act 1989. In M. Hill & J. Aldgate (Eds.), *Child Welfare Services. Developments in Law, Policy, Practice and Research* (pp. 147–159). London: Jessica Kingsley.

Aldridge, J., & Becker, S. (2003). *Children Caring for Parents with Mental Illness. Perspectives of young carers, parents and professionals*. Bristol: The Policy Press.

Alison, L. (2000). What are the Risks to Children of Parental Substance Misuse? In F. Harbin & M. Murphy (Eds.), *Substance Misuse and Child Care. How to understand, assist and intervene when drugs affect parenting* (pp. 9–20). Lyme Regis: Russell House Publishing.

Ammerman, R. T., Kolko, D. J., Kirisci, L., Blackson, T. C., & Dawes, M. A. (1999). Child Abuse Potential in Parents with Histories of Substance Use Disorder. *Child Abuse and Neglect, 23*(12), 1225–1238.

Armstrong, K. L., Frazer, J. A., Dodds, M. R., & Morris, J. (2000). Promoting secure attachment, maternal mood and child health in a vulnerable population: a randomized controlled trial. *Journal of Paediatrics and Child Health, 36*, 555–562.

Audit Commission. (1994). *Seen But Not Heard Co-ordinating Community Child Health and Social Services for Children in Need*.

Australian Institute of Health and Welfare. (2004). *Child Protection Australia 2002–2003*. Canberra: AIHW.

Ayre, P. (2001). Child protection and the media: lessons from the last three decades. *British Journal of Social Work, 31*(6), 887–891.

Baginsky, M. (2000). *Child Protection and Education*. London: NSPCC.

Bannon, M. J., Carter, Y. H., Jackson, N. R., & Blair, M. (2003). The training needs care of primary health teams in child protection. In M. J. Bannon & Y. H. Carter (Eds.), *Protecting Children from Abuse and Neglect in Primary Care*. Oxford: Oxford University Press.

Bannon, M. J., Carter, Y. H., Jackson, N. R., Pace, M., & Thorne, W. (2001). Meeting the Training Needs of GP Registrars in Child Abuse and Neglect. *Child Abuse Review*, *10*, 254–261.

Barnes, L. L. & Plotnikopf, G. A. et al. (2000). Spirituality, religion and pediatrics: intersecting worlds of healing. *Paediatrics*, 16, p. 899–908

Barnes, G., & Farrell, M. (1992). Parental Support and Control as Predictors of Adolescent Drinking, Delinquency and Relate Problem Behaviour. *Journal of Marriage and the Family*, *54*, 763–776.

Barton, A. (2002). *Managing Fragmentation. An Area Child Protection Committee in a Time of Change*. Aldershot: Ashgate.

Batchelor, J. A. (1999). *Failure to Thrive in Young Children. Research and Practice Evaluated*. London: The Children's Society.

BBC. (2005). *Young Fathers*. Retrieved 21/2/2005, from www.bbc.co.uk/inside

Behl, L., Conyngham, H. and May, P. (2003). Trends in Child Maltreatment Literature. *Child Abuse & Neglect*, *27*(2), 215–229.

Bellis, M. D. D. (2005). The Psychobiology of Neglect. *Child Maltreatment*, *10*(2), 150–172.

Benedict, M., Wulff, L., & White, R. (1992). Current parental stress in maltreating and nonmaltreating families of children with multiple disabilities. *Child Abuse and Neglect*, *16*, 155–163.

Bentovim, A. (1998). Significant Harm in Context. In M. Adcock & R. White (Eds.), *Significant Harm: its management and outcome* (pp. 57–90). Croydon: Significant Publications.

Bentovim, A., & Miller, L. B. (2001). *The Family Assessment. Assessment of Family Competence, Strengths and Difficulties*. Brighton: Pavilion Publishing.

Beresford, B., & Oldman, C. (2000). *Making Homes Fit for Children*. York: Joseph Rowntree

Berliner, L. (1994). The Problem with Neglect. *Journal of Interpersonal Violence*, *9*(4), 556–560.

Biehal, N. (2005). *Working with adolescents. Supporting families, preventing breakdown*. London: BAAF Adoption and Fostering.

Bifulco, A., & Moran, P. (1998). *Wednesday's Child. Research into Women's Experience of Neglect and Abuse in Childhood, and Adult Depression*. London: Routledge.

Bigelow, K. M., & Lutzker, J. R. (2000). Training Parents Reported for or at Risk for Child Abuse and Neglect to Identify and Treat Their Children's Illnesses. *Journal of Family Violence*, *15*(4), 311–330.

Birchall, E., & Hallett, C. (1995). *Working Together in Child Protection.* London: HMSO.

Birmingham Area Child Protection Committee. (2004). *Special Cases Review Group. Summary Report. Chapter 8 Case Review Toni-Ann Byfield.* Birmingham: Birmingham ACPC.

Bonner, B. L., Crow, S. M., & Logue, M. B. (1999). Fatal Child Neglect. In H. Dubowitz (Ed.), *Neglected Children. Research, Practice and Policy* (pp. 156–173). Thousand Oaks: Sage.

Booth, T., & Booth, W. (1994). *Parenting Under Pressure: Mothers and Fathers with Learning Difficulties.* Buckingham: Open University.

Booth, T., & Booth, W. (1997). *Exceptional Childhoods, Unexceptional Children: Growing up with parents who have learning difficulties.* London: Family Policy Studies Centre in association with Joseph Rowntree Foundation.

- Bowcott, O. (2002). *'Series of errors' behind child abuse death.* Retrieved 09/06/2004, from www.guardian.co.uk/child/story/0,7369,675074,00

Bowlby, J. (1951). *Maternal Care and Mental Health.* Geneva: World Health Organisation.

Bowlby, J. (1969). *Attachment and Loss. Vol. 1: Attachment.* London: Hogarth Press.

Bowlby, J. (1979). *The making and Breaking of Affectional Bonds.* London: Tavistock.

Boxer, G. H., Carson, J., & Miller, B. (1988). Neglect Contributing to Tertiary Hospitalization in Childhood Asthma. *Child Abuse and Neglect, 12,* 491–501.

Brayden, R., Atlemeier, W., Tucker, D., Dietrich, M., & Vietze, P. (1992). Antecedents of child neglect in the first 2 years of life. *Journal of Pediatrics, 120,* 426–429.

The Bridge Child Care Consultancy Service. (1995). *Paul. Death through Neglect.* London: Islington Area Child Protection Committee.

Briggs, F., & Hawkins, R. (1998). *Child Protection. A Guide for Teachers and Child Care Professionals.* St Leonards: Allen & Unwin.

Bross, D. C. (1982). Medical care neglect. *Child Abuse and Neglect, 6,* 375–381.

Brown, R. (1996). *Group Processes. Dynamics within and between groups.* Oxford: Blackwells.

Browne, K., & Lynch, M. (1998). The Challenge of Child Neglect. *Child Abuse Review, 8*(2), p. p75.

Buchanan, A. (1996). *Cycles of Child Maltreatment. Facts, Fallacies and Interventions.* Chichester: Wiley.

Buckley, H., Skehill, C., & O'Sullivan, E. (1997). *Child Protection Practices in Ireland.* Dublin: Oak Tree Press.

Buckley, H. (2002). *Child Protection and Welfare Innovations and Interventions.* Dublin: Institute of Public Administration.

Buckley, H. (2003). *Child Protection Work. Beyond the Rhetoric.* London: Jessica Kingsley.

Buckley, H. (2005). Neglect. No Monopoly on Expertise. In J. Taylor & B. Daniel (Eds.), *Child Neglect. Practice Issues for Health and Social Care* (pp. 113–130). London: Jessica Kingsley.

Buckley, H., Horwath, J., Whelan, S., & Health Service Executive. (2006). *A Framework for Assessing Vulnerable Children and their Families.* Children's Research Centre.

Buckley, H., Whelan, S., & Holt, S. (2006). *Listen to Me! Children's Experience of Domestic Violence.* Dublin: Children's Research Centre and Mayo Women's Support Services.

Budd, K. S., Poindexter, L. M., Felix, E. D., & Naik-Polan, A. T. (2001). Clinical Assessment of Parents in Child Protection Cases: An Empirical Analysis. *Law and Human Behavior, 25*(1), 93–108.

Burke, J., Chandy, J., Dannerbeck, A., & Watt, J. W. (1998). The Parental Environment cluster model of Child Neglect: An Integrative Conceptual Model. *Child Welfare, lXXVII*(4), 389–405.

Burton, K. (1996). *Child Protection Issues in General Practice: An action research project to improve interprofessional practice.* Essex: Essex Child Protection Committee.

Calder, M. C., & Horwath, J. (Eds.). (1999). *Working for Children on the Child Protection Register: an inter-agency guide.* Aldershot: Arena.

Carter, H. (2004, 20 March). Mother on drinking binge left baby in car. *The Guardian*, p. 13.

Carter, Y., & Bannon, M. (2003). *The role of Primary Care in the Protection of Children from Abuse and Neglect.* London: Royal College of General Practitioners.

Cassell, D., & Coleman, R. (1995). Parents with psychiatric problems. In P. Reder & C. Lucey (Eds.), *Assessment of parenting psychiatric and psychological contributions.* London: Routledge.

Castleton, P. (2004). Personal communication on brain development with author.

CDC. (2003). *Nutrition and Physical Activity.* Retrieved 10/10/2003, from http://www.cdc.gov/nccdphp/dnpa/physical/index.htm

Cemlyn, S. (2000). From Neglect to Partnership? Challenges for Social Services in Promoting the Welfare of Traveller Children. *Child Abuse Review, 9*, 349–363.

Chaffin, M., Kelleher, K., & Hollenberg, J. (1996). Onset of physical abuse and neglect: psychiatric, substance abuse and social risk factors from prospective community data. *Child Abuse and Neglect, 20*(3), 191–204.

Charles, M., & Hendry, E. (Eds.). (2000). *Training Together to Safeguard Children. Guidance on inter-agency training.* London: NSPCC.

Childhelp USA. (2003). *National Child Abuse Statistics.* Retrieved 26/3/2004, from http://www.childhelpusa.org/abuseinfo-stats.htm

Cleaver, H., & Freeman, P. (1995). *Parental Perspectives in Cases of Suspected Child Abuse.* London: HMSO.

Cleaver, H., Unell, I., & Aldgate, J. (1999). *Children's Needs – Parenting Capacity. The impact of parental mental illness, problem alcohol and drug use, and domestic violence on children's development.* London: The Stationery Office.

Cleaver, H., Walker, S., with, & Meadows, P. (2004). *Assessing Children's Needs and Circumstances.* London: Jessica Kingsley.

Cleaver, H., & Walker, S. (2004). From policy to practice: the implementation of a new framework for social work assessments of children and families. *Child and Family Social Work, 9,* 81–90.

Cleaver, H., & Nicholson, D. (2005). *Children who live with a parent with learning disabilities.* Paper presented at the Xth ISPCAN European Regional Conference, Berlin, Germany.

Cm (5730). (2003). *The Victoria Climbié Inquiry Report.* London: TSO.

Cm (5860). (2003). *Every Child Matters.* London: TSO.

Coleman, R., & Cassell, D. (1995). Parents who misuse drugs and alcohol. In P. Reder & C. Lucey (Eds.), *Assessment of parenting psychiatric and psychological contributions* (pp. 182–193). London: Routledge.

Coles, J. (2003). The neglect of neglect. *The Lancet, 361*(9367), 1475–1476.

Commission for Social Care Inspection. (2005). *Safeguarding Children. The Second Joint Chief Inspectors' Report on Arrangements to Safeguard Children.* London: Commission for Social Care Inspection.

Connell-Carrick, K. (2003). A Critical Review of the Empirical Literature: Identifying Correlates of Child Neglect. *Child and Adolescent Social Work Journal, 20*(5), 389–425.

Coohey, C. (1995). Neglectful Mothers, their Mothers, and Partners: The Significance of Mutual Aid. *Child Abuse and Neglect, 19*(8), 885–895.

Coohey, C. (1996). Child maltreatment: Testing the social isolation hypothesis. *Child Abuse and Neglect, 20,* 241–254.

Coohey, C. (1998). Home Alone and Other Inadequately Supervised Children. *Child Welfare, LXXVII*(3), 291–310.

Coohey, C. (2003). Making judgements about risk in substantiated cases of supervisory neglect. *Child Abuse and Neglect, 27,* 821–840.

Corby, B. (2002). Child Abuse and Child Protection. In B. Goldston, M. Lavalette & J. McKechnie (Eds.), *Children, Welfare and State* (pp. 136–151). London: Sage.

Corden, J., & Somerton, J. (2004). The Trans-Theoretical Model of Change:

A Reliable Blueprint for Assessment in Work with Children and Families? *British Journal of Social Work* (34), 1025–1044.

Cox, A. D. (1988). Maternal depression and impact on children's development. *Archives of Disease in Childhood, 63,* 90–95.

Cox, A. D., Puckering, C., Pound, A., & Mills, M. (1987). The impact of maternal depression in young children. *Child Psychology and Psychiatry, 22*(6), 917–928.

Cox, A., & Bentovim, A. (2000). *Framework for the Assessment of Children in Need and their Families. The Family Pack of Questionnaires and Scales.* London: The Stationery Office.

Cox, A., & Walker, S. (2002). *The HOME Inventory: A training approach for the UK.* Brighton: Pavilion Publishing.

Craft, J. L., & Staut, M. M. (1991). Reporting and Founding of Child Neglect in Urban and Rural Communities. *Child Welfare, LXX*(3), 359–370.

Crittenden, P. (1996). Research on maltreating families: implications for intervention. In J. Briere, L. Berliner & J. Bulkley (Eds.), *The APSAC Handbook on Child Maltreatment* (pp. 158–174). Thousand Oaks: Sage.

Crittenden, P. M. (1992). Children's Strategies for Coping with Adverse Home Environments: An Interpretation Using Attachment Theory. *Child Abuse and Neglect, 16,* 329–343.

Crittenden, P. M. (1999). Child Neglect: Causes and Contributors. In H. Dubowitz (Ed.), *Neglect Children. Research, Practice and Policy.* Thousand Oaks: Sage.

Crittenden, P. M., & Ainsworth, M. D. S. (1987). Child Maltreatment and Attachment Theory. In D. Cicchetta & V. Carton (Eds.), *Child Maltreatment – Theory and Research* (pp. 432–462). Cambridge: Cambridge University Press.

Cullingford, J., & Morrison, J. (1997). The relationship between criminality and home background. *Children and Society, 20,* 27–48.

Curtis Committee. (1946). *Report of the care of children committee.* London: HMSO.

Dale, P., Davies, M., Morrison, T., & Waters, J. (1989). *Dangerous Families – Assessment and Treatment of Child Abuse* (Third Ed.). London: Routledge.

Daley, B. J. (1999). Novice to Expert: An Exploration of How Professionals Learn. *Adult Education Quarterly, 49* (summer), 133–147.

Daniel, B. & Taylor, J. (2005). The Role of Fathers in Cases of Child Neglect. In J. Taylor & B. Daniel, (Eds.). *Child Neglect Practice Issues for Health and Social Care.* London: Jessica Kingsley, pp. 263–279.

Daniel, B. M., & Baldwin, N. (2002). Assessment practice in cases of child neglect: a developmental project. *Practice, 13*(4), 21–38.

Daniel, B., & Baldwin, N. (2001). Assessment practice in cases of child neglect: a developmental project. *Practice, 13*(4), 21–38.

Daniel, B., & Taylor, J. (2001). *Engaging with Fathers. Practice Issues for Health and Social Care.* London: Jessica Kingsley.

Daro, D. (1988). *Confronting Child Abuse.* New York: New York Free Press.

Davies, M. (2002). A few thoughts about the mind, the brain, and a child with early deprivation. *Journal of Analytical Psychology, 47*, 421–435.

D'Cruz, H. (2004). The Social Construction of Child Maltreatment: The Role of Medical Practitioners. *Journal of Social Work, 4*(1), 99–123.

De Bellis, M. (2005). The Psychology of Neglect. *Child Maltreatment, 10*(2), 150–172.

DePanfilis, D. (1999). Intervening with Families When Children Are Neglected. In H. Dubowitz (Ed.), *Neglected Children. Research, Practice and Policy* (pp. 211–236). London: Sage.

DePanfilis, D., & Dubowitz, H. (2005). Family Connections: A Program for Preventing Child Neglect. *Child Maltreatment, 10*(2), 108–123.

Department for Education and Skills, Department for Health, & Home Office. (2003). *Keeping Children Safe. The Government's response to the Victoria Climbié Inquiry Report and Joint Inspectors' Report Safeguarding Children.* London: The Stationery Office.

Department for Education and Skills. (2004a). *Outcomes Framework.* Retrieved 11/01/2005, from www.everychildmatters.gov.uk/-content/docu-ments/Outcomes

Department for Education and Skills. (2004b). *Referrals, Assessments and Children and Young People on Child Protection Registers, England – Year Ending 31 March 2003.* Retrieved 10/5/2005, from http://www.dfes.gov.uk/rsgateway/DB/VOL/v000444/index.shtml

Department for education and skills. (2004c). *Common Core of Skills and Knowledge.* Retrieved 2/02/2005 from www.everychildmatters.gov.uk/deliveringservices/commoncore

Department for Education and Skills. (2005). *Referrals, Assessments and Children and Young People on Child Protection Registers, England – Year Ending 31 March 2005.* Retrieved 10/2/2006, from http://www.dfes.gov.uk

Department for Education and Skills. (2005). *The Common Assessment Framework for Children and Young People.* www.everychildmatters.gov.uk accessed 16/1/2005.

Department for Work and Pensions. (2004). *Housholds below Average Income 1994/5–2002–3.* London: Corporate Document Services.

Department of Health (Ed.). (1998). *Modernising Health and Social Services: National Priorities Guidance*: Department of Health.

Department of Health and Children (1999). *Children First National Guidelines for the Protection and Welfare of Children.* Dublin: department of Health and education.

Department of Health, Home Office, & Department for Education and Employment. (2000). *Framework for the Assessment of Children in Need and their Families.* London: The Stationery Office.

Department of Health, Home Office, & Department for Education and Employment. (1999). *Working Together to Safeguard Children. A guide to inter-agency working to safeguard and promote the welfare of children.* London: The Stationery Office.

Department of Health, Home Office, & Department for Education. (1991). *Working Together under the Children Act 1989: A guide to arrangements for inter-agency cooperation for the protection of children from abuse.* London: HMSO.

Department of Health, Home Office, Department for Education and Skills, DCMS, Office of the Deputy Prime Minister, & Lord Chancellor. (2003). *What to Do If You're Worried a Child Is Being Abused.* London: TSO.

Department of Health (1988) *A draft guide for arrangements for inter-agency co-operation for the protection of children from abuse.* London: HMSO.

Department of Health (1988) *A guide for social workers undertaking a comprehensive assessment.* London: HMSO.

Department of Health (1991) *A guide to arrangements for inter-agency cooperation for the protection of children from abuse.* London: HMSO.

Department of Health. (1991). *Child Abuse. A Study of Inquiry Reports 1980–1989.* London: HMSO.

Department of Health. (1995). *Child Protection Messages From Research.* London: HMSO.

Department of Health. (1995a). *The Challenge of Partnership in Child Protection: Practice Guide.* London: HMSO.

Department of Health. (2000). *Assessing Children in Need and their Families: Practice Guidance.* London: Stationery Office.

Department of Health. (2000). *framework for the Assessment of Children in Need and Their Families, The Family Pack of Questionnaires and Scales.* London: Stationery Office.

Department of Health. (2002). *The Integrated Children's System.* London: Department of Health.

Detailed Evidence and Guidelines for Managers and Practitioners. London: HMSO.

Department of Health. (2005). *Obesity among children under 11.* London: Department of Health. www.departmentofhealth.gov.uk accessed 13/3/2006

DHSS. (1970). *The Battered Baby.* CMOZ/70.

DHSS. (1974). Non-accidental Injury to Children.

DHSS. (1980). *Child Abuse: Central Register Systems.*

DHSS. (1982a). *Child Abuse: A Study of Inquiry Reports.* London: HMSO.

DHSS. (1982b). *Child Abuse: A study of Inquiry Reports 1973–1981.* London: HMSO.

DHSS. (1985). *Social Work Decisions in Child Care: Recent Research Findings and their Implications.* London: HMSO.

DHSS. (1986). *Child Abuse and Working Together:*

DHSS. (1988). *Working Together:*

DiLenonardi, J. (1993). Families in Poverty and Chronic Neglect of Children. *Journal of Contemporary Human Services, 74*, 557–562.

Donohue, B. (2004). Coexisting child neglect and drug abuse in young mothers: specific recommendations for treatment based on a review of the outcome literature. *Behavior Modification, 28*(2), 206–233.

Donzelot, J. (1980). *The Policing of Families.* London: Hutchinson.

Dowdney, L., & Skuse, D. (1993). Parenting Provided by Adults with Mental Retardation. *Journal of Child Psychology and Psychiatry, 14*(1), 25–47.

Dowling, M., Gupta, A., & Aldgate, J. (2006). The Impact of Community and Environmental Factors. In J. Aldgate, D. Jones, W. Rose & C. Jeffery (Eds.), *The Developing World of the Child* (pp. 141–160). London: Jessica Kingsley.

Doyle, C. (2003). A Framework for Assessing Emotional Abuse. In M. C. Calder & S. Hackett (Eds.), *Assessment in child care* (pp. 247–262). Lyme Regis: Russell House Publishing.

Drake, B., & Pandey, S. (1996). Understanding the relationship between neighborhood poverty and specific types of child maltreatment. *Child Abuse and Neglect, 20*(11), 1003–1018.

Dube, S. R., Anda, R. F., Felitti, V. J., Croft, J. B., Edwards, V. J., & Giles, W. H. (2001). Growing up with parental alcohol abuse: exposure to childhood abuse, neglect and household dysfunction. *Child Abuse and Neglect, 25*, 1627–1640.

Dubowitz, H. (1999a). Neglect of Children's Health Care. In H. Dubowitz (Ed.), *Neglected Children. Research, Practice and Policy* (pp. 109–131). Thousand Oaks: Sage.

Dubowitz, H. (2000). How Do I Determine Whether A Child's Nutritional Needs Are Being Met? In H. Dubowitz & D. DePanfilis (Eds.), *Handbook for Child Protection Practice* (pp. 134–136). Thousand Oaks: Sage.

Dubowitz, H. (Ed.). (1999b). *Neglected Children. Research, Practice and Policy.* Thousand Oaks: Sage.

Dubowitz, H. A., Starr, R. H., & Black, M. M. (1998). Community and Professional Definitions of Child Neglect. *Child Maltreatment, 3*(3), 235–243.

Dubowitz, H., Black, M., Kerr, M., Starr, R., & Harrington, D. (2000). Fathers and child neglect. *Archives of Pediatric and Adolescent Medicine*, *154*, 135–141.

Dubowitz, H., Black, M., Starr, R. & Zuravin, S. (1993). A conceptual definition of child neglect. *Criminal Justice A Behaviour*, (20), 8–26.

Dubowitz, H., Giardino, A., & Gustavson, E. (2000). Child neglect: guidance for pediatricians. *Pediatrics Review*, *21*(4), 111–116.

Dubowitz, H., Newton, R. R., Litrownik, A. J., Lewis, T., Briggs, E. C., Thompson, R., English, D., Lee, L. & Feen, M. M. (2005). Examination of a Conceptual Model of Child Neglect. *Child Maltreatment*, *10*(2), 173–189.

Duriez, B. & Soenens, B. Reconsidering the relationship between parenting and religiosity. *Psychological Reports*, *4*(2), 545–546.

Dunn, M. G., Tarter, R. E., Mezzich, A. C., Vanukov, M., Kirisci, L., & Kirillova, G. (2002). Origins and consequences of child neglect in substance abuse families. *Clinical Psychology Review*, *22*, 1063–1090.

Dwivedi, K., & Varma, V. P. (1996). *Meeting the Needs of Ethnic Minority Children. A Handbook for Professionals*. London: Jessica Kingsley.

Edleston, J. L. (1999). Children Witnessing of Adult Domestic Violence. *Journal of Interprofessional Violence*, *14*(8), 839–870.

Egeland, B., Sroufe, A., & Erickson, M. (1983). The Developmental Consequences of Different Patterns of Maltreatment. *Child Abuse and Neglect*, *7*, 459–469.

English, D. J. (1999). Evaluation and Risk Assessment of Child Neglect in Public Child Protection Services. In H. Dubowitz (Ed.), *Neglected Children. Research, Practice and Policy* (pp. 191–210). Thousand Oaks: Sage.

English, D. J., Graham, J. C., Litrownik, A. J., Everson, M., & Bangdiwala, S. I. (2005). Defining maltreatment chronicity: Are there differences in child outcomes? *Child Abuse and Neglect*, *29*, 575–595.

Erickson, M. & Egeland, B. (1996). Child Neglect. In J. Myers, L. Beiliner, J., Briere, C. Hendnx, et al., (Eds.), *The APSAC Handbook on Child Maltreatment*, 2nd Ed (pp. 4–20). Thousand Oaks: Sage.

Erickson, M. F., & Egeland, B. (2002). Child Neglect. In J. E. B. Myers, L. Berliner, J. Briere, C. T. Hendrix, C. Jenny & T. A. Reid (Eds.), *The APSAC Handbook on Child Maltreatment* (pp. 3–20). Thousand Oaks: Sage.

Erickson, M. F., Egeland, B., & Pianta, R. (1989). The effects of maltreatment on the development of young children. In D. Cicchetti & V. Carlson (Eds.), *Child Maltreatment* (pp. 647–684). New York: Cambridge University Press.

Ertem, I. O., Bingoler, B. E., Ertem, M., Uysal, Z., & Gozdasoglu, S. (2002). Medical neglect of a child: challenges for pediatricians in developing countries. *Child Abuse and Neglect*, *26*, 751–761.

Fahlberg, V. I. (1994). *A Child's Journey through Placement* (UK Edition ed.): British Agencies for Adoption and Fostering.

Falkov, A. (1996). *Study of Working Together 'Part 8' Reports. Fatal Child Abuse and Parental Psychiatric Disorder: An Analysis of 100 Area Child Protection Committee Case Reviews Conducted under the Terms of Part 8 of Working Together Under the Children Act 1989*: Department of Health.

Farmer, E., & Owen, M. (1995). *Child Protection Practice Private Risks and Public Remedies.* London: HMSO.

Feldman, A. L., Leger, M., & Walton-Allen, N. (1997). Stress in Mothers with Intellectual Disabilities. *Journal of Child and Family Studies, 6*(4), 471–485.

Feldman, K. W., Monastersky, C., & Feldman, G. K. (1993). When is childhood drowning neglect? *Child Abuse & Neglect, 17*, 329–336.

Fellow-Smith, L. (2000). Impact of parental anxiety disorder on children. In P. Reder, M. McClure & A. Jolley (Eds.), *Family Matters. Interfaces between Child and Adult Mental Health* (pp. 96–106). London: Routledge.

Ferguson, H., & O'Reilly, M. (2001). *Keeping Children Safe. Child Abuse, Child Protection and the Promotion of Welfare.* Dublin: A&A Farmar.

Ferrari, A. M. (2002). The impact of culture upon child rearing practices and definitions of maltreatment. *Child Abuse and Neglect, 26*, 793–813.

Fiddy, A. (2002). *Education Act 2002: Safeguarding and promoting the welfare of children.* London: Children's Legal Centre.

Fisher, I. (2004). *Deprivation and Discrimination faced by Traveller Children: Implications for Social Policy and Social Work.* Norwich: University of East Anglia.

Flaherty, J., Vert-Wilson, J., & Doman, P. (2004). *Poverty: The Facts* (Fifth Ed.). London: Child Poverty Action Group.

Flouri, E., & Buchanan, A. (2003). The Role of Father Involvement and Mother Involvement in Adolescents' Psychological Well-being. *British Journal of Social Work, 33*, 399–406.

Fongey, P., Steele, M., Steele, H., Higgitt, A., & Target, M. (1994). The theory and practice of resilience. *Journal of Child Psychology and Psychiatry, 35*, 231–257.

Forna, A. (1998). *Mothers of All Myths.* London: Harper Collins.

Forrester, D. (2000). Parental substance misuse and child protection in a British sample. A survey of children on the child protection register in an inner London district office. *Child Abuse Review, 9*(4), 235–246.

Foss, L. A., Hirose, T., & Barnard, K. E. (1999). Relationship of three types of parent-child interaction in depressed and non-depressed mothers and their children's mental development at 13 months. *Nursing and Health Sciences, 1*, 211–219.

Foster, P., & Wilding, P. (2000). Whither Welfare Professionals? *Social Policy and Administration, 34*(2), 143–159.

Gambrill, E., & Shlonsky, A. (2000). Risk Assessment in Context. *Children and Youth Services Review, 22*(11–12), 813–837.

Garbarino, J. (1987). The abuse and neglect of special children: An introduction to the issues. In J. Garbarino, P. Brookhouse & K. Autrier (Eds.), *Special Children Special Risks. The Maltreatment of Children with Disabilities* (pp. 3–14). New York: Gruyer.

Garbarino, J., & Collins, C. (1999). Child Neglect: The family with a hole in the middle. In h. Duberwitz (Ed.), *Neglected Children. Research, Practice and Policy* (pp. 1–23). Thousand Oaks: Sage.

Garbarino, J., & Kostlny, K. (1992). Child Maltreatment as a Community Problem. *Child Abuse and Neglect, 16*, 455–464.

Garbarino, J., Gutteman, E., & Seeley, J. W. (1986). *The Psychologically Battered Child: Strategies for identification, assessment and intervention.* San Francisco: Jossey-Bass.

Gaudin, J. M. (1993). *Child Neglect: A Guide for Intervention.* Washington DC: US Department of Health and Human Services Administration for Children and Families.

Gaudin, J. M. (1999). Child Neglect: Short-Term and Long-Term Outcomes. In H. Dubowitz (Ed.), *Neglected Children. Research, Practice and Policy* (pp. 89–108). Thousand Oaks: Sage.

Gaudin, J. M., Polansky, N. A., Kilpatrick, A. C., & Shilton, P. (1996). Family Functioning in Neglectful Families. *Child Abuse and Neglect, 20*(4), 363–377.

Gaudin, J., & Polansky, N. (1986). Distancing of the neglectful family. *Child and Youth Services Review, 8*, 1–12.

Gauthier, L., Stollak, G., Messe, L., & Aronoff, J. (1996). Recall of Childhood Neglect and Physical Abuse as Differential Predictors of Current Functioning. *Child Abuse and Neglect, 20*(7), 549–599.

Gelles, R. J. (1982). Problems in defining and labelling child abuse. In R. H. Starr (Ed.), *Child abuse predictions: Policy implications* (pp. 1–30). Cambridge MA: Ballinger.

Gelles, R. J. (1999). Policy Issues in Child Neglect. In H. Dubowitz (Ed.), *Neglected Children. Research, Practice and Policy.* Thousand Oaks: Sage.

Gershater-Molko, R. M., Lutzker, J. R., & Sherman, J. A. (2003). Assessing child neglect. *Aggression and Violent Behaviour, 8*, 563–585.

Ghate, D., & Hazel, N. (2002). *Parenting in Poor Environments.* London: Jessica Kingsley.

Gibbons, J., Conroy, S., & Bell, C. (1995). *Operating the Child Protection System*: HMSO.

Gibbons, J., Gallaher, B., Bell, C., & Gordon, D. (1995). *Development after Physical Abuse in Early Childhood*. London: HMSO.

Gill, P. K. (2005 unpublished). *Community Partnership Project 2004–2005. Final Report*. London: Metropolitan Police.

Gilligan, R. (1998). The importance of schools and teachers in child welfare. *Child and Family Social Work*, *3*, 13–25.

Gilligan, R. (1999). Working with Social Networks: Key Resources in Working with Children at Risk. In M. Hill (Ed.), *Effective Ways of Working with Children and their Families* (pp. 70–91). London: Jessica Kingsley.

Gilligan, R. (2001). Promoting Positive Outcomes for Children in Need: the Assessment of Protective Factors. In J. Horwath (Ed.), *The Child's World: Assessing Children in Need* (pp. 180–193). London: Jessica Kingsley.

Giovannoni, J., & Becerra, R. (1979). *Defining Child Abuse*. New York: Free Press.

Glaser, D. (2000). Child Abuse and Neglect and the Brain – A Review. *Journal of Child Psychology and Psychiatry*, *41*(1), 97–116.

Glaser, D., Prior, V., & Lynch, M. A. (2001). *Emotional abuse and emotional neglect: antecedents, operational definitions and consequences*. York: British Association for the Study and Prevention of Child Abuse and Neglect.

Glennie, S., & Norman, J. (2000). Delivering inter-agency training: the development of alternative structures. In M. Charles & E. Hendry (Eds.), *Training Together to Safeguard Children*. London: NSPCC.

Glisson, C., & Hemmelgarten, A. (1998). The effects of organisational climate and interorganisational coordination on the quality and outcomes of children's service systems. *Child Abuse and Neglect*, *22*(5), 401–421.

Goldberg, S. (1999). *Attachment and Development*. London: Arnold.

Golden, M. H., Samuels, M. P. & Southall, D. P. (2003). How to distinguish between neglect and deprivational abuse. *Archive of Diseases in Childhood*, *88*, 105–107.

Goldson, E. (1998). Children with disabilities and child maltreatment. *Child Abuse and Neglect*, *22*(7), 663–667.

Graham, J., & Bowling, B. (1995). *Young People and Crime*. Home Office Research Study 145. London: Home Office.

Graham, B. (1998). Overwhelmed or underwhelmed? The response of an area social work team to neglect. In H. Buckley (Ed.), *Child protection and Welfare. Innovations and Interventions*. Dublin: Institute of Public Administration.

Greenough, W. T., Black, J. E., & Wallace, C. S. (1987). Experience and brain development. *Child Development*, *58*, 539–559.

Guterman, N. B., & Lee, Y. (2005). The Role of Fathers in Risk for Physical Child Abuse and Neglect: Possible Pathways and Unanswered Questions. *Child Maltreatment*, *10*(2), 136–149.

Haeringen, A. R. V., Dadds, M., & Armstrong, K. L. (1998). The Child Abuse Lottery – Will the Doctor Suspect and Report? Physicians' Attitudes Towards and Reporting of Suspected Child Abuse and Neglect. *Child Abuse and Neglect, 22*(3), 159–169.

Hall, D. K., & Pearson, J. (2003). *Resilience – giving children the skills to bounce back.* Ontario: Reaching IN, Reaching OUT Project, Toronto and Guelph.

Hallett, C. (1995). *Interagency Coordination in Child Protection.* London: HMSO.

Hallett, C., & Birchall, E. (1992). *Coordination in Child Protection.* London: HMSO.

Hanafin, S. (1998). Deconstructing the role of the public health nurse in child protection. *Journal of Advanced Nursing, 28*(1), 178–184.

Hansen, D. J., Pallotta, G. M., Tishelman, A. C., Conaway, L. P., & MacMillan, V. M. (1989). Parental problem-solving skills and child behavior problems. A comparison of physically abusive, neglectful, clinic and community families. *Journal of Family Violence, 4*(4), 353–368.

Harbin, F., & Murphy, M. (Eds.). (2000). *Substance misuse and child care. How to understand, assist and intervene when drugs affect parenting.* Lyme Regis: Russell House Publishing.

Hart, D. (2001). Assessment prior to birth. In J. Horwath (Ed.), *The Child's World. Assessing Children in Need* (pp. 234–252). London: Jessica Kingsley.

Hawes, D., & Perez, B. (1995). *The Gypsy and the State. The Ethnic Cleansing of Bisect Society.* Bristol: SAUS Publications.

Hendry, E. (1997). Engaging General Practitioners in Child Protection Training. *Child Abuse Review, 6*, 60–64.

Herrenkohl, E., Herrenkohl, R., Egolf, B. and Russo, M. (1998). The Relationship between Early Maltreatment and Teenage Parenthood. *Journal of Adolescence, 21*(3), 291–303.

Hester, M., Pearson, C., & Harwin, N. (1999). *Making an Impact: Children and Domestic Violence.* London: Jessica Kingsley.

Hildyard, C., & Wolfe, D. (2002). Child neglect: developmental issues and outcomes. *Child Abuse and Neglect, 26*, 679–695.

Hill, P. and Pargamount, K. (2003). Advances in the Capitalisation and Measurement of Religion and Spirituality. Implications for Physical and Mental Health Research. *American Psychologist, 58*(1), 64–74.

HM Government (1933). *The Children and Young Person Act 1933* www.???.co.uk/acts/1933 call accessed 16/11/2004.

HM Government. (2006). *Working together to safeguard children. A guide to inter-agency working to safeguard and promote the welfare of children.* London: HM Government.

HMSO. (1974). *Report of the committee of inquiry into the care and supervision provided in relation to Maria Colwell.* London: HMSO.

Hobbs, C. J., & Wynne, J. M. (2002). Neglect of neglect. *Current Paediatrics*, *12*, 144–150.

Hogan, C., & Murphy, D. (2002). *Outcomes: Reframing responsibility for well-being*. Baltimore: The Annie Casey Foundation.

Holland, S. (2000). The Assessment Relationship: Interactions between Social Workers and Parents in Child Protection Assessments. *British Journal of Social Work*, *30*, 149–163.

Holland, S. (2004). *Child and Family Assessment in Social Work Practice*. London: Sage.

Hollows, A. (2003). Making Professional Judgements in the Framework for the Assessment of Children in Need and Their Families. In M. C. Calder & S. Hackett (Eds.), *Assessment in Child Care* (pp. 61–74). Lyme Regis: Russell House publishing.

Home Office. (1960). *Report of the Committee on Children and Young Persons*. London: HMSO.

Home Office, Department for Constitutional Affairs and Youth Justice Board. (2004). *Circular Parenting Orders and Contracts for Criminal Conduct and Anti-social Behaviour*. Retrieved 13/3/2006. www.youth-justice-board.gov.uk

Horner, N. (2003). *What is Social Work? Context and Perspectives*. Exeter: Learning Matters.

√Horwath, J. (2002). Maintaining a Focus on the Child? First Impressions of the 'Framework for the Assessment of Children in Need and their Families' in cases of Child Neglect. *Child Abuse Review*, *11*(4), 195–213.

√ Horwath, J. (2005). Identifying and assessing cases of child neglect: learning from the Irish experience. *Child and Family Social Work*, *10*(2), 99–110.

Horwath, J. (2005a). The Influences of Differences in Perceptions of Child Neglect in Social Work Practice. In J. Taylor & B. Daniel (Eds.), *Child Neglect. Practice Issues for Health and Social Care*. London: Jessica Kingsley.

Horwath, J. (forthcoming). Managing Difference: Working Effectively in a Multi-Agency Context. In P. Cawson, H. Cleaver & S. Walker (Eds.), *Safeguarding Children: A Shared Responsibility*. Chichester: Wiley.

Horwath, J. (2006). The Missing Assessment domain: practitioner subjectivity when identifying and referring child neglect. *British Journal of Social Work*. access published 4 May 2006. doi10.1093/bysu/bc1029

Horwath, J., & Bishop, B. (2001). *Child Neglect Is My View Your View?* Dunshaughlin: North Eastern Health Board and University of Sheffield.

Horwath, J., & Morrison, T. (1999). *Effective Staff Training in Social Care: from theory to practice*. London: Routledge.

Horwath, J., & Morrison, T. (2001). Assessment of Parental Motivation to Change. In J. Horwath (Ed.), *The Child's World. Assessing Children in Need* (pp. 98–113). London: Jessica Kingsley.

Horwath, J., & Saunders, T. (2004a). *Do you see what I see? Multi-professional perspectives on child neglect.* Dunshauglin: North Eastern Health Board.

Horwath, J., & Saunders, T. (2004b). *Do you see what I see? Multi-professional perspectives on child neglect.* Appendices Dunshauglin: North Eastern Health Board.

Howe, D. (1995). *Attachment Theory for Social Work Practice.* Basingstoke: Macmillan.

Howe, D. (2003). Assessments Using an Attachment Perspective. In M. C. Calder & S. Hackett (Eds.), *Assessment in Child Care* (pp. 373–387). Lyme Regis: Russell House Publishing.

Howe, D., (2005). *Child Abuse And Neglect. Attchment Development and Intervention.* Basingstoke: Palgrave Macmillan.

Howe, D., Brandon, M., Hinings, D., & Schofield, G. (1999). *Attachment Theory, Child Maltreatment and Family Support.* Basingstoke: Macmillan.

Howe, D., Dooley, T., & Hinings, D. (2000). Assessment and decision-making in a case of neglect and abuse using an attachment perspective. *Child and Family Social Work, 5,* 143–155.

Humphreys, C., & Mullender, A. (2003). Assessment and Role across Social Work Specialisms in Working with Domestic Violence. In J. Horwath & S. M. Shardlow (Eds.), *Making Links across Specialisms. Understanding Modern Social Work Practice.* Lyme Regis: Russell House Publishing.

Hunt, J., Macleod, A., & Thomas, C. (1999). *The Last Resort: Child Protection and the 1989 Children Act.* London: The Stationery Office.

The International Obesity Task Force. (2005). *Obesity in Europe.* London: International Association for the Study of Obesity.

Iwaniec, D. (1995). *The Emotionally Abused and Neglected Child. Identification, Assessment and Intervention.* Chichester: Wiley.

Iwaniec, D. (2003). A Framework for Assessing Failure-to-Thrive. In M. C. Calder & S. Hackett (Eds.), *Assessment in Child Care* (pp. 263–281). Lyme Regis: Russell House Publishing.

Iwaniec, D. (2004). *Children who fail to thrive. A practice guide.* Chichester: Wiley.

Iwaniec, D., & Sneddon, H. (2002). The Quality of Parenting of Individuals Who had Failed to Thrive as Children. *British Journal of Social Work, 32,* 283–298.

Iwaniec, D., & McSherry, D. (2002). *Understanding Child Neglect: Contemporary Issues and Dilemmas.* Belfast: Institute of Child Care Research Queen's University.

Iwaniec, D., & McSherry, D. (2002). *Understanding Child Neglect: Contemporary Issues and Dilemmas.* Belfast: Institute of Child Care Research Queen's University.

Jack, G. (2000). Ecological Influences on Parenting and Child Development. *British Journal of Social Work* (30), 703–720.

Jack, G. (2001). Ecological perspectives in assessing children and families. In J. Horwath (Ed.), *The Child's World: Assessing Children in Need.* (pp. 53–74). London: Jessica Kingsley.

Jack, G., & Gill, O. (2003). *The Missing Side of the Triangle.* London: Barnardo's.

Jackson, C. (1998). Listen to Mother. *Mental Health Care, 1*(7), 217–219.

Jackson, D. (2003). Broadening Constructions of Family violence: Mother Perspectives of Aggression form their Children. *Child and Family Social Work, 8,* 321–329.

James, H. (2004). Promoting Effective Working with Parents with Learning Disabilities. *Child Abuse Review, 13*(1), 31–42.

Janis, I. L. (1972). *Victims of Groupthink.* Boston: Houghton Mifflin.

Jaudes, P. K., Ekwo, E., & Voorhis, J. V. (1995). Association of drug abuse and child abuse. *Child Abuse and Neglect, 19*(9), 1065–1075.

Jay, M. S. (2004). Childhood obesity is not PHAT! *The Journal of Pediatrics, 144*(4), A1.

Jenner, S., & McCarthy, G. (1995). Quantitative measures of parenting: a clinical-developmental perspective. In P. Reder & C. Lucey (Eds.), *Assessment of parenting. Psychiatric and psychological contributions* (pp. 136–150). London: Routledge.

Jeor, S. S., Perumean-Chaney, S., Sigman-Grant, M., Williams, C., & Foreyt, J. (2002). Family-based interventions for the treatment of childhood obesity. *Journal of the American Diabetic Association, 102*(5), 640–644.

Johnson, C. F. (1993). Physicians and Medical Neglect: variables that affect reporting. *Child Abuse and Neglect, 17,* 605–612.

Johnson-Reid, M., & Barth, R. (2000). From maltreatment report to juvenile incarceration: the role of child welfare services. *Child Abuse and Neglect, 24,* 505–520.

Joint Chief Inspectors. (2002). *Safeguarding Children. A Joint Chief Inspectors' Report on Arrangements to Safeguard Children.* London: Department of Health.

Joint Chief Inspectors. (2002). *Safeguarding Children. A Joint Chief Inspectors' Report on Arrangements to Safeguard Children.* London: Department of Health.

Jones, C. (2001). Voices from the Front-Line: State Social Workers and New Labour. *British Journal of Social Work, 31,* 547–562.

Jones, D. P. H. (1996). Editorial: Parental Social Isolation. *Child Abuse and Neglect, 20*(3), 239–240.

Jones, J., & Gupta, A. (1998). The Context of Decision-Making in Cases of Child Neglect. *Child Abuse Review, 7,* 97–110.

Jones, P. (1997). *Parental lack of supervision*. Washington DC: Child Welfare League of America.

Jordan, B., & Jordan, C. (2000). *Social Work and the Third Way*. London: Sage.

Jouriles, E. (1998). *Children Exposed to Marital Violence. Theory, Research and Applied Issues*. Washington DC: American Psychological Association.

Kantor, G. K., & Little, L. (2003). Defining the Boundaries of Child Neglect. When Does Domestic Violence Equate With Failure to Protect? *Journal of Interpersonal Violence, 18*(4), 338–355.

Karr-Morse, R., & Wiley, M. S. (2000). *Ghosts from the Nursery. Tracing the Roots of Violence*. New York: The Atlantic Monthly Press.

Keen, J., & Alison, L. H. (2001). Drug misusing parents: key points for health professionals. *Archives of Disease in Childhood, 85*, 296–299.

Kelley, S. J. (1992). Parenting Stress and Child Maltreatment in Drug-Exposed Children. *Child Abuse and Neglect, 16*, 317–328.

Kempe, C. H., & Helfer, R. (1968). *The Battered Child*. Chicago: University of Chicago Press.

Kendall-Tackett, K. A., & Eckenrode, J. (1996). The Effects of Neglect on Academic Achievement and Disciplinary Problems: A Developmental Perspective. *Child Abuse and Neglect, 20*(3), 161–169.

Kennedy, M., & Wonnacott, J. (2003). Disabled Children and the Assessment Framework. In M. C. Calder & S. Hackett (Eds.), *Assessment in Child Care. Using and developing frameworks for practice* (pp. 172–192). Lyme Regis: Russell House Publishing.

Kennedy, M., & Wonnacott, J. (2005). Neglect of Disabled Children. In J. Taylor & B. Daniel (Eds.), *Child Neglect. Practice Issues for Health and Social Care* (pp. 228–248). London: Jessica Kingsley.

Kenwood, H. (2002). *Ainlee. Chapter 8 Review*. London: Newham Area Child Protection Committee.

Kerr, M., Black, M., & Krishnakumar, A. (2000). Failure to Thrive, Maltreatment and the Behaviour and Development of 6 Year Old Children from Low Income, Urban Families. *Child Abuse and Neglect, 24*, 587–598.

Knutson, J. F., DeGarmo, D., Koeppl, G., & Reid, J. B. (2005). Care Neglect, Supervisory Neglect, and Harsh Parenting in the Development of Children's Aggression: A Replication and Extension. *Child Maltreatment, 10*(2), 92–107.

Koenig, A. L., Cicchetti, D., & Rogosch, F. A. (2004). Moral Development: The Association between Maltreatment and Young Children's Prosocial Behaviour and Moral Transgressions. *Social Development, 13*(1), 87–106.

Korbin, J. E., & Spilsbury, J. C. (1999). Cultural Competence and Child Neglect. In H. Dubowitz (Ed.), *Neglected Children. Research, Practice and Policy* (pp. 69–88). Thousand Oaks: Sage.

Kotch, J. B., Browne, D. C., & Ringwelt, C. L. (1995). Risk of Child Abuse or Neglect in a Cohort of Low-Income Children. *Child Abuse and Neglect, 19*(9), 1115–1130.

Kozlowska, K., & Hanney, L. (2002). The Network Perspective: An Integration of Attachment and Family Systems Theories. *Family Process, 41*(3), 285–312.

Kurtz, P. D., Jnr, J. M. G., Wodarski, J. S., & Howing, P. T. (1993). Maltreatment and the school-aged child: School performance consequences. *Child Abuse and Neglect, 17*(5), 581–589.

Lacharite, C., Ethier, L., & Couture, G. (1996). The Influence of Partners on Parental Stress of Neglectful Mothers. *Child Abuse Review, 5*, 18–33.

Lagerberg, D. (2001). A descriptive survey of Swedish child health nurses' awareness of abuse and neglect. 1 Characteristics of the nurses. *Child Abuse and Neglect, 25*, 1583–1601.

Lamb, W. H. (2003). The neglect of child neglect. *The Lancet, 361*(9367), 1475.

Lavan, A. (1998). Social Work in Ireland. In S. Shardlow & M. Payne (Eds.), *Contemporary Issues in Social Work: Western Europe* (pp. 39–56). Aldershot: Arena.

Lawrence, R., & Irvine, P. (2004). Redefining fatal child neglect. *Child Prevention Issues* (21 spring, 5–9).

Lea-Cox, C., & Hall, A. (1991). Attendance of general practitioners at child protection case conferences. *British Medical Journal, 302*, 1378–1379.

Lee, B. J., & George, R. M. (1999). Poverty, Early Childbearing and Child Maltreatment: A Multinomial Analysis. *Child Abuse and Neglect, 21*(9/10), 755–780.

Levendosky, A., & Graham-Bermann, S. (2001). Parenting in Battered Women: The Effects of Domestic Violence on Women and their Children. *Journal of Family Violence, 16*(2).

Little, M. (1995). Child protection or family support? Finding a balance. *Family Matters, 40*, 18–21.

Livingstone, B. (2000). Epidemiology of Childhood Obesity in Europe. *European Journal of Paediatrics, 159*(Supplement 1), 14–34.

Llewellyn, G., Connell, D., & Bye, R. (1998). Perception of Service Needs by Parents with Intellectual Disability, their Significant Others and their Service Workers. *Research in Developmental Disabilities, 19*(3), 245–260.

Lord Laming. (2003). *The Victoria Climbié Inquiry Report.* Norwich: TSO.

Louis, A., Condon, J., Shute, R., & Elzinga, R. (1997). The Development of the Louis Macro (mother and child risk observation) Forms: Assessing Parent-Infant-Child Risk in the Presence of Maternal Mental Illness. *Child Abuse and Neglect, 21*(7), 589–606.

Lupton, C., North, N., & Khan, P. (2001). *Working Together or Pulling Apart?*

The National Health Service and child protection networks. Bristol: The Policy Press.

Lymbery, M. E. F. (2003). Negotiating the Contradictions between Competence and Creativity in Social Work Education. *Journal of Social Work*, *3*(1), 99–118.

Lyon, T. A. (1999). Are Battered Women Bad Mothers? Rethinking the Termination of Abused Women's Parental Rights for Failure to Protect. In H. Dubowitz (Ed.), *Neglected Children. Research, Practice and Policy* (pp. 237–260). Thousand Oaks: Sage.

Maccoby, E. (1980). *Social Development: Psychology Growth and the Parent–Child Relationship*. New York: Harcourt Brace Jovanovich.

Macdonald, G. (2001). *Effective Interventions for Child Abuse and Neglect*. Chichester: Wiley.

Macdonald, G. (2005). Intervening with Neglect. In J. Taylor & B. Daniel (Eds.), *Child Neglect. Practice Issues for Health and Social Care* (pp. 279–290). London: Jessica Kingsley.

Mackner, L., & Starr, R. (1997). The cumulative effect of neglect and failure to thrive on cognitive functioning. *Child Abuse and Neglect*, *21*, 691–700.

Margolin, L. (1990). Fatal child neglect. *Child Welfare*, *69*, 309–319.

McConnell, D., & Llewellyn, G. (2002). Stereotypes, parents with intellectual disability and child protection. *Journal of Social Welfare and Family Law*, *24*(3), 297–317.

McDevitt, S. (1996). The impact of news media on child abuse reporting. *Child Abuse and Neglect*, *20*, 261–272.

McGaha, C. G. (2002). Development of Parenting Skills in Individuals with an Intellectual Impairment: an epigenetic explanation. *Disability & Society*, *17*(1), 81–91.

McGaw, S., & Sturmey, P. (1994). Assessing Parents with Learning Disabilities: The Parenting Skills Model. *Child Abuse Review*, *3*, 36–51.

McGee, C. (2000). *Childhood Experiences of Domestic Violence*. London: Jessica Kingsley.

McGloin, J. M., & Widom, C. (2001). Resilience among abused and neglected children grown up. *Development and Psychopathology*, *13*, 1021–1038.

McIntosh, J. E. (2002). Thought in the face of violence: a child's need. *Child Abuse and Neglect*, *26*, 229–241.

McMahon, T. J., & Rounsaville, B. J. (2002). Substance abuse and fathering: adding poppa to the research agenda. *Addiction*, *97*, 1109–1115.

Melzak, S. (2005). *The Therapeutic Needs of Refugee Children and Adolescents*. Paper presented at the Safeguarding Refugee and Asylum-seeking Children, London 28th November 2005.

Milligan, C., & Dowie, A. (1998). *What Do Children Need from their Fathers?* Edinburgh: Centre for Theology and Public Issues.

Minty, B., & Pattinson, G. (1994). The Nature of Child Neglect. *British Journal of Social Work, 24,* 733–747.

Monckton, W. (1945). *Report by Sir Walter Monckton on the circumstances that led to the boarding out of Dennis and Terence O'Neill at Bank Farm, Minsterley, and the steps taken to supervise their welfare. Cmd. 6636.* London: HMSO.

Morrison, T. (1990). The Emotional Effects of Child Protection Work on the Workers. *Practice, 4,* 253–271.

Morrison, T. (1996). Partnership and Collaboration: Rhetoric and Reality. *Child Abuse and Neglect, 20*(2), 127–140.

Morrison, T. (2001). *Staff Supervision in Social Care. Making a Real Difference for Staff and Service Users.* Brighton: Pavilion.

Mounteney, J. (1998). *Highlight Children of drug-abusing parents.* London: National Children's Bureau.

Mullender, A. (1996). *Rethinking Domestic Violence. The social work and probation response.* London: Routledge.

Mullender, A., Hague, G., Iman, U., Kelly, L., Malos, E., & Regan, L. (2003). *Children's Perspectives on Domestic Violence.* London: Sage.

Munro, E. (2000). *Effective child protection.* London: Sage.

Murphy, J. M., Jellinek, M., Quinn, D., Smith, G., Poitrast, F. G., & Goshkorn, M. (1991). Substance abuse and serious child mistreatment: Prevalence, risk and outcome in a court sample. *Child Abuse and Neglect, 15,* 197–211.

Murphy, M. (1995). *Working Together In Child Protection* (First Ed.). Aldershot: Arena.

Murphy, M., & Harbin, F. (2003). The Assessment of Parental Substance Misuse and its Impact on Childcare. In M. C. Calder & S. Hackett (Eds.), *Assessment in child care* (pp. 353–361). Lyme Regis: Russell House Publishing.

Murphy-Berman, V. (1994). A Conceptual Framework for Thinking about Risk Assessment and Case Management in Child Protective Services. *Child Abuse and Neglect, 18*(2), 193–201.

Nadya, R. (2002). Influences on Registered Nurses' Decision-making in Cases of Suspected Child Abuse. *Child Abuse Review, 11,* 168–178.

Nair, P., Black, M. M., Schuler, M., Keane, V., Snow, L., Rigney, B. A., et al. (1997). Risk factors for disruption in primary caregiving among infants of substance abusing women. *Child Abuse and Neglect, 21*(11), 1039–1051.

National Center for Injury Prevention and Control. (2004). *Using Evidence-Based Parenting Programs to Advance the Disease Control and Prevention (CDC) Efforts in Child Maltreatment Prevention.* Atlanta (GA): Centers for Disease Control and Prevention.

National Clearing House on Child Abuse and Neglect. (2001). *Short and Long Term Consequences of Neglect.* Retrieved 13/08/2001, from www.calib.com/nccanch/pubs/usermanuals/negelct/conseq.cfm

National Clearing House on Child Abuse and Neglect. (No date). *Defining Neglect*. Retrieved 13/8/2001, from www.calib.com/nccanch/pubs/usermanuals/neglect/define.cfm

National Clearing House on Child Abuse and Neglect. (2001). *Understanding the Effects of Maltreatment on Early Brain Development*. Washington: National Clearinghouse on Child Abuse and Neglect.

Nelson, K. E., Saunders, E. J., & Landsman, M. J. (1993). Chronic Neglect in Perspective. *Social Work*, *38*(6), 661–671.

Newman, T. (2003). *Children of disabled parents. New thinking about the families affected by disability and illness*. Lyme Regis: Russell House.

Newton, M. (2003). *Savage Girls and Wild Boys. A History of Feral Children*. New York: Faber and Faber.

New Zealand Family Violence Clearing House (No date). Accessed 11/11/2005. www.nzfvc.org.nz.

Nicklas, T. A., Yang, S., Baranowski, T., Zakeri, I., & Berenson, G. (2003). Eating patterns and obesity in children. The Bogalusa Heart Study. *American Journal of Preventative Medicine*, *25*(1), 9–16.

North Eastern Health Board. (1994). *Child Protection Guidelines*. Dunshaughlin: North Eastern Health Board.

NSPCC. (1997, 11–17 September). Drunk in Charge: Substance Abuse. *Community Care*, 35.

O'Hagan, K., & Dillenburger, K. (1995). *The Abuse of Women within Childcare Work* (First Ed.). Buckingham – Philadelphia: Open University Press.

Olds, D. L., Henderson Jnr, C. R., Chamberlain, P., Kitxman, C. R., Ecknerode, J., Cole, R. C., & Tatelbaum, R. C. (1999). Prenatal and infancy home visitation by nurses: recent findings. *The Future for Children*, *9*(1), 44–65.

Olds, D. L., Henderson Jnr, C. R., Kitxman, C. R., Ecknerode, J., Cole, R. E., & Tatelbaum, R. (1998). The promise of home visitation: research from two randomized trials. *Journal of Community Psychology*, *26*(1), 5–21.

O'Neale, V. (2000). *Excellence Not Excuses: Inspection of Services for Ethnic Minority Children and Families*. London: Social Services Inspectorate.

Packman, J., & Jordan, B. (1991). The Children Act: Looking Forward, Looking Back. *British Journal of Social Work*, *21*, 315–327.

Panaccione, V., & Wahler, R. (1986). Child behaviour, maternal depression and social coercion as factors in the quality of child care. *Journal of Abnormal Child Psychology*, *14*, 273–284.

Parker, R. (1999). The Shaping of Child Care Policy and Practice: Past and Future. In B. Holman, R. Parker & W. Utting (Eds.), *Reshaping Child Care Practice* (pp. 42–71). London: National Institute for Social Work.

Parton, N. (1985). *The Politics of Child Abuse*. Basingstoke: Macmillan.

Parton, N. (1995). Neglect as child protection: the political context and the practical outcomes. *Children and Society*, *9*(1), 67–89.

Parton, N. (2004). From Maria Colwell to Victoria Climbie: Reflections on Public Inquires into Child Abuse a Generation Apart. *Child Abuse Review*, 13, 80–94.

Parton, N., Thorpe, D., & Wattam, C. (1997). *Child Protection. Risk and the Moral Order*. Houndsmill: Macmillan.

Pelcovitz, D. A. (1980). *Child abuse as viewed by suburban elementary teachers*. Saratoga CA: Century Twenty-One Publishing.

Perez, C. M., & Widom, C. S. (1994). Childhood victimization and long term intellectual and academic outcomes. *Child Abuse and Neglect*, 18, 617–633.

Perry, B. D. (2002). Childhood Experience and the Expression of Genetic Potential: What Childhood Neglect Tells Us About Nature and Nurture. *Brain and Mind*, 3, 79 –100.

Perry, B. D. (2004). *The Impact of Abuse and Neglect on the Developing Brain*. Retrieved 31/3/2004, from http://teacher.scholastic.com/professional/bruceperry/abuse_neglect.htm

Perry, B. D., & Pollard, D. (1997). *Altered brain development following global neglect in early child hood*. Paper presented at the Society for Neuroscience, New Orleans.

Peterson, S. L., Robinson, E. A., & Littman, I. (1983). Parent-child interaction training for parents with a history of mental retardation. *Applied Research in Mental Retardation*, 4, 329–342.

Pianta, R., Egeland, B., & Erikson, M. F. (1989). The antecedents of maltreatment: results of the Mother-Child Interaction Research Projects. In D. Cicchetti & V. Carlson (Eds.), *Child Maltreatment: Theory and Research on the Causes of Child Abuse and Neglect* (pp. 203–253). Cambridge: Cambridge University Press.

Polansky, N. A. (1998). Domestic Violence and Substance Abuse. An Integrated Approach. In A. Robert (Ed.), *Battered Women and their Families*. New York: Springer.

Polansky, N. A., Ammons, P. W., & Weathersby, B. L. (1983). Is There an American Standard of Child Care? *Social Work*, 28(5), 341–346.

Polansky, N. A., Chalmers, M. A., Buttenweiser, E., & Williams, D. P. (1981). *Damaged Parents*. Chicago: The University of Chicago Press.

Polansky, N. A., Gaudin, J. M., Ammons, P. W., & David, K. B. (1985). The psychological ecology of the neglectful mother. *Child Abuse and Neglect*, 9, 265–275.

Pollak, J., & Levy, S. (1989). Countertransference and Failure to Report Child Abuse and Neglect. *Child Abuse and Neglect*, 13, 515–522.

Pollak, S. D., Cicchetti, D., Hornung, K., & Reed, A. (2000). Recognizing emotion in faces: developmental effects of child abuse and neglect. *Developmental Psychology*, 36, 1140–1145.

Polnay, J. C. (2000). General practitioners and child protection case conference participation. *Child Abuse Review, 9,* 108–123.

Protchaska, J., & diClementi, C. (1982). Transtheoretical Therapy: Towards a more integrative model of change. *Psychotherapy: Theory, Research and Practice, 19*(3).

Pugh, G., De'Ath, E., & Smith, C. (1994). *Confident Parents, Confident Children. Policy and practice in parent education and support.* London: National Children's Bureau.

Pugh, R. (2000). *Rural Social Work.* Lyme Regis: Russell House.

Quinton, D. (2004). *Supporting Parents Messages from Research.* London: Department for Education and Skills.

Reder, P., & Duncan, S. (1999). *Lost Innocents? A follow-up study of fatal child abuse.* London: Routledge.

Reder, P., & Duncan, S. (2001). Abusive Relationships, Care and Control Conflicts and Insecure Attachments. *Child Abuse Review, 10,* 411–720.

Reder, P., & Duncan, S. (2004). Making the Most of the Victoria Climbié Inquiry Report. *Child Abuse Review, 13*(2), 95–114.

Reder, P., & Lucey, C. (2000). The Impact of Children on Their Parents. In P. Reder, M. McClure & A. Jolley (Eds.), *Family Matters: Interface between Child and Adult Mental Health.* London: Routledge.

Reder, P., Duncan, S., & Gray, M. (1993). *Beyond Blame – Child Abuse Tragedies Revisited* (First Ed.). London: Routledge.

Ringwelt, C. & Caye, J. (1989). The Effect of Demographic Factors on Perceptions of Child Neglect. *Child and Youth Service Review, 11,* 133–144.

Roditti, M. G. (2005). Understanding Communities of Neglectful Parents: Child Caregiving Networks and Child Neglect. *Child Welfare, LXXXIV*(2), 277–298.

Rose, S. J., & Meezan, W. (1996). Variations in Perceptions of Child Neglect. *Child Welfare, 75*(2), 139–160.

Rose, S., & Meezan, W. (1997). Defining Child Neglect: Evolution, influences and issues. In J. D. Berrick, R. Barth & N. Gilbert (Eds.), *Child Welfare Research Review* (Vol. 2). New York: Cambridge University Press.

Rose, S., & Selwyn, J. (2000). Child Neglect: An English Perspective. *International Social Work, 32,* 179–192.

Rose, W. (2001). Assessing Children in Need and their Families: An Overview of the Framework. In Horwath, (Ed.), *The Child's World. Assessing cildren in Need* (pp. 35–50). London: Jessica Kingsley.

Rosenberg, D., & Cantwell, H. (1993). The consequences of neglect – individual and society. In B. Tindall (Ed.), *Bailliere's Clinical Paediatrics,* (Vol. 1, no 1, pp. 185–210). London: Bailliere Tindall.

Royal College of Paediatrics and Child Health. (2004). Retrieved 21/06/2004, from www.rcph.ac.uk/publications/recent-publications. html

Royal College of Psychiatrists. (2002). *Patients as parents. Addressing, the needs, including safety, of children whose parents have mental illness.* London: Royal College of Psychiatrists.

Rutter, J. (2001). *Supporting refugee children in 21st century Britain. A compendium of essential information.* Stoke on Trent: Trentham Books.

Rutter, M. (1985). Resilience in the face of adversity: protective factors and resilience to psychiatric disorder. *British Journal of Psychiatry,* (147), 163–182.

Rutter, M., & and English and Romanian Adoptees study team. (1998). Developmental catch-up, and deficit, following adoption after severe global privation. *Journal of Child Psychology and Psychiatry,* 465–476.

Rutter, M., & Quinton, D. (1984). Parental psychiatric disorder: effects on children. *Psychological Medicine, 14,* 853–880.

Rutter, M., Anderson-Wood, L., Beckett, C., Bredenkamp, D., Castle, J., Grootheus, C., et al. (1999). Quasi-autistic patterns following severe early global privation. *Journal of Child Psychology and Psychiatry, 40,* 537–549.

Sabin, M. A., Crowe, E. C., & Shield, J. P. H. (2004). The prognosis in childhood obesity. *Current Paediatrics, 14*(2), 110–114.

Salmelainen, P. (1996). *Child Neglect: Its Causes and Its Role in Delinquency.* Retrieved 21/08/2001, from http://www.lawlink.nsw.gov.au/bocsar1.nsf/pages/childneglecttext

Samra-Tibbetts, C., & Raynes, B. (1999). Assessment and planning. In M. C. Calder & J. Horwath (Eds.), *Working for Children on the Child Protection Register* (pp. 81–118). Aldershot: Ashgate.

Sanders, M. R. (1999). Triple P-Positive Parenting Program: towards an empirically validated multilevel parenting and family support strategy for the prevention of behavior and emotional problems in children. *Clinical Child and Family Psychology Review,* (2), 71–90.

Scannapieco, M., & Connell-Carrick, K. (2005). Focus on the first years: Correlates of substantiation of child maltreatment for families with children 0 to 4. *Children and Youth Services Review, 27*(12), 1307–1323.

Schaffer, H. R. (2004). *Introducing Child Psychology.* Oxford: Blackwell.

Schore, A. N. (2002). Dysregulation of the right brain: a fundamental mechanism of traumatic attachment and the psychopathogenesis of post-traumatic stress. *Australian and New Zealand Journal of Psychiatry, 36,* 9–30.

Schumacher, J., Slep, A., & Heyman, R. (2001). Risk Factors for Child Neglect. *Aggression and Violent Behaviour, 6,* 231–254.

SCODA (Standing Conference on Drug Abuse). (1997). *Drug Using Parents:*

Policy Guidelines for Inter-Agency Working. London: Local Government Association.

Scott, D. (1997). Inter-agency conflict: an ethnographic study. *Child and Family Social Work, 2*, 73–80.

Scourfield, J. (2000). The rediscovery of child neglect. *The Sociological Review, 48*(3), 365–382.

Scourfield, J. B. (2001). Constructing women in child protection work. *Child and Family Social Work, 6*, 77–87.

Seaman, P., Turner, K., Hill, M., Stafford, A., & Walker, M. (2006). *Parenting and children's resilience in disadvantaged communities*. York: Joseph Rowntree Foundation.

Sheffield Area Child Protection Committee. (2005). *Executive Summary of the W Children Serious Case Review*. Retrieved 16/1/2006 from www.sheffield.gov.uk

Shelter. (2004). *Toying with their Future. The hidden costs of the housing crisis*. Retrieved 16/2/2006, from http://england.shelter.org.uk

Shelter. (2005). *Full House? How over-crowding housing affects families*. Retrieved 16/2/2006, from http://england.shelter.org.uk

Sheridan, M. J. (1995). A Proposed Intergenerational Model of Substance Abuse, Functioning, and Abuse/Neglect. *Child Abuse and Neglect, 10*(5), 519–530.

Shipman, K., Edwards, A., Brown, A., Swisher, L., & Jennings, E. (2005). Managing emotion in a maltreating context: A pilot study examining child neglect. *Child Abuse & Neglect, 29*, 1015–1029.

Shor, R. (1998). Paediatricians in Israel: Factors which Affect the Diagnosis and Reporting of Maltreated Children. *Child Abuse and Neglect, 22*(2), 143–153.

Sinclair, R., & Bullock, R. (2002). *Learning from Past Experience-A Review of Serious Case Reviews*. London: Department of Health.

Sinclair, R., & Bullock, R. (2002). *Learning from Past Experience – A Review of Serious Case Reviews*. London: Department of Health.

Skuse, D., Reilly, S., & Wolke, D. (1994). Psychosocial adversity and growth during infancy. *European Journal of Clinical Nutrition, 48*(Supplement 1), 113–130.

Smith, C. A., Ireland, T. O., & Thornberry, T. P. (2005). Adolescent maltreatment and its impact on young adult antisocial behaviour. *Child Abuse and Neglect, 29*, 1099–1119.

Smith, M., Nursden, J., & McMahon, L. (2004). Social Workers' Responses to Experiences of Fear. *British Journal of Social Work, 34*, 541–559.

Socolar, R. R. S., & Reives, P. (2002). Factors that facilitate or impede physicians who perform evaluations for child maltreatment. *Child Maltreatment, 7*(4), 377–381.

Soetendorp, D. (2005). *A Sense of Belonging Addressing the Loss.* Paper presented at the Safeguarding Refugee and Asylum-Seeking Children, London 28th November 2005.

Speak, S., Cameron, S., & Gilroy, R. (1997). *Young single fathers: Participation in fatherhood – bridges and barriers.* Bristol: Family Policy Studies Centre.

Spicer, D. (2004). Personal communication.

Srivastava, P., Fountain, R., Ayre, P., & Stewart, J. (2003). The Graded Care Profile: A Measure of Care. In M. C. Calder & S. Hackett (Eds.), *Assessment in Child Care* (pp. 227–246). Lyme Regis: Russell House Publishing.

Srivastava, O. P., Stewart, J., Fountain, R., & Ayre, P. (2005). Common Operational Approach Using the 'Graded Care Profile' in Cases of Neglect. In J. Taylor & B. Daniel (Eds.), *Child Neglect. Practice Issues for Health and Social Care* (pp. 131–146). London: Jessica Kingsley.

Stanley, J., & Goddard, C. (2002). *In The Firing Line. Violence and Power in Child Protection Work.* Chichester: Wiley.

Stanley, N., Penhale, B., Rioran, D., Barbour, R. S., & Holden, S. (2003). *Child Protection and Mental Health Services.* Bristol: The Policy Press.

Stephens, D. L. (1999). Battered women's views of their children. *Journal of Interpersonal Violence, 14*(7), 731–746.

Stern, D. (1995). *The Interpersonal World of the Infant: A View from Psychoanalysis and Developmental Psychology.* New York: Basic Books.

Stevenson, O. (1998). *Neglected Children: Issues and Dilemmas.* Oxford: Blackwell Science.

Stevenson, O. (1998a). Neglect: Where Now? Some Reflections. *Child Abuse Review, 7,* 111–115.

Stevenson, O. (2005). Foreward. In J. Taylor & B. Daniel (Eds.), *Child Neglect. Practice Issues for Health and Social Care* (pp. 9–10). London: Jessica Kingsley.

Stevenson, O. (2005). Working Together in Cases of Neglect: Key Issues. In J. Taylor & B. Daniel (Eds.), *Child Neglect. Practice Issues for Health and Social Care* (pp. 97–112). London: Jessica Kingsley.

Stevenson, O. (Ed.). (1998b). *Child Welfare in the UK.* Oxford: Blackwell Science.

Stone, B. (1998). *Child Neglect. Practitioners Perspectives.* London: NSPCC.

Stone, B. (2003). A Framework for Assessing Neglect. In M. C. Calder & S. Hackett (Eds.), *Assessment in Child Care. Using and developing frameworks for practice* (pp. 214–226). Lyme Regis: Russell House Publishing.

Stowman, S., & Donohue, B. (2005). Assessing Child Neglect: A Review of Standardized Measures. *Aggression and Violent Behaviour, 10*(4), 491–512.

Strauss, M. A. & Kaufman, G. K. (2005). Definition and measurement of neglect. Some general principles and their application to self report measures. *Child Abuse and Neglect, 29*(1), 19–29.

Straus, M. A., & Savage, S. A. (2005). Neglectful Behavior by Parents in the Life History of University Students in 17 Countries and Its Relation to Violence against Dating Partners. *Child Maltreatment, 10*(2), 124–135.

Sullivan, S. (2000). *Child Neglect: Current Definitions and Models. A review of the literature.* Ottawa: Family Violence Prevention Unit.

Sullivan, P., & Knutson, J. F. (2000). Maltreatment and Disabilities: A Population-Based Epidemiological Study. *Child Abuse and Neglect, 24*(10), 1257–1273.

Swift, K. J. (1995). An Outrage to Common Decency: Historical Perspectives on Child Neglect. *Child Welfare, LXXXIV*(1), 71–91.

Tanner, K., & Turney, D. (2003). What do we know about child neglect? A critical review of the literature and its application to social work practice. *Child and Family Social Work, 8*, 25–34.

Taylor, C., & White, S. (2001). Knowledge, Truth and Reflexivity. The problem of judgement in social work. *Journal of Social Work, 1*(1), 37–59.

Taylor, J., & Daniel, B. (1999). Interagency Practice in Children with Non-Organic Failure to Thrive: Is There a Gap Between Health and Social Care? *Child Abuse Review, 8*, 325–338.

Thoburn, J. (2002). Out-of-home care for the abused or neglected child: research, planning and practice. In K. Wilson & A. James (Eds.), *The Child Protection Handbook* (pp. 514–537). Edinburgh: Bailliere Tindall.

Thoburn, J., Wilding, J., & Watson, J. (2000). *Family Support in Cases of Emotional Maltreatment and Neglect.* London: The Stationery Office.

Thompson, R. (1995). *Preventing Child Mistreatment through Social Support: A critical analysis.* California: Sage.

Thorn, W., & Bannon, M. J. (2003). The Child Protection Case Conference. In M. J. Bannon & Y. H. Carter (Eds.), *Protecting Children from Abuse and Neglect in Primary Care* (pp. 177–186). Oxford: Oxford University Press.

Thorpe, D. (1994). *Evaluating Child Protection.* Buckingham: Open University Press.

Tite, R. (1993). How Teachers Define and Respond to Child Abuse: The Distinction between Theoretical and Reportable Cases. *Child Abuse and Neglect, 17*, 591–603.

Tomison, A. M. (1995). *Spotlight on Child Neglect.* Retrieved 13/8/2001, from http://www.aifs.org.au/nch/issues4.html

Torode, R., Walsh, T., & Woods, M. (2001). *Working with Refugees and Asylum-Seekers. A Social Work Resource Book.* Dublin: Trinity College.

The Treasury. (2003). *Every Child Matters.* Norwich: TSO.

Trocme, N., Fallon, B., MacLaurin, B., Dacuik, J., Felstiner, C., & Black, T. (2003). *Canadian Incidence Study of Reported Child Abuse and Neglect.* Ottawa: Minister of Public Works and Government Services Canada.

Trocme, N., MacLaurin, B., Fallon, B., Daciuk, J., Billingsley, D., Tourigny, M., Mayer, M., Wright, J., Baxter, K., Bulford, G., Itomick, J., Sullivan, R. & McKenzie, B. (2001). *Canadian Incidence Study of Reported Child Abuse and Neglect: Final Report.* Ottawa: Canada Health.

Trocme, N., Fallon, B., MacLaurin, B., Daciuk, J., Felstiner, C., Black, T. (2005). *The Canadian Incidnt Study of Reported Child Abused Neglect 2005.* Ottawa: National Clearing House on Family Violence.

Trocme, N., Tourigny, M., MacLaurin, B., & Fallon, B. (2003). Major findings from the Canadian incidence study of reported child abuse and neglect. *Child Abuse and Neglect, 27,* 1427–1439.

Truman, P. (2004). Problems in identifying cases of child neglect. *Nursing Standard, 18*(29), 33–38.

Tunnard, J. (2002). *Parental Drug Misuse – A Review of Impact and Intervention Studies.* Dartington: Research in Practice.

Turney, D. (2000). The feminizing of neglect. *Child and Family Social Work, 5,* 47–56.

Turney, D. (2005). Who Cares? The Role of Mothers in Cases of Child Neglect. In J. Taylor & B. Daniel (Eds.), *Child Neglect. Practice Issues and Social Care* (pp. 263–278). London: Jessica Kingsley.

Tymchuk, A., & Andron, L. (1990). Mothers with mental retardation who do or do not abuse or neglect their children. *Child Abuse and Neglect, 14,* 313–323.

Tymchuk, A., & Andron, L. (1994). Rationale, approaches, results and resource implications of programmes to enhance parenting skills of people with learning disabilities. In A. Craft (Ed.), *Practice Issues in Sexuality and Learning Disabilities* (pp. 202–216). London: Routledge.

U.S. Department of Health and Human Services. (2003). *Emerging Practices in the Prevention of Child Abuse and Neglect.* Washington DC: Children's Bureau's Office on Child Abuse and Neglect.

UNICEF. (2001). *A League Table of Child Deaths by Injury in Rich Nations.* Florence: UNICEF Innocenti Research Centre.

Upton, D. (1999). How can we achieve evidence-based practice if we have a theory-practice gap in nursing today? *Journal of Advanced Nursing, 29*(3), 549–555.

Utting, D. (1995). *Family and Parenthood: Supporting Families, Preventing Breakdown.* York: Joseph Rowntree.

Valios, N. (2004a). 25 March. The Big Issue. *Community Care,* 34–36.

Valios, N. (2004b, 1–7 July). Haringey criticised over scalding case. *Community Care,* 11.

Vinson, T., Baldry, E., & Hargreaves, J. (1996). Neighbourhoods, Networks and Child Abuse. *British Journal of Social Work, 26,* 523–543.

Vulliamy, A. P., & Sullivan, R. (2000). Reporting Child Abuse: Pediatricians' Experiences with the Child Protection System. *Child Abuse and Neglect*, *24*(11), 1461–1470.

Wachs, T. D. (2000). Nutritional deficits and behavioural development. *International Journal of Behavioural Development*, *24*(4), 435–441.

Walker, M., & Glasgow, M. (2005). Parental Substance Misuse and the Implications for Children. In J. Taylor & B. Daniel (Eds.), *Child Neglect. Practice Issues for Health and Social Care* (pp. 206–227). London: Jessica Kingsley.

Ward, H. (2001). The developmental needs of children: implications for assessment. In J. Horwath (Ed.), *The Child's World. Assessing Children in Need* (pp. 167–179). London: Jessica Kingsley.

Watson, G. (2005). The theoretical and Practical issues in Attachment and Neglect: The Case of Very Low Birth Weight Babies. In J. Taylor & B. Daniel (Eds.), *Child Neglect. Practice Issues for Health and Social Care Conference* (pp. 186–205). London: Jessica Kingsley.

Wattenberg, E., & Boisen, L. (no date). *Testing the Community Standard on Neglect: Are We There Yet? Findings from a First-Stage Survey of Professional Social Services Workers.* Retrieved 21/8/2001, from http://www.umn.edu/Children/sh3.html

Webb, E., Maddocks, A., & Bongilli, J. (2002). Effectively Protecting Black and Minority Ethnic Children from Harm: Overcoming Barriers to the Child Protection Process. *Child Abuse Review*, *11*, 394–410.

Wekerle, C., & Wolfe, D. A. (1993). Prevention of child physical abuse and neglect. Promising new directions. *Clinical Psychology Review*, *13*(6), 501–540.

West, M. O., & Prinz, R. J. (1987). Parental alcoholism and childhood psychopathology. *Psychological Bulletin*, *102*(2), 204–218.

Westcott, H. (1993). *Abuse of Children and Adults with Disabilities.* London: NSPCC.

Westcott, H., & Cross, M. (1996). *This Far and No further. Towards ending the abuse of disabled children.* Birmingham: Venture Press.

Wilding, B., & Thoburn, J. (1997). Family Support Plans for Neglected and Emotionally Maltreated Children. *Child Abuse and Neglect*, *22*(343–356).

Williams, A. (1994). Ensuring a healthy start: preventing failure to thrive in infants. *Child Health*, *2*(2), 68–72.

Wilson, D., & Horner, W. (2005). Chronic Child Neglect: Needed Developments in Theory and Practice. *Families in Society: The Journal of Contemporary Social Services*, *86*(4), 471–481.

Winnicott, D. W. (1965). *The Family and Individual Development.* London: Tavistock.

Wolock, I., & Horowitz, B. (1984). Child Maltreatment as a social problem: the neglect of neglect. *American Journal of Orthopsychiatry, 54,* 530–543.

Woodhouse, A. E., Green, G., & Davies, S. (2001). Parents with learning disabilities: Service audit and development. *British Journal of Learning Disabilities, 29,* 128–132.

Woodhouse, D., & Pengelly, P. (1991). *Anxiety and the Dynamics of Collaboration.* Aberdeen: Aberdeen University Press.

World Health Organisation. (2002). *World Report on Violence and Health.* Geneva: World Health Organisation.

Wright, C. M. (1995). A population approach to weight monitoring and failure to thrive. In T. J. David (Ed.), *Recent Advances in Paediatrics,* (Vol. 13, pp. 73–78). Edinburgh: Churchill Livingstone.

Wright, C., & Birks, E. (2000). Risk factors for failure to thrive: a population-based survey. *Child: Care, Health and Development, 26*(1), 5–16.

Zellman, G. L. (1990). Child abuse reporting and failure to report among mandated reporters: Prevalence, incidence and reasons. *Journal of Interpersonal Violence, 5,* 3–22.

Index